STUDY GUIDE TO ACCOMPANY
GARRETT & HOUGH'S

Brain&Behavior

An Introduction to
Behavioral Neuroscience
FIFTH EDITION

Bob Garrett
California Polytechnic State University, San Luis Obispo

Gerald Hough
Rowan University

Prepared by **Meghan C. Kahn**
Indiana University Southeast

Los Angeles | London | New Delhi
Singapore | Washington DC | Melbourne

FOR INFORMATION:

SAGE Publications, Inc.
2455 Teller Road
Thousand Oaks, California 91320
E-mail: order@sagepub.com

SAGE Publications Ltd.
1 Oliver's Yard
55 City Road
London EC1Y 1SP
United Kingdom

SAGE Publications India Pvt. Ltd.
B 1/I 1 Mohan Cooperative Industrial Area
Mathura Road, New Delhi 110 044
India

SAGE Publications Asia-Pacific Pte. Ltd.
3 Church Street
#10-04 Samsung Hub
Singapore 049483

Acquisitions Editor: Abbie Rickard
Content Development Editor: Lucy Berbeo
Editorial Assistant: Jennifer Cline
Production Editor: David C. Felts
Copy Editor: Amy Marks
Typesetter: C&M Digitals (P) Ltd.
Proofreader: Jeff Bryant
Cover Designer: Gail Buschman
Marketing Manager: Katherine Hepburn

Printed in the United States of America

Library of Congress Control Number: 2017952744

ISBN 978-1-5063-9247-9

This book is printed on acid-free paper.

SUSTAINABLE FORESTRY INITIATIVE
Certified Chain of Custody
At Least 10% Certified Forest Content
www.sfiprogram.org
SFI-01028

19 20 21 10 9 8 7 6 5 4

Brief Contents

Detailed Contents

Acknowledgments

Revising and updating this guide has been a rewarding, yet time-intensive project. I would first like to thank my husband, Sean, and children, Everett and Rosalind for providing support and understanding during this project. I acquired my first understanding of teaching through observing my mother, Mary, in the years she taught high school social studies. I hope this guide and my other endeavors in teaching reflect the care and thought that she always put into her work. Along the way, I have been able to develop my teaching and research skills due to support from several mentors: Ms. Cheryl Schulte at Port Byron High School, who showed me that a woman could be a scientist; Dr. Nancy Furlong at Alfred University, who mixed high teaching standards with personal support; and Dr. Gerald Hough and Dr. Tammy Jechura, who were both incredibly patient in teaching me as a young graduate student. Lastly, I would like to thank my amazing students at Indiana University Southeast who continue to teach me so much about how learning really happens. So many of my students have inspired me over the years, but in particular, I would like to acknowledge the following former students for the ways they have affected me: Brittany Sizemore, BethAnn Rice, Leamon Daniel, Alex Tinsley, and Deanna Kaparo. I am a better teacher and person for knowing each of you.

—Meghan C. Kahn

1 What Is Behavioral Neuroscience?

Learning Objectives

After reading this chapter, you will be able to

1. Define the mind-brain problem in behavioral neuroscience
2. Describe the contributions of philosophers and scientists to the development of behavioral neuroscience as a field of study
3. Identify the role of physiologists in the establishment of modern-day behavioral neuroscience
4. Compare the relative contributions of genes and environment in the development of behavioral characteristics
5. Critique the fixed nature of heredity in shaping behavior

The Origins of Behavioral Neuroscience

Summary and Guided Review

After studying this section in the text, fill in the blanks of the following summary.

___Neuroscience___ (1) is the multidisciplinary study of the nervous system and its role in behavior. During the 1990s, also known as the Decade of the ___brain___ (2), intensive research into the role of biology in behavioral problems led to new treatments for depression, addiction, and age-related memory impairment. Advances were also made in the area of genetics, including a greater understanding of the genes involved in diseases such as ___Schizophrenia___ (3) and a(n) ___map___ (4) of all human genes.

___Behavioral___ (5) neuroscience is the branch of psychology that studies the relationships between behavior and the body, and it attempts to answer questions about the biological basis of diverse phenomena such as mental illness, emotions, perception, cognition, and consciousness. Psychology emerged as a separate discipline in 1879 when ___Wilhelm Wundt___ (6) established the first psychology laboratory, and behavioral neuroscience arose as a distinct subfield of psychology some time after this.

Behavioral neuroscience addresses the ___mind - brain___ (7) problem, which concerns the nature of the relationship between the physical brain and the mind. Most modern neuroscientists believe that the ___mind___ (8) is not a real thing but rather is a concept we use to explain our awareness of experience. This position is known as materialistic ___monism___ (9) and assumes that everything is physical. The position that the mind is nonmaterial and separate from the physical brain is called ___dualism___ (10). This issue of lack of consensus on the mind-brain problem is not a new one: Among the ancient Greek philosophers, Democritus and ___Aristotle___ (11) were monists, whereas ___Plato___ (12) was a dualist.

Scientists often use ___models___ (13) to help them explain how things work. The hydraulic model of behavior was developed by the 17th-century French philosopher ___Descartes___ (14) to explain the physical basis of behavior. According to this model, when the mind willed the body to action, the ___pineal___ (15) gland pumped animal spirits through the nerves (believed to be hollow tubes) to the muscles, resulting in movement. The pineal gland, therefore, was considered the seat of the ___soul___ (16). This model was ultimately shown to be wrong based on the approach of ___empiricism___ (17), which involves use of the methods of observation and experimentation.

Important principles of nervous system anatomy and physiology were discovered during the 1700s and 1800s. Work by several physiologists showed that nerves operated via ___electricity___ (18), not "animal spirits." However, the German physiologist ___Helmholtz___ (19) performed experiments that indicated that nerve conduction was not as fast as electricity conducted through wires, which suggested that something more than just electricity was operating in the nervous system.

In the 1800s, well-documented cases of brain injury suggested that specific parts of the brain have specific functions, a concept known as ___localization___ (20). For example, railroad worker ___Phineas___ ___Gage___ (21) underwent extreme changes in personality following an accident in which an iron rod was driven through his skull and ___frontal___ (22) lobes. Another case was reported by the French physician ___Broca___ (23); his patient was unable to speak, and after the patient died, it was discovered that he had damage in the ___left___ (24) hemisphere of his brain. Gall took the localization concept to an extreme in his theory of ___phrenology___ (25), which stated that several emotional and intellectual faculties were located in specific areas of the brain based on bumps on the skull. On the other extreme, Lashley's theory of ___equipotentiality___ (26) argued that brain functions are evenly distributed across the brain. Currently, brain researchers know that brain functions are both localized and ___distributed___ (27), which means that several brain areas interact to produce specific experiences such as learning or emotion.

While not common, evidence that the mind-brain problem is still debated comes from researchers who are interested in ___conscious___ ___experience___ (28), which they believe cannot be explained by materialism. These scientists study nonmaterial neuroscience and point to studies in which ___behavior___ ___therapy___ (29) altered brain function in patients as evidence for their position. Material neuroscientists interpret these findings as the ___brain___ (30) changing the brain.

Short Answer and Essay Questions

Answer the following questions.

1. Give two examples of the types of research questions that behavioral neuroscientists might ask. For each, explain how someone from a neuroscience background might approach each research question differently than someone from a behavioral psychology background.

2. Regarding the mind-brain question, compare monism and dualism. What are (or were) the problems with each position? How do most modern neuroscientists explain the relationship between the brain and mind?

3. Why was the case of Phineas Gage important for brain science? What did it reveal about the localization of function issue?

4. Compare the theories of localization and equipotentiality. What is the current position of brain researchers on this issue?

Nature and Nurture

Summary and Guided Review

After studying this section in the text, fill in the blanks of the following summary.

The question of ___nature___ (31) versus ___nurture___ (32) asks how important genes and environment, respectively, are in influencing behavior. Evidence is accumulating that many behaviors have a genetic or ___hereditary___ (33) component. ___Genes___ (34), which direct cellular processes and transmit inherited characteristics, are located mostly on ___chromosomes___ (35), which are paired in all cells, with the exception of some in the sex cells. The sex of an individual is determined by the sex chromosomes: Females have ___two___ (36) X chromosome(s), and males have ___one___ (37) X chromosome(s) and one Y chromosome. Most body cells have ___46___ (38) chromosomes, but _____sperm_____ (39) and egg cells have 23. When conception occurs, the fertilized egg, or _____zygote_____ (40), contains half of each parent's genetic material. For the first eight weeks following conception, the developing baby is considered a(n) _____embryo_____ (41), and then it is called a(n) _____fetus_____ (42) until it is born.

Genes are composed of a double strand of molecules known as _____DNA_____ (43), or deoxyribonucleic acid. The strands are connected by pairs of nucleotides (adenine, _____thymine/cytosine_____ (44), guanine, and _____cytosine/thymine_____ (45) that carry instructions for producing _____protein_____ (46), which are used in the construction of the body or act as _____enzymes_____ (47). Researchers are building computers out of _____DNA_____ (48) due to its small size and computing speed. Chemists at North Carolina State University are using DNA to detect genes for _____cancer_____ cells (49).

Different versions of a gene are called _____alleles_____ (50). In some cases the effects of the two alleles blend to produce a combined result; one example of this would be type _____AB_____ (51) blood. A(n) _____dominant_____ (52) allele will produce its effects regardless of which allele it is paired with. In order for a(n) _____recessive_____ (53) trait to be expressed, there must be a copy of the same allele on each chromosome. Individuals who possess two copies of a dominant allele are _____homozygous_____ (54) for that gene and will have the same _____phenotype_____ (55), or appearance, as those who possess one dominant and one recessive allele, who are _____heterozygous_____ (56). An X-linked trait is produced by a gene on the X chromosome that is not paired with one on the Y chromosome. If a recessive gene is located on the X chromosome, the trait it influences is more likely to be seen in _____males_____ (57); red-green color blindness is an example of a(n) _____X (sex)-linked_____ (58) trait. Traits such as height and intelligence are _____polygenic_____ (59), meaning they are influenced by more than one gene.

For some time, psychologists focused on _____learning_____ (60) as the main source of behavior, rather than genes. This emphasis on the role of the environment began changing in the 1960s, and a more balanced view was adopted. Psychologists now believe that genes influence many human behavioral traits, and _____intelligence_____ (61) is the behavioral trait whose genetic origins have received the most research attention. However, it is important to remember that genes control only the production of proteins, so they influence behavior indirectly through physiological systems.

Locating genes that influence traits is difficult and time-consuming. However, in 2000, several genetics laboratories published a rough draft of the human _____genome_____ (62), which will be useful in locating specific genes. This effort, known as the International Human Genome Project, has revealed that humans have only _____21,000_____ (63) individual genes that encode proteins, and that 97% of the genome is made up of "_____junk_____" (64) DNA, which are sections of chromosomes whose function is uncertain, though 80% of them control _____gene expression_____ (65). Although the map does not tell scientists what each gene does, it will allow them to more easily locate specific genes that contribute to specific traits. For example, although researchers in the 1980s knew that the gene for Huntington's disease was located on chromosome 4 near two _____marker_____ (66) genes, it took them 10 more years to locate the specific gene. Scientists now predict that they can locate important genes much more quickly because of the map. Such knowledge is expected to lead to genetic-based treatment of many more disorders. Encyclopedia of

The _____DNA elements_____ (67) (ENCODE) Project began after completion of the Human Genome Project and is focused on determining the function of the human genome.

Scientists at 32 different international institutions are now working to identify the short sequences of DNA, or ___exons___ (68), that are responsible for protein creation and are likely areas where mutations result in conditions such as blindness and movement disorders.

The notion that offspring are like clones of their parents is incorrect. Children inherit _____half_____ (69) of each parent's DNA, and because of the 60–70 trillion possible ___combinations___ (70) of genes resulting from sexual reproduction, no two individuals are genetically exactly alike (unless they are identical twins). This variability of traits is the cornerstone of Darwin's theory of ___natural___ ___selection___ (71), which states that organisms possessing traits that are most conducive to survival are more likely to pass their genes on to offspring. In addition, the effects of genes are not ___rigid___ (72). They are not all active at the same time, and they may produce more proteins at some times than at others. They may also become active during certain ___experiences___ (73), such as when an organism is learning. Clearly genes are not the sole dictators of behavior. Instead, they give us predispositions for certain characteristics.

Comparisons between identical and ___fraternal___ (74) twins allow researchers to estimate the percentage of variation in characteristics due to heredity, or ___heritability___ (75). It appears that heritability for intelligence is about _____50_____% (76). Personality characteristics show a heritability of _____40___%–___50_____% (77). If half of the variation in behaviors is due to genetics, then the other half must be due to ___environment___(78). However, it is important to understand that the more similarity there is between people's environments, the ___higher___ (79) the degree of heritability.

Scientists now argue that genes contribute to our predisposition or ___vulnerability___ (80) for certain traits. The genes we inherit may result in a predisposition for a disorder such as schizophrenia, but the disorder will emerge only under certain environmental conditions. Clearly both factors are important.

Short Answer and Essay Questions

Answer the following questions.

5. What is the immediate function of genes? Explain how genes can indirectly influence behavior. Describe the ways in which the actions of genes can be variable.

6. What is the rationale for comparing identical and fraternal twins in order to measure the heritability of traits?

7. Angelina Jolie tested positive for a defective gene (*BRCA1*) that triggers breast cancer in 87% of women with that particular defect. As a result, she removed all of her natural breast tissue through a procedure called a double mastectomy despite not having any symptoms of cancer. Do you agree with her decision? Using information gleaned in this section, explain both points of view.

8. Janet and Charles are expecting their first baby. They are both highly intelligent, and they assume that their child will inherit their intelligence through the genes it shares with them. They feel that the environment has little or no impact on intelligence. After having read the section "Heredity: Destiny or Predisposition?" what would you tell this couple about the scientific evidence for their claim? (Be sure to address the concept of *predisposition* in your answer.)

Post-test

Use these multiple-choice questions to check your understanding of the chapter.

1. Which of the following did NOT occur during the Decade of the Brain (1990s)?
   a. Genes contributing to the development of schizophrenia were identified.
   b. It was discovered that neurons conduct electricity.
   c. Drugs that block addiction were discovered.
   d. New treatments for depression were developed.

2. Who among the following is credited with establishing the first psychology laboratory in Germany in 1879?
   a. Wilhelm Wundt
   b. Hermann von Helmholtz
   c. Gustav Fritsch
   d. Franz Gall

3. Dr. Locke is a philosopher who believes that there is no distinction between the physical brain and the mind. This position is known as
   a. materialistic monism.
   b. idealistic monism.
   c. dualism.
   d. materialistic dualism.

4. _____ was a dualist.
   a. Aristotle
   b. Plato
   c. Democritus
   d. Descartes

5. According to the hydraulic model of the nervous system,
   a. nerves were like electrical wires that conducted electricity.
   b. nerves were hollow tubes that allowed animal spirits to flow through them.
   c. nerves were not responsible for behavior.
   d. none of the above

6. Descartes believed that the "seat of the soul" was located in
   a. the frontal lobes of the brain.
   b. animal spirits.
   c. the pineal gland.
   d. the left hemisphere.

7. Through their experiments, Fritsch and Hitzig showed that
   a. the muscle in a frog's leg can be made to move by stimulating the nerve connected to it.
   b. the rate of nerve conduction is about 90 feet per second.
   c. the left hemisphere controls speech.
   d. muscle movement is the result of brain stimulation.

8. Who discovered that nerves conduct electricity at a rate significantly slower than the speed of light?
   a. Hermann von Helmholtz
   b. Rene Descartes

    c. Luigi Galvani

    d. Phineas Gage

9. Broca's mute patient had damage to his
    a. pineal gland.
    b. frontal lobes.
    c. left hemisphere.
    d. motor cortex.

10. Which of the following can be taken as evidence for the idea that different functions are localized in different portions of the brain?
    a. Lashley's theory of equipotentiality
    b. Phineas Gage's personality change following frontal lobe damage
    c. Gall's theory of phrenology
    d. Galvani's demonstration that electricity could move the leg of a dead frog

11. With the exception of egg and sperm cells, all human body cells have
    a. 23 chromosomes.
    b. 46 chromosomes.
    c. 23 genes.
    d. 46 genes.

12. If you underwent a procedure to test for a particular disease that is triggered by a defective protein inherited from your parents, what SPECIFIC genetic component will they be looking for?
    a. a particular chromosome in your genome
    b. a particular gene on a chromosome
    c. a particular allele of a gene
    d. a particular base in an allele

13. Female humans have
    a. two X chromosomes.
    b. two Y chromosomes.
    c. one X and one Y chromosome.
    d. one X chromosome.

14. At six weeks after conception, a developing human is known as a(n)
    a. zygote.
    b. ova.
    c. embryo.
    d. fetus.

15. How many different bases make up DNA?
    a. 20
    b. 10
    c. 5
    d. 4

16. Enzymes
    a. are proteins.
    b. are produced as a result of genetic mechanisms.
    c. modify chemical reactions in the body.
    d. all of the above

17. John has type B blood, and Sue has type A blood. If they have a child, what blood type is impossible for that child to have?
    a. type A
    b. type O
    c. type AB
    d. All of the above are possible types.

18. If John and Sue have a baby with type A blood, which of the following statements is TRUE?
    a. The baby is homozygous for the dominant A allele.
    b. The baby is heterozygous for the dominant A allele.
    c. The baby has a recessive B allele.
    d. The baby has a dominant O allele.

19. Which of the following is FALSE regarding red-green color blindness?
    a. It is an X-linked trait.
    b. A female cannot be red-green color blind.
    c. Males are more likely to have it.
    d. It is a recessive trait.

20. A trait is polygenic if
    a. it is influenced by a gene on the X chromosome.
    b. it is influenced by a gene on the Y chromosome.
    c. it is influenced by more than one gene.
    d. it is influenced only by a single gene.

21. Which of the following is believed to have a genetic basis?
    a. sexual orientation
    b. drug addiction
    c. personality
    d. all of the above

22. Which of the following is TRUE of the human genome?
    a. Nearly all of the base-pair sequences have been mapped.
    b. Most of our DNA is directly involved in coding for proteins.
    c. The functions of all genes are well documented.
    d. There are about 80,000 genes.

23. The differential survival of organisms with more adaptive traits is known as
    a. sexual reproduction.
    b. predisposition.
    c. natural selection.
    d. heritability.

24. Which of the following is NOT true of gene activity?
    a. Once a gene becomes inactive, it remains inactive.
    b. Genes may fluctuate in the amount of protein they code for at different times.
    c. A gene may become active at only a certain time of the life cycle.
    d. The activity of a gene may be influenced by experience.

25. Which of the following traits has the HIGHEST degree of heritability?
    a. intelligence
    b. personality
    c. height
    d. occupational interests

26. If people from similar environments are sampled, estimates of heritability for traits will be _____ people from different environments are sampled.
    a. lower than if
    b. higher than if
    c. the same as when
    d. either a or b

27. The BEST way to think about the relationship among genes, environment, and intelligence is that
    a. environment is more important than genetic inheritance.
    b. our genes are more important than the environment.
    c. a person's intelligence is equally influenced by each parent's genes.
    d. genes set the potential range and environment determines the actual capacity.

Answers

Guided Review

1.	Neuroscience	41.	embryo
2.	Brain	42.	fetus
3.	schizophrenia	43.	DNA
4.	map	44.	thymine or cytosine
5.	Behavioral	45.	cytosine or thymine
6.	Wilhelm Wundt	46.	proteins
7.	mind-brain	47.	enzymes
8.	mind	48.	DNA
9.	monism	49.	cancer
10.	dualism	50.	alleles
11.	Aristotle	51.	AB
12.	Plato	52.	dominant
13.	models	53.	recessive
14.	Descartes	54.	homozygous
15.	pineal	55.	phenotype
16.	soul	56.	heterozygous
17.	empiricism	57.	males
18.	electricity	58.	X-linked (or sex-linked)
19.	Helmholtz	59.	polygenic
20.	localization	60.	learning
21.	Phineas Gage	61.	intelligence
22.	frontal (or prefrontal)	62.	genome
23.	Broca	63.	21,000
24.	left	64.	junk
25.	phrenology	65.	gene expression
26.	equipotentiality	66.	marker
27.	distributed	67.	Encyclopedia of DNA Elements
28.	conscious experience	68.	exons
29.	behavior therapy	69.	half
30.	brain	70.	combinations
31.	nature	71.	natural selection
32.	nurture	72.	rigid
33.	hereditary	73.	experiences
34.	Genes	74.	fraternal
35.	chromosomes	75.	heritability
36.	two	76.	50
37.	one	77.	40–50
38.	46	78.	environment
39.	sperm	79.	higher
40.	zygote	80.	vulnerability

Short Answer and Essay Questions

1. There are several possible answers, but all must mention that behavioral neuroscientists look for a connection between the nervous system and a specific behavior or set of behaviors. Though not completely separate in approaches, neuroscientists will tend to approach questions using molecular, genetic, functional, mechanistic, or physiological methods, whereas behavioral psychologists might use interviews, questionnaires, or therapeutic or cognitive methods.

2. Monism assumes that the mind and brain are composed of the same thing or substance. Most monists are materialistic, meaning that they believe everything, including the mind, is physical and therefore has no separate existence. Dualists, however, believe that while the brain is physical, the mind is also real, although not material, and exists separately from the brain. The problem with dualism is that it cannot explain how something nonphysical (the mind) can affect something physical (the body). The problem with materialistic monism is explaining how the brain causes subjective, mental experience. Most modern neuroscientists are materialistic monists. They believe that the mind is not a real entity but rather a concept we use to describe what our brains are doing. Therefore, the mind really is the brain or, more precisely, the activity of the brain. However, nonmaterial neuroscientists are keeping the brain-body debate alive by arguing that if behavior therapy can change brain function, then the mind must exist to have an impact on the brain. Material monists would argue that this phenomenon demonstrates that the brain affects the brain.

3. It was important because it showed that damage to a particular part of the brain resulted in disruption of some types of functions but not others. Following his accident, Gage was still able to speak and move normally, and he showed no change in memory or intelligence, but his personality changed, and he became impulsive and hard to deal with. This suggested that the part of the brain damaged by his injury was involved in some types of behaviors but not in others.

4. Localization is the theory that different brain areas are in control of different functions. Equipotentiality assumes that the brain as a whole contributes to all functions. Most brain researchers now believe that while specific functions are located in specific brain regions, several different brain areas work together to produce behaviors and experiences; thus, the brain's functions are both localized and distributed.

5. Genes direct the production of proteins. Those proteins can then influence behavior through their role as enzymes or in creating parts of the body. Genes are variable in their effects because they may not always be active and because they can vary the amount of a protein that is produced. They may also change functioning as the body ages. Alleles are different forms of genes, which necessarily make different proteins. An allele that encodes for an abnormal or nonfunctional protein (such as sickle cell anemia and its characteristically misshapen hemoglobin molecule) is what we look for when performing a genetic screening test on an individual.

6. Identical twins have the same genes, whereas fraternal twins have about 50% of their genes in common. If we compare identical twins and fraternal twins on some trait such as intelligence, and we find that identical twins are more similar than fraternal twins, then we can assume that genes are responsible for some of the similarity between the identical twins.

7. Individual answers will vary, but the following points need to be understood: (a) The presence (or absence) of a particular allele never completely corresponds with the presence (or absence) of a particular disorder. (b) Environmental factors play a key role in expression of defective genes. (c) Removing potentially cancerous tissue (that is currently healthy) does not completely remove the risk of developing the disease. (d) Surgical procedures carry their

own inherent risks—does the benefit gained through surgery outweigh the risks or costs of that procedure?

8. The evidence suggests that genes and environment are both important. The heritability of intelligence is around 50%, so this means that the environment contributes just as much as genes do. Furthermore, what genes contribute is better thought of as a predisposition; the environment will always have a significant impact.

Post-test

1. b 2. a 3. a 4. b 5. b 6. c 7. d 8. a 9. c 10. b 11. b 12. c 13. a 14. c
15. d 16. d 17. d 18. b 19. b 20. c 21. d 22. a 23. c 24. a 25. c 26. b 27. d

2 Communication Within the Nervous System

Learning Objectives

After reading this chapter, you will be able to

1. Identify the cells of the nervous system

2. Name the structures of neurons

3. Compare the functions of sensory, motor, and interneurons

4. Explain the roles of ions and the cell membrane in nervous system communication

5. Demonstrate how neurotransmitters are involved in communication between nervous system cells

6. Discuss how neurons work together to generate your experiences of the world

7. Illustrate the ways that excitation and inhibition are important to the functioning of the nervous system

The Cells That Make Us Who We Are

Summary and Guided Review

After studying this section in the text, fill in the blanks of the following summary.

The human brain consists of about 86 billion _____ (1) that carry messages and underlie our thoughts, feelings, and behaviors. It also contains many _____ (2) cells, which have a variety of functions and make up the other half of the cells in the brain. Neurons exist in many different forms, but they share similar structures and functions. The _____ (3), or cell body, is where the cell's nucleus containing DNA is located as well as other _____ (4) in the cytoplasm that carry out the functions of the neuron. Branching out from the cell body are _____ (5), structures that receive messages from other cells. A single tail-like structure called the _____ (6) extends away from the cell body and carries messages to other neurons. The axon _____ (7) contain chemical messengers called _____ (8) that enable the neuron to communicate with other cells. Although axons are quite thin (at most 0.1 mm in mammals), they can be up to _____ (9) m long. _____ (10) neurons, which are multipolar, carry information to muscles and organs, whereas _____ (11) neurons, which are either unipolar or bipolar, are stimulated by internal or environmental events and transmit information about those events to the brain and spinal cord. Neurons with short or no axons that transmit information between adjacent neurons in the same area of the brain are called _____ (12), and they are the most abundant type.

The membrane of a neuron is composed of a double layer of lipid molecules and contains _____ (13) molecules. Fluid is found both inside and outside the cell. Some molecules, such as oxygen, can pass through the membrane, while others are prevented from getting in; this property is known as selective _____ (14). Because ions (charged particles) are distributed in different concentrations on each side of the membrane, the membrane is _____ (15) (electrically charged). When the neuron is at rest, the inside is negatively charged relative to the outside, typically around _____ mV (16). This is known as the _____ (17) potential. _____ (18) and chloride ions are more concentrated outside the cell, and potassium ions and protein anions are more concentrated inside. Ions are attracted to the side of the membrane where their type is less abundant by the force of _____ (19). Because of _____ (20), ions are also attracted to the side of the membrane with the opposite charge (so positively charged ions are attracted to the negative side of the neuron). The _____-_____ (21) pump helps to maintain the balance of ions within and outside of the neuron.

Sodium ions are attracted inside the cell by both _____ (22) and _____ (23), but they are kept out because they cannot pass through the membrane. However, if the membrane is depolarized sufficiently by an activating stimulus past _____ (24), then the neuron will generate a(n) _____ (25) potential. Voltage-gated _____ (26) channels in the membrane open, allowing that ion to enter the neuron so rapidly that the cell becomes suddenly positively charged at the site of the depolarization. Shortly after this, the sodium channels close, and _____ (27) channels open and those ions leave the neuron, which hyperpolarizes the membrane. The potassium channels then close, and the membrane returns to resting potential as the small number of ions that moved diffuse away into the surrounding fluid. All of this occurs in about 1 _____ (28). Once it occurs, the depolarization spreads down the axon, and it causes adjacent voltage-gated sodium channels to open and _____ (29) another portion of the membrane. This wave of action potentials travels down the length of the axon until it reaches the axon _____ (30) and is converted into a neurotransmitter signal described later.

Depolarizations and action potentials are not identical. Whereas the initial depolarization or local potential is _____ (31), the action potential is not. Action potentials occur according to the _____-or-_____ (32) law, which means that a cell's action potentials are all of the same strength. Also, unlike local potentials, action potentials are _____ (33), meaning they maintain their full strength until they reach the axon terminal.

Immediately after an action potential occurs, the sodium channels are unable to open again, and therefore the cell is unable to produce another action potential right away. This is known as the _____ (34) refractory period. The cell is also subject to a relative refractory period, when the _____ (35) channels are still open and the inside is slightly more _____ (36) charged for a short time. In order for an action potential to occur at this time, the stimulus must be _____ (37) than normal. More intense stimuli will produce earlier and, therefore, more frequent action potentials; this is the _____ (38) law.

Puffer fish, scorpion, and snake venoms contain _____ (39) that affect potassium and sodium channels; other animal toxins also affect calcium channels. Sometimes blocking sodium channels can be useful, as is the case with _____ _____ (40), whereas opening potassium channels (causing hyperpolarizations) is one way that _____ _____ (41) work. A new strategy called _____ (42) uses light to control ion channels allows more precise targeting of neurons; potential applications range from tracing neural pathways to identifying circuits involved in a variety of behaviors.

Glial cells are an important component of the nervous system. For example, the fatty substance _____ (43) insulates axons and also increases conduction speed, which allows the nervous system to transmit signals faster without having to produce larger axons. In the central nervous system, myelin is made by _____ (44), while _____ (45) cells produce myelin for the rest of the nervous system. Action potentials occur only at the gaps between myelin cells known as nodes of _____ (46), where most of the cell's voltage-gated channels are located. The action potential jumps from one gap to the next rather than traveling smoothly down the entire length of the axon; this is known as _____ (47) conduction; it is faster and uses less _____ (48) than conduction in unmyelinated neurons. When myelin is destroyed, as in the disease _____ _____ (49), the neurons cease to function properly.

Glial cells, which are far more numerous than neurons, also perform a number of important functions. By acting as a scaffold, they _____ (50) developing neurons to their destinations. They support and keep mature neurons functioning properly. When deprived of glial cells, neurons lose some of their _____ (51) with other neurons. Glial cells that play an important role in learning are_____ (52).

Short Answer and Essay Questions

Answer the following questions.

1. Identify the key parts of a typical neuron and describe their functions.

2. How are sensory and motor neurons different in terms of their functions and structure?

3. What does it mean that the neural cell membrane is selectively permeable? How do water, oxygen, and carbon dioxide molecules enter the cell? How do ions and other substances necessary for functioning enter the cell?

4. Of all the ions involved in neuronal depolarization, sodium (Na^+) ions are most strongly attracted across the membrane. Give two reasons for this.

5. Identify the two "key players" or ions in the action potential. Describe the sequence of events that occur during the action potential.

6. When an axon is depolarized to threshold, it fires an action potential at the site of depolarization. How does that action potential spread to the rest of the axon? Why does that action potential spread in only one direction (toward the axon terminals)?

7. One way in which the intensity of a stimulus is coded or represented in the sensory neuron is by the frequency with which action potentials are generated. For example, a more intense stimulus produces more action potentials per second than a less intense one, although the action potentials themselves are of the same strength. What role does the relative refractory period play in this effect?

8. Explain why action potentials are conducted more quickly, and more efficiently in terms of energy used, in myelinated cells than in unmyelinated cells.

9. What are some functions (other than myelination) of glial cells?

How Neurons Communicate With Each Other

Summary and Guided Review

After studying this section in the text, fill in the blanks of the following summary.

The fact that neurons are not physically attached to one another was discovered by Spanish anatomist _____ (53) in the 19th century with the help of _____ (54) stain that identifies a small number of particular neurons. In the 20th century, _____ (55) showed that neurons communicate with one another chemically. He did this by first stimulating the vagus nerve of a frog heart, which resulted in the heart rate _____ (56). Then he collected the salt solution he had placed in the heart and administered it to another heart, which also _____ (57) its rate of beating. Later research has shown that neurons can also communicate by electricity and by gas. At chemical synapses the _____ (58) are located in small sacs in the axon terminals called _____ (59). When an action potential reaches the axon terminal, _____ (60) ions enter the cell and cause the vesicles to fuse with the presynaptic cell membrane, dumping their contents into the synaptic cleft. The neurotransmitter molecules then attach to receptors on the _____ (61) membrane, causing ion channels to open and producing a graded potential. An immediate response in the postsynaptic cell is seen when _____ (62) receptors are opened, while prolonged effects follow the opening of _____ (63) receptors.

Neurotransmitters can affect the postsynaptic cell by causing hyperpolarization (inhibition) or _____ (64) (excitation). Inhibition in the nervous system is important for many reasons, including its role in controlling excitation. Neurotransmitters that cause _____ (65) channels to open lead to EPSPs of the soma and dendrites, whereas those that cause potassium and/or chloride channels to open lead to _____ (66). Both of these are called _____ (67) potentials, and when they reach the voltage-sensitive axonal _____ (68), they either increase or decrease the rate of action potentials. EPSPs may ultimately have inhibitory effects, if they increase output to inhibitory neurons. The stimulant drug _____ (69) is believed to calm hyperactive children by increasing frontal lobe activation, which in turns inhibits behavior.

A single neuron is continuously receiving messages from as many as _____ (70) other cells, most of which have only very small effects on the cell voltage. The incoming information is integrated in the soma of the postsynaptic neuron. When two or more postsynaptic potentials arrive simultaneously but at different parts of the cell, _____ (71) summation occurs. Because the effect of a graded potential takes a while to dissipate, when postsynaptic potentials arrive in close succession, _____ (72) summation can occur. A good way of thinking about the neuron is that it serves as both an information integrator in handling information from a variety of sources and as a(n) _____ (73) maker about whether it will fire and at what rate.

Once it has attached to the postsynaptic receptor and had its effect on the postsynaptic cell, the neurotransmitter is _____ (74) in one of three ways. In the first, the presynaptic cell reabsorbs the neurotransmitter using a process called _____ (75). In the second, the neurotransmitter is broken down by an _____ (76), such as acetylcholinesterase for the neurotransmitter acetylcholine. In the third, glial cells actively absorb excess transmitters. Drugs may affect behavior by interfering with these mechanisms in some way.

Synaptic transmission can be altered by a third neuron's _____ (77) synapses onto the presynaptic neuron's terminals, which affect the release of the neurotransmitter from the presynaptic neuron through presynaptic excitation or _____ (78). Additionally, _____ (79) on the presynaptic axon terminals can monitor the amount of neurotransmitters in the synapse and adjust the cell's release of it, and the postsynaptic membrane regulates the number and _____ (80) of its receptors. _____ (81) cells also regulate synaptic activity in a number of ways, including absorbing free neurotransmitters from the synapse and releasing their own neurotransmitters.

There are many different neurotransmitters, and each may have different effects through different receptor types. For example, acetylcholine has an excitatory effect at _____ (82) receptors, whereas at _____ (83) receptors, it may have excitatory, inhibitory, or more complex long-term effects. A single neuron can release more than one type of neurotransmitter at the same synapse. One of these may be _____ (84) and have an immediate effect on the postsynaptic cell; the others (such as neuropeptides) enhance the effects of the first through more prolonged mechanisms. Some cells appear to release two fast-acting transmitters at the same time, and some release both excitatory and inhibitory transmitters at different _____ (85).

Many drugs affect neural functioning by acting like neurotransmitters at the synapse. Nicotine, for example, is a(n) _____ (86) at acetylcholine receptors. Amazonian Indians tip their darts with an acetylcholine antagonist, _____ (87), to paralyze animals. Thankfully, this toxin is destroyed when the animals are cooked and eaten.

It is difficult to understand how neural activity controls behavior if we limit ourselves to simple trains of impulses in a chain of individual neurons. However, researchers have been able to record temporal variations in firing during taste stimulation that form a(n) _____ (88) that can then be duplicated as electrical pulses to produce the same behavior in other animals. Complex processing such as color vision or sound discrimination requires groups of neurons that function together as a(n) _____ (89). An exciting new initiative focused on mapping the brain's connections is the _____ _____ (90) Project. This collaborative effort among scientists at multiple universities hopes to better understand disorders such as schizophrenia and _____ (91).

Short Answer and Essay Questions

Answer the following questions.

10. Describe the experiment by Otto Loewi. How did he arrive at the conclusion that neurons communicate via chemical transmission?

11. What happens to a cell's polarity and firing rate when an IPSP occurs? Why does the firing rate change?

12. Why is the model consisting of a single chain of neurons inadequate for explaining how the brain works? Give two reasons. (Hint: In your answer, consider both postsynaptic integration and how synaptic activity may be regulated.)

13. Explain temporal and spatial summation in terms of what happens at the synapse, and how these processes impact the initiation of an action potential.

Post-test

Use these multiple-choice questions to check your understanding of the chapter.

1. Scientists estimate that there are about _____ neurons in the brain.
   a. 1 million
   b. 86 million
   c. 1 billion
   d. 86 billion

2. Neurons account for _____ of all the cells in the nervous system.
   a. 10%
   b. 25%
   c. 50%
   d. 75%

3. The nucleus of a neural cell is located in the
   a. axon.
   b. dendrites.

    c. soma.

    d. axon hillock.

4. A neuron that transmits information between the central nervous system and a muscle is called a(n)

    a. motor neuron.

    b. sensory neuron.

    c. interneuron.

    d. projection neuron.

5. A _____ neuron has an axon and numerous dendrites projecting away from the cell body.

    a. bipolar

    b. multipolar

    c. unipolar

    d. monopolar

6. Which of the following statements regarding interneurons is TRUE?

    a. They receive input directly from the external environment.

    b. They send information across long distances.

    c. They may have no axon at all.

    d. They are found only in the brain.

7. The neural membrane is selectively permeable to all of the following substances EXCEPT

    a. sodium.

    b. potassium.

    c. oxygen.

    d. chloride.

8. When a neuron is at rest, _____ ions are more plentiful outside of the cell.

    a. Na^+

    b. K^+

    c. anions

    d. all of the above

9. The TYPICAL resting potential of a neuron is

    a. −70 V.

    b. −35 mV.

    c. 70 mV.

    d. −70 mV.

10. When the cell is at rest, K^+ ions are strongly attracted across the cell membrane to the outside of the cell

    a. mostly because of electrostatic pressure.

    b. mostly because of the force of diffusion.

    c. equally because of electrostatic pressure and force of diffusion.

    d. by neither electrostatic pressure nor force of diffusion.

11. All of the following are able to pass through the membrane under certain conditions EXCEPT

    a. Na^+

    b. Cl^-

    c. K^+

    d. A^-

12. Which of the following statements regarding the sodium-potassium pump is FALSE?
    a. It requires a lot of energy.
    b. It works against diffusion.
    c. It pumps sodium into the cell.
    d. It helps maintain the resting potential.

13. Neurons undergo depolarization when
    a. K^+ ions enter the cell.
    b. Na^+ ions enter the cell.
    c. either K^+ or Na^+ ions enter the cell.
    d. Cl^- ions leave the cell.

14. Depolarization is MOST similar to
    a. hypopolarization.
    b. hyperpolarization.
    c. action potential.
    d. electrical gradient.

15. When the neuron is at resting potential, Na^+ ions are strongly attracted across the cell membrane because of
    a. electrostatic pressure.
    b. diffusion.
    c. both electrostatic pressure and diffusion.
    d. neither electrostatic pressure or diffusion.

16. A neuron will fire an action potential when it is
    a. depolarized by 10 mV.
    b. hyperpolarized by 10 mV.
    c. depolarized by 15 mV.
    d. depolarized to its threshold.

17. The outflow of K^+ ions during an action potential results in
    a. hypopolarization.
    b. hyperpolarization.
    c. depolarization.
    d. another action potential.

18. The action potentials generated by a specific neuron are all the same strength, yet humans experience events that vary in intensity (i.e., strong versus weak smells). What helps to account for this variation in experience?
    a. the length of individual action potentials
    b. the distance that an action potential travels along one neuron's axon
    c. the number of action potentials generated by a single neuron in a period of time
    d. the degree of depolarization that occurs during a neuron's action potential

19. Which of the following statements regarding the absolute refractory period is FALSE?
    a. The potassium channels are closed and cannot be opened.
    b. The sodium channels are closed and cannot be opened.
    c. An action potential cannot be generated.
    d. It ensures that the action potential will travel only in one direction.

20. During the relative refractory period,
    a. the neuron is hyperpolarized.
    b. a stronger stimulus may result in another action potential.

    c. potassium channels are open.

    d. all of the above

21. The _____ the axon, the _____ the action potential.

    a. thicker; slower

    b. thicker; faster

    c. longer; slower

    d. thinner; faster

22. In the central nervous system, myelin is formed by

    a. Schwann cells.

    b. protein.

    c. oligodendrocytes.

    d. vesicles.

23. In myelinated axons,

    a. action potentials occur along the entire length of the axon.

    b. action potentials occur only at the nodes of Ranvier.

    c. action potentials occur only where the myelin is in contact with the axon.

    d. action potentials travel more slowly than on unmyelinated axons.

24. Myelination results in all of the following EXCEPT

    a. increased capacitance.

    b. increased speed of conduction.

    c. saltatory conduction.

    d. less work required by the sodium-potassium pump.

25. Which of the following was not mentioned as a function of glial cells?

    a. storing neurotransmitters

    b. guiding developing axons

    c. assisting in the development of synapses

    d. transmitting action potentials

26. Who discovered that neurons are separate cells and are NOT in contact with each other?

    a. Ramón y Cajal

    b. Golgi

    c. Loewi

    d. Dale

27. Who demonstrated that synaptic transmission is chemical?

    a. Ramón y Cajal

    b. Golgi

    c. Loewi

    d. Dale

28. What scientific evidence supported the conclusion that chemical signals are used for communication across the synapse in most neurons?

    a. the observation of action potentials in response to Na+ channels opening

    b. the observation that fluid surrounding the heart of a frog could produce heart rate changes when injected into another frog

    c. the observation that tetrodotoxin prevents an action potential from being generated

    d. the observation that local and general anesthetics produce different effects

29. When an action potential reaches an axon terminal, _____ ions enter the cell and trigger the release of the neurotransmitter.
    a. Na^+
    b. K^+
    c. Cl^-
    d. Ca^{2+}

30. Fast-acting receptors involved in muscle activity and sensory processing are referred to as
    a. metabotropic.
    b. autoreceptors.
    c. ionotropic.
    d. presynaptic.

31. Under normal circumstances, the neurotransmitter molecules released by a *single* neuron can do all of the following EXCEPT
    a. cause ion channels to open.
    b. trigger a graded depolarization.
    c. trigger an action potential.
    d. inhibit the postsynaptic cell.

32. An IPSP will occur if
    a. sodium channels open.
    b. potassium channels open.
    c. chloride channels open.
    d. b or c

33. Action potentials are first produced
    a. at the axon hillock.
    b. in the soma.
    c. in the dendrites.
    d. in the axon terminals.

34. In order for spatial summation to occur,
    a. several EPSPs must arrive at the same time from different inputs.
    b. several EPSPs and/or IPSPs must arrive at the same time from different inputs.
    c. several EPSPs must arrive in quick succession from a single input.
    d. EPSPs and IPSPs must arrive in quick succession from a single input.

35. If a neuron has a resting potential of −70 mV and a threshold of −60 mV, which of the following combinations of simultaneous postsynaptic potentials will result in an action potential?
    a. 15 EPSPs of 1 mV each and 20 IPSPs of 1 mV each
    b. 50 EPSPs of .5 mV each and 20 IPSPs of .5 mV each
    c. 50 EPSPs of .2 mV each and 15 IPSPs of .2 mV each
    d. 25 EPSPs of 1 mV each and 20 IPSPs of 1 mV each

36. Acetylcholine is removed from the synapse by
    a. reuptake by the presynaptic neuron.
    b. absorption by the postsynaptic neuron.
    c. enzymatic deactivation.
    d. absorption by glial cells.

37. Neurotransmitters interact with receptor sites like a
    a. key into a lock.
    b. slip cover over a sofa.
    c. bird sitting next to another bird on a wire.
    d. train passing another train in the night.

38. Which of the following statements regarding nicotinic receptors is FALSE?
    a. They are inhibitory.
    b. They are stimulated by acetylcholine.
    c. They are found in the brain.
    d. They are found in muscles.

39. Regarding the types of neurotransmitters that a neuron can release, which of the following statements is FALSE?
    a. A neuron may release more than one fast-acting neurotransmitter.
    b. There are neurons that are incapable of releasing any neurotransmitters at all.
    c. A neuron may release one fast-acting and one slower-acting neurotransmitter.
    d. A neuron may release one fast-acting and several slower-acting neurotransmitters.

40. Which of the following is an antagonist at opiate receptors?
    a. nicotine
    b. muscarine
    c. naloxone
    d. curare

41. Sammy has just taken a drug that acts as an agonist at GABA receptors. Which of the following is Sammy most likely to experience?
    a. increased alertness
    b. greater calmness
    c. increased pain sensitivity
    d. extreme hunger

42. The ability of neurons to carry information is increased by
    a. variations in the size of the neural impulse.
    b. its maintenance of the same firing rate regardless of the stimulus.
    c. the neuron's consistency in producing excitation or inhibition.
    d. varied time intervals of neural bursts.

43. The solution to the problem that chains of single neurons are inadequate to handle the brain's tasks is
    a. neural networks.
    b. artificial neural networks.
    c. labeled lines.
    d. temporal coding.

Answers

Guided Review

1.	neurons	38.	rate
2.	glial	39.	neurotoxins
3.	soma	40.	local anesthetics
4.	organelles	41.	general anesthetics
5.	dendrites	42.	optogenetics
6.	axon	43.	myelin
7.	terminals	44.	oligodendrocytes
8.	neurotransmitters	45.	Schwann
9.	5	46.	Ranvier
10.	Motor	47.	saltatory
11.	sensory	48.	energy
12.	interneurons	49.	multiple sclerosis
13.	protein	50.	guide
14.	permeability	51.	synapses or terminals
15.	polarized	52.	astrocytes
16.	−70	53.	Ramón y Cajal
17.	resting	54.	Golgi's
18.	Na^+ or Sodium	55.	Loewi
19.	diffusion	56.	decreasing
20.	electrostatic pressure	57.	decreased
21.	sodium-potassium	58.	neurotransmitters
22.	diffusion or electrostatic pressure	59.	vesicles
23.	electrostatic pressure or diffusion	60.	calcium or Ca
24.	threshold	61.	postsynaptic
25.	action	62.	ionotropic
26.	sodium	63.	metabotropic
27.	potassium	64.	depolarization or hypopolarization
28.	millisecond	65.	Na^+ or sodium
29.	depolarize or hypopolarize	66.	IPSPs
30.	terminals	67.	graded
31.	graded or decremental	68.	hillock
32.	all-or-none	69.	Ritalin
33.	ungraded or nondecremental	70.	1,000
34.	absolute	71.	spatial
35.	K^+ or potassium	72.	temporal
36.	negatively	73.	decision
37.	stronger	74.	inactivated

75. reuptake

76. enzyme

77. axoaxonic

78. inhibition

79. autoreceptors

80. sensitivity

81. Glial

82. nicotinic

83. muscarinic

84. fast-acting

85. terminals or synapses

86. agonist

87. curare

88. code

89. neural network

90. Human Connectome

91. autism

Short Answer and Essay Questions

1. A typical neuron has a cell body or soma, containing the nucleus (which contains the genetic material) and organelles that keep the cell alive and functioning. Dendrites are the receiving components of the cell, whereas the axon carries information to the terminals. The terminals contain transmitters that communicate with the next cell.

2. Sensory neurons carry information about internal and environmental stimuli to the central nervous system, whereas motor neurons carry messages away from the central nervous system to the muscle and glandular cells of the body. Structurally, sensory neurons are usually bipolar or unipolar. Motor neurons are usually multipolar, with dendritic branches extending in several directions.

3. A membrane that is selectively permeable allows only certain substances to pass through it. Neurons can be readily permeated by water, oxygen, and carbon dioxide but not by other substances that they need for proper functioning. Protein channels embedded within the membrane control the flow of ions and various kinds of molecules. These substances can get in only when the protein channels are open.

4. Na^+ ions are more concentrated on the outside of the cell, so they are attracted across the membrane by the force of diffusion. And, because they are positively charged, they are also attracted into the cell because the inside of it is negative relative to the outside (electrostatic pressure).

5. If the excitatory inputs exceed the inhibitory inputs to an adequate degree, the cell will depolarize to a threshold at which sodium channels will open, and sodium will enter, further depolarizing the cell. Potassium channels will also open, and as potassium leaves the axon the cell will return to the resting potential and actually become hyperpolarized for a time.

6. The action potential spreads because it causes the sodium channels near it to open, thereby depolarizing the adjacent part of the membrane to threshold. This propagates the action potential across the length of the axon. The action potential cannot spread backward toward the soma because once the sodium channels at the site of depolarization close, they cannot be opened for a brief period (the absolute refractory period).

7. During the relative refractory period, a neuron is slightly more negative inside than while at rest, and so it requires a stronger stimulus to initiate an action potential. Therefore, stimuli of stronger intensities will have a greater effect than those of weak intensities. A stronger stimulus will cause the neuron to fire again earlier in the recovery period and, therefore, more frequently.

8. The axons of myelinated cells contain gaps between the myelin where the action potential actually occurs. In between those gaps, the cell undergoes a graded depolarization that spreads more quickly than an action potential. This depolarization then triggers the action potential at the next gap. Because the action potential is generated at fewer points along the axon and transmission is faster between nodes, it travels more quickly. Furthermore, fewer ions are exchanged; therefore, the cell does not have to work as hard (via the sodium-potassium pump) to restore the resting potential.

9. Glial cells provide support and guidance for developing neurons. They also support synapses (neurons lose synapses in the absence of glial cells). They absorb and recycle neurotransmitters from the synapse. They release glutamate into the synapse, which may alter the function of neurons.

10. First, Loewi isolated the hearts of two frogs and kept them beating. Then he stimulated the vagus nerve of one heart, which caused it to slow down. He transferred fluid from this heart to the other heart, which also slowed down. Then he caused the first heart to speed up and repeated the procedure of transferring fluid. The second heart also increased its rate of contractions. He concluded that something in the fluid, some chemical released by the nerve he stimulated, had caused the change in heart rate.

11. The cell becomes slightly hyperpolarized, and this makes it more difficult for the neuron to fire. This is because in order for the cell to be depolarized to threshold, a stronger than normal stimulus (perhaps in the form of several additional EPSPs) is required.

12. First of all, a single postsynaptic neuron usually receives information from more than one presynaptic neuron. Therefore, its activity is a result of the integration of excitatory and inhibitory information it receives from all of these different sources. Second, synaptic activity may be modulated by a number of mechanisms, including glial cells, autoreceptors, and presynaptic excitation or inhibition from a third neuron.

13. Temporal summation occurs when two or more postsynaptic potentials occurring in close temporal (time) proximity have a cumulative effect on a neuron. For example, while a single EPSP will not cause a neuron to fire or increase a cell's firing rate, several EPSPs occurring very close together in time will have a cumulative effect, increasing the chances that an action potential will occur. Spatial summation occurs when simultaneous postsynaptic potentials arriving at nearby locations influence the likelihood of firing or the firing rate of a neuron. For example, although a single IPSP may not have much effect on the postsynaptic cell, several IPSPs occurring together may reduce the frequency of action potentials. An example in real life: A child may clean up his or her room after being asked several times in a row by the same person (temporal) or after several family members asking at the same time (spatial).

Post-test

1. d 2. c 3. c 4. a 5. b 6. c 7. c 8. a 9. d 10. b 11. d 12. c 13. b 14. a
15. c 16. d 17. b 18. c 19. a 20. d 21. b 22. c 23. b 24. a 25. d 26. a
27. c 28. b 29. d 30. c 31. c 32. d 33. a 34. b 35. b 36. c 37. a 38. a
39. b 40. c 41. b 42. d 43. a

3 The Organization and Functions of the Nervous System

Learning Objectives

After reading this chapter, you will be able to

1. Identify the components of the central nervous system

2. Name the structures in the forebrain, midbrain, and hindbrain

3. Predict how damage to specific brain structures will impact specific behaviors

4. Describe the components that protect the brain from damage

5. Examine the functions of the peripheral nervous system divisions

6. Explain how the peripheral and central nervous systems interact in generating experiences and behavior

7. Summarize the changes that the nervous system undergoes during typical development

8. Illustrate the changes that occur in the nervous system as the result of experiences

The Central Nervous System

Summary and Guided Review

After studying this section in the text, fill in the blanks of the following summary.

The central nervous system (CNS) includes the __Brain__ (1) and the __Spinal__ __cord__ (2). In the CNS a bundle of axons is called a(n) __tract__ (3) and a group of cell bodies is known as a(n) __nucleus__ (4). In the peripheral nervous system (PNS), an axon bundle is called a(n) __nerve__ (5) and a group of cell bodies is referred to as a(n) __ganglion__ (6). Early in development, the CNS begins as a hollow tube and quickly differentiates into a spinal cord and three brain areas, the __forebrain__ (7) (which in humans becomes the largest area), the __midbrain__ (8), and the most ventral area called the __hindbrain__ (9).

The forebrain contains two __cerebral__ (10) hemispheres; the __thalamus__ (11), which receives sensory information; and the underlying __hypothalamus__ (12). The hemispheres are separated by the longitudinal __fissure__ (13). For the most part, each hemisphere receives information from and controls movement in the __opposite__ (14) side of the body. The outer layer of the cerebral hemispheres, the __cortex__ (15), is wrinkled in appearance and contains many __gyri__ (16) (ridges) and __sulci/fissures__ (17) (grooves). The surface is composed mostly of cell __bodies__ (18), which accounts for its gray appearance. Its convoluted structure allows for greater __surface__ (19) area and more efficient connections for axons. The interior of the cortex, composed mostly of axons, appears __white__ (20). Furthermore, the cortex is arranged in six __layers__ (21) in most areas. The layers are organized in __columns__ (22) that run perpendicular to the cortical surface area; these provide a vertical unity to the layers and are considered the primary __information__ (23) processing unit in the cortex.

Among humans, having a larger brain is not usually an indication of superior __intelligence__ (24). In a comparison of different species, the overall size of the brain is in proportion to the body, with larger animals having larger brains. The intelligence of a species appears to be more related to the ___convolutions___ (25) of the brain rather than its size. Among the most intelligent species, the cortex is ___larger___ (26) in proportion to other brain areas. The nervous system itself is arranged in a(n) ___hierarchy___ (27), with complexity in structure and in the behaviors controlled increasing from the spinal cord up to the cortex.

Each hemisphere is divided into four lobes, and each lobe contributes to somewhat different functions. One function that the ___frontal___ (28) lobes are involved in is movement, as well as some of the most complex human capabilities. Different parts of the body are mapped onto areas of the ___precentral gyrus___ (29), the location of the primary motor cortex, in the form of a(n) ___homunculus___ (30), such that the parts of the body that are capable of fine motor movements (such as the fingers) are represented by a larger portion of the brain. The primary motor cortex also works with neighboring ___secondary___ (31) motor areas and subcortical structures such as the ___basal ganglia___ (32) in the control of movement. ___Broca's___ (33) area, another frontal lobe structure, is involved in ___speech___ (34) production and grammar.

The ___prefrontal___ (35) cortex, which is the anterior portion of the frontal lobe and the largest area of the human brain, contributes to a number of cognitive functions. Damage to this area can lead to many types of problems, including an inability to plan or organize actions, learn from experience, control impulsive behavior, or make decisions. It is also believed to be involved in mental illnesses such as schizophrenia and ___depression___ (36). In the 1940s and 1950s, it was common practice to "disconnect" the prefrontal cortex from the rest of the brain through a procedure known as a(n) ___lobotomy___ (37). Over 40,000 of these were performed in the United States on people with mental illnesses of various types. The success of this procedure was limited, and it eventually fell into disfavor, especially when effective ___drug___ (38) treatments became available in the 1950s. The importance of the frontal lobes was clearly demonstrated in the case of ___Phineas Gage___ (39), who suffered specific deficits as a result of an accident in which a dynamite tamping iron pierced his skull and brain.

The parietal lobe contains the postcentral gyrus, which includes the ___somatosensory___ (40) cortex, onto which the body senses are projected. This area is structured to represent the body in much the same way as the primary motor cortex. The parietal lobe ___association areas___ (41) provide further processing of sensory information, integrating several different types of sensory input. A person with damage to this area may experience ___neglect___ (42), a condition in which objects, people, and activity on the side opposite the damage are ignored.

The ___temporal___ (43) lobe contains the auditory cortex and (on the left hemisphere) ___Wernicke's___ (44) area, which is involved in language comprehension and production. Visual identification of objects is carried out in the ___inferior___ (45) temporal cortex; people with damage to this area have difficulty recognizing objects by sight, including familiar people. People have reported experiencing specific events or memories when parts of the temporal cortex have been stimulated during brain surgery. Most of this brain stimulation research was conducted by the neurosurgeon ___Penfield___ (46).

The entire occipital lobe is devoted to the sense of ___vision___ (47). The primary projection area is organized like a map of the retina (the back part of the eye). The remainder of the occipital cortical areas process different components of images, such as color, form, and movement.

Other major structures of the forebrain include the ___thalamus___ (48), which serves as a relay station for sensory information, and the ___hypothalamus___ (49), which is important in emotions and motivated behavior. The hypothalamus controls the ___pituitary___ (50) or master gland, which in turn controls all other glands in the body. Bodily cycles such as sleep are controlled in part by the _____Pineal_____ (51) gland.

    One way in which the hemispheres communicate with each other is via structures such as the corpus _Callosum_ (52), which is found at the bottom of the longitudinal fissure. In cases of severe epilepsy, the corpus callosum may be surgically disconnected. People who have had this procedure can lead normal lives, but they show that, to a certain extent, the two hemispheres have different functions: The left hemisphere is more involved in _language_ (53) and the right in _spatial_ (54) tasks and recognizing faces. Fluid-filled cavities called _ventricles_ (55) are located in the brain. They contain _cerebrospinal_ (56) fluid, which transports nutrients to and wastes away from the CNS.

    The midbrain contains several important structures. The superior and inferior _colliculi_ (57) are involved in eye movements and locating sounds, respectively. The midbrain also contains areas involved in movement; degeneration of cells in the _substantia nigra_ (58) is implicated in Parkinson's disease. The ventral _tegmental_ (59) area plays a role in reward. The tube-shaped midbrain and hindbrain make up the brain _stem_ (60). The hindbrain includes the _medulla_ (61), which is involved in vital functions such as respiration and keeping the heart beating, and the _pons_ (62), which is involved in sleep and arousal. The _reticular_ (63) formation is a collection of nuclei running through the core of the midbrain and hindbrain. On the back of the brain stem is the _cerebellum_ (64), which physically resembles the cerebral cortex and is essential in a number of motor and cognitive activities.

    The spinal cord communicates between the brain and the body; it contains _pattern generators_ (65), which are motor programs for repetitive behaviors such as walking, and is responsible for certain reflexive behaviors. The spinal cord contains ascending _sensory_ (66) tracts, which enter the spinal cord through the _dorsal_ (67) roots, and descending _motor_ (68) tracts, which exit the spinal cord through the _ventral_ (69) roots. Some of the sensory neurons form connections directly or indirectly with motor neurons, which allow for spinal _reflexes_ (70).

    The CNS is protected in a number of ways. It is covered by the _meninges_ (71) (three-layered membrane), and the _cerebrospinal_ (72) fluid cushions the brain. Harmful substances are prevented from entering the brain by the _blood-brain_ (73) barrier. The cells making up the walls of many of the _capillaries_ (74) serving the brain are tightly joined, which keeps many substances from passing through them. One area of the brain that is not protected in this way is the area _postrema_ (75); when toxins are detected here, vomiting occurs.

Short Answer and Essay Questions

Answer the following questions.

1. What is a major advantage of the convoluted structure of the cerebral cortex?

2. Why is brain size alone not a good indication of intelligence of different species of animals (e.g., humans and elephants)? Explain what characteristics of an animal's brain are found to correlate with intelligence.

3. How are the primary motor and somatosensory cortices organized in relation to the body areas they receive information from or send information to? What determines how much space on the cortex is devoted to a particular area of the body?

4. What is the condition known as *neglect?* What is the likely cause of it?

5. Identify three of the many functions of the temporal lobe.

6. Name three areas in the midbrain and hindbrain that are involved in motor function.

7. Why is the blood-brain barrier important? Explain how the structure of the blood-brain barrier helps keep some harmful substances out of the brain. Why is it advantageous that the area postrema NOT be protected by the barrier?

The Peripheral Nervous System

Summary and Guided Review

After studying this section in the text, fill in the blanks of the following summary.

The peripheral nervous system (PNS) is composed of spinal and __Cranial__ (76) nerves; it can be divided into the __Somatic__ (77) nervous system, which is involved in the control of movement and carries sensory information to the CNS, and the autonomic nervous system (ANS), which is involved in the control of smooth muscles, __organs__ (78), and glands. Two of the cranial nerves are sometimes considered part of the brain: the __olfactory__ (79) nerve, which carries information about smell, and the __optic__ (80) nerve, which carries information about vision.

The ANS has two divisions: the __sympathetic__ (81), which mobilizes bodily resources, and the __parasympathetic__ (82), which helps to restore energy. The sympathetic nervous system is highly coordinated due to the sympathetic __ganglionic__ __chains__ (83). Most of the affected organs are stimulated together when this system is activated. In general, the two branches of the ANS have opposite effects on organs. For example, sympathetic activation __increases__ (84) heart rate, while parasympathetic activation __decreases__ (85) it. However, both branches are active at the same time, but one may have a stronger effect at one time than the other.

Short Answer and Essay Questions

Answer the following questions.

8. From the information provided in Figure 3.20, which cranial nerves appear to be involved in eye movement? Which are probably involved in speaking?

9. Why is the sympathetic nervous system able to act in a more coordinated fashion than the parasympathetic? What advantage is there for the coordinated action of the sympathetic nervous system?

Development and Change in the Nervous System

Summary and Guided Review

After studying this section in the text, fill in the blanks of the following summary.

Once the neural tube has formed, the nervous system develops in stages. During the first stage, __proliferation__ (86), new neurons are formed at a high rate in the

Ventricular (87) zone of the neural tube. In the second stage, the new neurons migrate toward the outer layers of the tube with the support of *radial* (88) glial cells. During this time, the neurons have the potential to become many different types of neurons. The next stage is *circuit formation* (89), during which axons find their way to target cells and form synapses with them. The chemical environment of the developing nervous system is detected by *growth cones* (90) on the ends of the axons; they are attracted to certain locations and repelled from others by the chemicals. The genes *Robo* (91) 1 and 3 are involved in getting neurons to their final destination. The nervous system produces many more neurons than it needs, and during the next stage of development, *circuit pruning* (92), synapses are eliminated and neurons die, leaving only those that are functional and useful. A neuron is more likely to survive this stage if it fires at the same time as its neighbors, in part because postsynaptic neurons release *neurotrophins* (93) that enhance the development of presynaptic neurons. Circuit pruning may occur before birth, even in the absence of environmental input. In the visual system, for example, waves of activity sweep through the *retina* (94), strengthening the connections that have been formed. As synapses are formed, most neurons lose *plasticity* (95), or the ability to undergo modification, while others remain flexible throughout the life span.

During the formation of the nervous system, disruption of development can have serious consequences. For example, periventricular *heterotopia* (96), a genetic disorder, produces a smooth cortex, which usually results in severe epilepsy and mental retardation. Prenatal exposure to *alcohol* (97) consumed by the mother may result in neurons migrating to the wrong place or failing to become appropriately organized. Babies with fetal alcohol syndrome often have small and malformed *brains* (98) and are mentally impaired. Ionizing *radiation* (99) is another environmental agent that can interfere with proliferation and migration, particularly if the mother is exposed between the 8th and 15th weeks of pregnancy. The nervous system is not considered fully mature until *myelination* (100) is complete, which happens sometime in late *adolescence* (101) or adulthood. This process begins with the lower areas of the brain, and the last areas to mature are the *frontal* (102) lobes.

Throughout the life span, the nervous system may undergo *reorganization* (103) in response to experience. Through this process, some synapses may be lost while new ones are formed, and areas of the brain devoted to specific functions may actually expand. Reorganization can even violate the doctrine of specific *nerve energies* (104), which states that input to a particular sensory area will always result in the same type of sensation. In the blind, for example, some of the visual cortex may be taken over by the *somatosensory* (105) system, so the visual cortex actually participates in reading Braille. Sometimes reorganization can have detrimental effects, such as when a limb is amputated and the somatosensory neurons from nearby body parts take over the part of the cortex that was devoted to the missing limb; this is thought to be responsible for *phantom* (106) pain that amputees sometimes experience. Experiments with cats have revealed that if an animal sees only vertical stripes during early development, it will not be able later to detect objects that are oriented *horizontally* (107).

Two common causes of damage in the adult brain are *strokes* (108), brain damage caused by a lack of blood supply to part of the brain, and *traumatic brain injuries* (109), which often occur in a car accident or fall. Mild TBIs can occur through head injuries that are sustained in sports activities and can have long-lasting effects on memory and *attention* (110). Although the National Football League has received a great deal of attention for retired players showing signs of TBI, this type of brain injury occurs in other sports, such as woman's soccer. Repeatedly hitting a soccer ball with the head has been correlated with abnormalities in brain _____white_____ _____matter_____ (111).

Recovery from damage in the nervous system is limited. Although in some species, such as _____amphibians_____ (112), damaged neurons easily regenerate, this is not true in all animals. In mammals, regeneration involving the regrowth of severed _____axons_____ (113) occurs in the peripheral nervous system with the help of myelin. In the CNS, however, regrowth is unlikely because of the chemical environment, scar tissue, and the presence of glial and _____immune_____ (114) cells. Also, in most parts of the nervous system, new cells are not produced once proliferation ends. However, new cell production, or _____neurogenesis_____ (115) can be induced in the hippocampus and olfactory bulb by disease-related damage, and is visible when researchers stain the brain with (BrdU) bromodeoxyuridine (116). It may be possible to enhance regeneration as a treatment for brain damage. bromodeoxyuridine

Many people who suffer brain damage do recover some of the functions lost initially from the damage through the process of _____compensation_____ (117), in which healthy neurons take over the connections that were lost due to the damage. reorganization (118) may also occur, such as in the case of aphasia (language impairment). Occasionally, researchers encounter a person who suffers from profound structural damage but who shows no apparent behavioral impairment. Examples from the text include cases of periventricular heterotopia, which has been discussed previously, and _____hydrocephalus_____ (119), a condition in which blockage of cerebrospinal fluid can lead to severe retardation if untreated. These cases demonstrate that the nervous system is capable of compensating for even extensive damage, although the processes involved are not understood.

There are some other promising forms of therapy that may result in repairing CNS damage, including spinal cord injury and brain damage. One promising molecule, when given to rats with induced stroke, blocks glutamate-induced _____excitotoxicity_____ (120), reducing the area of brain damage by 40%. Embryonic _____stem_____ (121) cells are pluripotent and may be used in the mature brain to replace cells damaged by injury or disease.

Short Answer and Essay Questions

Answer the following questions.

10. During neural development, axons often have to grow over extensive distances, and sometimes across hemispheres, in order to reach their target postsynaptic cells. How is this accomplished? Include in your answer the roles of growth cones and the *Robo1* and *Robo3* genes.

11. It is clear that the nervous system starts out with a lot more neurons than it needs. Why do you think it is advantageous for the nervous system to have so many neurons to start with, if many of them are only going to be lost? Keep in mind that the environment an animal encounters is at least somewhat unpredictable.

12. Maria was exposed to high levels of ionizing radiation during her 32nd week of pregnancy. She is concerned that this will have profound negative effects on her fetus, particularly its nervous system. What would you tell her?

13. What is syndactyly? What does surgical correction of syndactyly and the resulting changes in the brain demonstrate about the role of experience in shaping the brain?

14. Describe some ways in which the CNS can compensate at the level of the synapse for the loss of neurons in specific locations.

15. Discuss some possible treatments that may be used in the future to correct brain and spinal cord injuries.

Post-test

Use these multiple-choice questions to check your understanding of the chapter.

1. A _____ is the name for a bundle of neurons in the PNS.
   a. nerve
   b. tract
   c. nucleus
   d. ganglion

2. The spinal cord is part of the _____ nervous system.
   a. central
   b. autonomic
   c. peripheral
   d. sympathetic

3. Which of the following is the largest division of the mature CNS in humans?
   a. forebrain
   b. midbrain
   c. hindbrain
   d. spinal cord

4. The space separating the cerebral hemispheres is called the
   a. lateral fissure.
   b. corpus callosum.
   c. central sulcus.
   d. longitudinal fissure.

5. The surface of the cortex appears gray because it is composed mostly of
   a. unmyelinated axons.
   b. unmyelinated cell bodies.
   c. myelinated axons.
   d. myelinated cell bodies.

6. In the cortex, a ridge is called a
   a. fissure.
   b. gyrus.
   c. tract.
   d. sulcus.

7. What is the name of the 19th-century European anatomist who argued that because women have smaller brains than men, they are less intelligent?
   a. Penfield
   b. Ramón y Cajal
   c. Bischoff
   d. Sperry

8. Animal species that are the MOST intelligent tend to have
   a. bigger brains overall.
   b. more convolutions on the cortex.
   c. a proportionately larger forebrain.
   d. b and c

9. The directional term *anterior* means
   a. in front of.
   b. behind.
   c. above.
   d. below.

10. The brain area controlling fine motor movement is located on the
    a. prefrontal cortex.
    b. precentral gyrus.
    c. postcentral gyrus.
    d. central sulcus.

11. The area of the motor cortex devoted to which of the following body areas is probably the smallest?
    a. lips
    b. tongue
    c. thumb
    d. thigh

12. Damage to the prefrontal cortex is LEAST likely to result in problems with
    a. decision making.
    b. planning.
    c. speech comprehension.
    d. impulse control.

13. Who among the following was a proponent of lobotomies as a treatment for mental illness?
    a. Penfield
    b. Gage
    c. Freeman
    d. Bischoff

14. The somatosensory cortex is located in the _____ lobe.
    a. frontal
    b. occipital
    c. temporal
    d. parietal

15. Identifying objects by touch is a function of the
    a. somatosensory cortex.
    b. parietal association cortex.
    c. visual cortex.
    d. inferior temporal cortex.

16. Modern computer studies of the skull of Phineas Gage have revealed the extent of damage to the
    a. frontal lobes.
    b. corpus callosum.

    c. parietal lobes.

    d. brain stem.

17. Which of the following is NOT a function of the temporal lobes?

    a. processing auditory information

    b. language comprehension

    c. fine motor control

    d. visual identification of objects

18. Electrical stimulation of the association areas of the temporal lobe may result in the patient experiencing

    a. intense pain.

    b. buzzing sounds.

    c. bright lights.

    d. vivid memories.

19. The occipital lobe processes _____ information.

    a. visual

    b. auditory

    c. somatosensory

    d. a and b

20. The thalamus receives information from all of the sensory systems EXCEPT the system for

    a. vision.

    b. hearing.

    c. smell.

    d. taste.

21. The hypothalamus is located _____ the thalamus.

    a. above

    b. below

    c. behind

    d. in front of

22. The _____ is the body's "master" endocrine gland.

    a. pituitary

    b. pineal

    c. hypothalamus

    d. pons

23. The sleep-inducing hormone melatonin is released by the

    a. pituitary gland.

    b. pineal gland.

    c. hypothalamus.

    d. pons.

24. Which statement regarding the corpus callosum is FALSE?

    a. It consists of neuron tracts connecting the two hemispheres.

    b. It is the only place in the brain where information crosses from one side to the other.

    c. It may be severed in order to help control epileptic seizures.

    d. It allows the left side of the brain to share information with the right.

25. Which of the following structures is NOT part of the brain stem?
    a. lateral ventricle
    b. midbrain
    c. pons
    d. medulla

26. All of the following structures are located in the midbrain EXCEPT the
    a. superior colliculi.
    b. ventral tegmental area.
    c. pons.
    d. substantia nigra.

27. Heart rate and breathing are controlled by the
    a. pons.
    b. cerebellum.
    c. superior colliculi.
    d. medulla.

28. A person with damage to the cerebellum may
    a. be blind.
    b. be unable to recognize familiar objects.
    c. be insensitive to pain.
    d. have problems with movement.

29. The cerebrospinal fluid protects the brain in all of the following ways EXCEPT that it doesn't
    a. provide nourishment to brain cells.
    b. cushion the brain.
    c. remove waste products from the CNS.
    d. prevent toxins from entering the CNS.

30. The skeletal muscles are MOST directly controlled by the _____ nervous system.
    a. autonomic
    b. somatic
    c. sympathetic
    d. central

31. Which of the following cranial nerves is sometimes considered part of the CNS rather than the PNS?
    a. oculomotor
    b. auditory
    c. vagus
    d. optic

32. Following escape from a stressor, for example, once you have finished a presentation in your class, your heart rate will go down, your breathing rate will decrease, and you will start to feel your stomach grumbling. What portion of the nervous system is responsible for these changes?
    a. parasympathetic
    b. sympathetic
    c. somatic
    d. spinal cord

33. The stage of neural development in which axons grow toward their target connections is called
    a. proliferation.
    b. migration.
    c. circuit formation.
    d. circuit pruning.

34. Cell proliferation occurs
    a. in the innermost layer of the neural tube.
    b. in the outermost layers of the neural tube.
    c. throughout the neural tube.
    d. in the location of a neuron's final destination.

35. Cells that form a scaffold for neural migration are called
    a. astrocytes.
    b. radial glial cells.
    c. myelin cells.
    d. ladder cells.

36. During the first three weeks after birth, the neurons in a monkey's corpus callosum
    a. triple in number each day.
    b. increase by about 8 million per day.
    c. decrease by about 8 million per day.
    d. undergo very little change.

37. Neural plasticity is retained to the greatest extent in adulthood in which of the following brain areas?
    a. primary visual cortex
    b. somatosensory cortex
    c. primary motor cortex
    d. association cortex

38. Which of the following is NOT a result of fetal exposure to alcohol?
    a. improper migration of cells
    b. failure of cells to form myelin
    c. small brain size
    d. mental retardation

39. Teenagers are commonly criticized for being impulsive and not fully considering the consequences of their actions. What portion of their brain might still be undergoing myelination, which can help to explain this behavior?
    a. frontal cortex
    b. occipital cortex
    c. spinal nerves
    d. medulla

40. Which of the following is NOT an example of brain reorganization?
    a. larger area of the somatosensory cortex devoted to the index finger in people who read Braille
    b. the occipital cortex of people blind from birth responding to somatosensory information
    c. phantom limb pain following amputation of a leg
    d. regrowth of a severed spinal motor neuron

41. Regeneration is LEAST likely to occur in the
    a. CNS of a frog.
    b. PNS of a frog.
    c. CNS of a mammal.
    d. PNS of a mammal.

42. In the adult mammal, neurogenesis is MOST likely to occur in the
    a. spinal cord.
    b. medulla.
    c. hippocampus.
    d. hypothalamus.

43. Which of the following is NOT true of hydrocephalus?
    a. It results from a blockage of the cerebrospinal fluid.
    b. It can be treated using a drainage shunt.
    c. Even without treatment, individuals usually have normal intelligence.
    d. It affects the development of the CNS.

44. Which of the following is NOT a problem following stroke?
    a. edema
    b. abnormal protein deposits
    c. excitotosis
    d. paralysis

45. Which of the following is FALSE regarding traumatic brain injury?
    a. It can produce Alzheimer-like effects even in young brains.
    b. It includes concussion as one of its mild forms.
    c. It requires a severe blow, due to the brain's cushioning.
    d. It can be minimized by three weeks of rest.

Answers

Guided Review

1.	brain	38.	drug
2.	spinal cord	39.	Phineas Gage
3.	tract	40.	somatosensory
4.	nucleus	41.	association areas
5.	nerve	42.	neglect
6.	ganglion	43.	temporal
7.	forebrain	44.	Wernicke's
8.	midbrain	45.	inferior
9.	hindbrain	46.	Penfield
10.	cerebral	47.	vision
11.	thalamus	48.	thalamus
12.	hypothalamus	49.	hypothalamus
13.	fissure	50.	pituitary
14.	opposite	51.	pineal
15.	cortex	52.	callosum
16.	gyri (plural of gyrus)	53.	language
17.	sulci (plural of sulcus) or fissures	54.	spatial
18.	bodies	55.	ventricles
19.	surface	56.	cerebrospinal
20.	white	57.	colliculi
21.	layers	58.	substantia nigra
22.	columns	59.	tegmental
23.	information	60.	stem
24.	intelligence	61.	medulla
25.	convolutions	62.	pons
26.	larger	63.	reticular
27.	hierarchy	64.	cerebellum
28.	frontal	65.	pattern generators
29.	precentral gyrus	66.	sensory
30.	homunculus	67.	dorsal
31.	secondary	68.	motor
32.	basal ganglia	69.	ventral
33.	Broca's	70.	reflexes
34.	speech	71.	meninges
35.	prefrontal	72.	cerebrospinal
36.	depression	73.	blood-brain
37.	lobotomy	74.	capillaries

75. postrema
76. cranial
77. somatic
78. organs
79. olfactory
80. optic
81. sympathetic
82. parasympathetic
83. ganglion chains
84. increases
85. decreases
86. proliferation
87. ventricular
88. radial
89. circuit formation
90. growth cones
91. *Robo*
92. circuit pruning
93. neurotrophins
94. retina
95. plasticity
96. heterotopia
97. alcohol
98. brains

99. radiation
100. myelination
101. adolescence
102. frontal
103. reorganization
104. nerve energies
105. somatosensory
106. phantom
107. horizontally
108. strokes
109. traumatic brain injuries (TBIs)
110. attention
111. white matter
112. amphibians
113. axons
114. immune
115. neurogenesis
116. BrdU (bromodeoxyuridine)
117. compensation
118. reorganization
119. hydrocephalus
120. excitotoxicity
121. stem

Short Answer and Essay Questions

1. One advantage is that it increases the surface area of the brain without increasing its size a great deal. This means more cortex can be packed into a small area.

2. If we compare between species, brain size is more related to body size than intelligence; the largest animals tend to have the largest brains. A good way of representing the connection between brain and intelligence is its complexity, particularly the degree to which the forebrain is developed. Humans' forebrains are larger and more extensively convoluted than apes' brains, which are larger and more convoluted than monkeys' brains, etc.

3. These areas of the brain are organized like maps of the body. Sensory neurons from adjacent areas of the body project to adjacent areas of the somatosensory cortex, and neurons from adjacent parts of the motor cortex control movement in adjacent areas of the body. Areas of the body that are either especially sensitive (because they contain a lot of sensory receptors) or capable of fine motor movement are represented by a larger area of the cortex than areas that are less sensitive or not involved in fine motor movement. For example, the fingers are represented to a greater extent in both cortices than is the back.

4. This is usually the result of damage to the association cortex in the parietal lobe. It occurs because this part of the brain is involved in various spatial tasks, such as being able to tell

where things are in the environment and being able to locate one's own body in space. Persons who suffer damage to this area in the right hemisphere may not pay attention to things on the left side of the body; such an individual may not even recognize that an arm or leg belongs to her or him.

5.   The temporal lobes are where auditory information is initially processed and most of language comprehension occurs; the lobes also contain auditory and visual association areas responsible for tasks such as recognition of faces and other visual objects.

6.   Three areas with a role in motor function in the midbrain and hindbrain are the substantia nigra, the cerebellum, and the reticular formation.

7.   The main route for toxins and other substances to get into organs is through the bloodstream. The brain is especially vulnerable (because most adult CNS neurons do not replicate), so it is especially important to keep toxins out of the brain. In many parts of the brain, the capillaries are structured to do just that. The cells that make up the capillary walls are packed together tightly, so that very few substances can pass through them without going through special channels, and the special channels are selective in what they allow through. However, not all brain areas are protected in this manner. In the area postrema, toxins can get in, and it is actually beneficial that they do in some cases. If a toxin is detected in this area, it triggers the vomiting response, and if the source of the toxin is in the stomach, it will be removed from the body.

8.   Cranial nerves III (oculomotor), IV (trochlear), and VI (abducens) control eye movement. Cranial nerves X (vagus) and XII (hypoglossal) are probably involved in speech.

9.   The sympathetic nervous system consists of components of several of the spinal nerves serving various internal organs. The activity of its neurons is coordinated because many of them are interconnected within the sympathetic ganglion chain just outside the spinal cord, which allows for a coordinated response. No such structure exists in the parasympathetic division. The advantage of the coordination of the sympathetic division is that it provides a mobilization of most of the body's resources in times of stress.

10.   First of all, axons contain a growth cone, which is used to find the correct pathway. The cone is sensitive to the external chemical environment, and it is attracted to certain places and repelled from others. The sensitivity of the growth cone to different chemicals can also change over time as the axon grows into different areas. The *Robo1* gene produces a chemical that repels axons; when it is active, axons do not grow across the midline of the brain. Activation of the *Robo3* gene leads to axons being attracted across the midline. Once it is deactivated, the axon is no longer attracted to the midline and continues to grow in that side of the brain.

11.   By initially overproducing neurons, the nervous system allows for streamlining (elimination of unused and retention of used connections) to eliminate errors in circuit formation. The alternative to overproduction would be more precise circuit formation, which would require complex chemical and genetic codes. In addition, this strategy allows for adaptation to varied environmental conditions that could not be predicted in advance. An example of such selection occurred in the experiment in which kittens were reared seeing only horizontal or only vertical stripes.

12.   Although there may be some detrimental effects, they would probably be worse if she had been exposed earlier, between 8 and 15 weeks of gestation, because that is when proliferation and migration of neurons are occurring at high rates.

13.   Syndactyly is a condition in which the fingers are connected by a web of tissue, are of limited usefulness, and are mapped onto overlapping areas of the somatosensory cortex.

Within a week following surgical separation, patients' brains showed dramatic changes in that the separated fingers were now represented in distinct locations on the somatosensory cortex. This indicates that the brain can quickly respond to changes in a person's experiences.

14. Healthy presynaptic neurons can form new terminals to create replacement connections. Postsynaptic cells can create new receptors to compensate for reduced presynaptic input. And "silent" collaterals, terminals that were inactive, may become active almost immediately following injury.

15. One possibility is introducing new neurons, either from fetal cells or stem cells. The other possibilities involve manipulating the environment of the mature CNS so that it does not inhibit axon regeneration. These mechanisms include providing the nervous system with substances that can promote neural growth, inhibit those substances that inhibit neural growth, serve as scaffolds for developing axons, and/or block the immune response that may be harmful to developing axons. Use of glial and stem cells from the person's own olfactory mucosa may also be helpful in restoration or improvement in function.

Post-test

1. d   2. a   3. a   4. d   5. b   6. b   7. c   8. d   9. a   10. b   11. d   12. c   13. c   14. d
15. b   16. a   17. c   18. d   19. a   20. c   21. b   22. a   23. b   24. b   25. a   26. c
27. d   28. d   29. d   30. b   31. d   32. a   33. c   34. a   35. b   36. c   37. d   38. b
39. a   40. d   41. c   42. c   43. c   44. b   45. c

4 The Methods and Ethics of Research

Learning Objectives

After reading this chapter, you will be able to

1.   Explain how scientific theories are generated

2.   Demonstrate how scientists test hypotheses

3.   Describe the differences between correlational and experimental studies

4.   Assess the methods that scientists have for studying the role of brain structures in behavior

5.   Compare the methods that scientists use to investigate the structure and function of brain cells

6.   Identify the ethical protections that are in place for human participants

7.   Summarize the ethical protections that exist for research animals

8.   Examine the ethical concerns that have been raised about stem cell and gene therapy research

Science, Research, and Theory

Summary and Guided Review

After studying this section in the text, fill in the blanks of the following summary.

Science requires that information be derived from observation, a concept known as __empiricism__ (1). Scientific observations should be objective so that two or more people watching the same event will describe it in the same way.

Like many other scientists, neuroscientists are careful about the way they interpret their research results. Knowledge often undergoes __changes__ (2) over time; what is thought of as a "fact" today may be shown to be incorrect in the future. For example, it was recently discovered that axon regrowth and __neurogenesis__ (3) may occur in the mature primate central nervous system. Many scientists use __theories__ (4) to explain observations and guide their research. They generate __hypothesis__ (5), which are testable predictions derived from theories. If a hypothesis is found to be incorrect, then the theory must be revised. The __dopamine__ (6) theory of schizophrenia is a good example of a theory that was modified when new data became available.

An experiment is a study in which the researcher manipulates at least one __independent__ (7) variable and measures its effects on one or more __dependent__ (8) variables. Experimenters also eliminate __extraneous__ (9) variables, extra variations in a study that might influence behavior, or equate them across subjects. __experimental__ (10) studies are most useful for determining cause-and-effect relationships, since researchers control one or more variables directly. In contrast, if a researcher measured the extent of frontal lobe impairment in a large group of people and then examined their records for criminal behavior, they might find that criminals are more likely to have frontal lobe deficits than other individuals. This would be an example of a(n) __correlational__ (11) study. This relationship could not be studied as an experimental study, because inducing brain damage in humans would violate __ethical__ (12) research practices. Researchers could, however, disrupt frontal lobe functioning using _transcranial_ _magnetic_ _stimulation_ (13), then assess how aggression is affected by presence or absence of frontal lobe function.

Short Answer and Essay Questions

Answer the following questions.

1. Why do researchers avoid using words like *truth* and *proof* when they discuss the results of their work?

2. If experimental studies are the only ones that allow us to determine cause-and-effect relationships, why are other studies used at all? What are the limitations of experimental studies?

3. Discuss how the dopamine theory of schizophrenia has evolved. What observations led to the dopamine theory? How was it tested? What were the results of these tests? What is the current status of the theory?

Research Techniques

Summary and Guided Review

After studying this section in the text, fill in the blanks of the following summary.

Brain researchers use a variety of techniques to study brain tissue, including staining and imaging neurons. An early method, invented by Camillo _Golgi_ (14) and used by Santiago Ramón y Cajal to examine individual neurons, involved staining brain tissue so that about 5% of the neurons would stand out from the rest. Neural pathways (bundles of axons) can be identified by using _myelin_ (15) stains, whereas groups of cell bodies can be identified with _Nissl_ (16) stains. Injection of fluorescent substances such as _fluorogold_ (17), which is transferred between neurons, also allows researchers to trace pathways between neurons. Injecting radioactively labeled glucose allows researchers to see which brain areas are most active during particular activities; this technique is known as _autoradiography_ (18). Candace Pert used a similar technique to identify _opiate_ (19) receptors in brain tissue. Immunocytochemistry involves attaching a dye, which is usually fluorescent, to _antibodies_ (20) to make receptors, neurotransmitters, or other cellular components visible. Using in situ _hybridization_ (21), in which radioactive DNA is paired with messenger RNA, researchers have been able to locate specific sites of gene activity.

Light microscopes magnify cells so that their larger components such as cell bodies, some organelles, axons, and _dendrites_ (22) are discernible. Electron microscopes can magnify images up to _250,000_ (23) times. Transmission electron microscopes work by passing electrons through objects and onto photographic film. This technique allows researchers to see such things as synaptic _vesicles_ (24). A(n) _scanning_ (25) electron microscope produces a three-dimensional image by inducing the object being observed to emit electrons. Two of the newest examples of advances in microscopic technology are the _Confocal_ _laser_ _scanning_ (26) microscope and the _two_-_photon_ (27) microscope.

Brain activity in the form of waves may be measured using electrodes attached to the scalp; the record of this activity is called a(n) _electroencephelogram_ (28). This technique has excellent _temporal_ (29) resolution but poor spatial resolution, meaning it is difficult to locate the exact area in which changes are occurring. Researchers can present a specific stimulus multiple times; the EEGs are recorded and then averaged to cancel out the "noise" from the rest of the brain, producing a(n) _event_-_related_ (30) potential.

When researchers want to target a specific brain area for recording or manipulation, a(n) _stereotaxic_ (31) instrument is used to insert an electrode or cannula, in a location determined from a brain _atlas_ (32). A stimulating _microelectrode_ (33) may be inserted into a particular area of the brain to determine the effects on the subject's behavior, or a recording one will capture neuronal activity while the subject is presented with different stimuli or engages in a certain behavior. Another method for stimulating groups of neurons is _optogenetics_ (34), which involves creating light-sensitive channels in targeted neurons; this method can also be used to study membrane voltage and _neurotransmitter_ (35) release. A narrow _cannula_ (36) tube may be inserted for delivering chemicals to a brain area, or to remove fluid samples to test for levels of various substances; this technique is called _microdialysis_ (37).

The study of people with brain injury or damage may give scientists clues about which brain areas are involved in which functions, but more precise methods require experimentally damaging specific areas and observing the effects under controlled conditions in animals. A procedure called _ablation_ (38) involves removing brain tissue; this may be done using a vacuum to remove the desired tissue, a technique known as _aspiration_ (39). Neural tissue may also be _lesioned_ (40), or damaged by the use of electricity, heat, or chemicals. Chilling a brain region or using certain chemicals produces a(n) _reversible_ (41) lesion, allowing the researcher to make comparisons before injection, during inactivation, and following recovery. A relatively new noninvasive technique called _transcranial_ _magnetic_ _stimulation_ (42) uses a magnetic coil to induce changes in electrical activity in the brain. Although this procedure shows some promise as a therapeutic tool, at the moment it is most likely to be useful for _research_ (43). A related technique, which activates astrocytes in the brain, is called _transcranial_ _direct_ _current_ (44) stimulation.

Brain _imaging_ (45) techniques allow for the examination of intact brains; they can reveal areas of damage as well as show which areas are active in response to specific stimulation or during specific behaviors. The first modern imaging technique was the _computed_ _tomography_ (46) scan, which takes sequential X-ray "slices" of the brain and combines the different images using a computer; the horizontal scans thus form a composite view of the entire brain. Another technique is _magnetic_ _resonance_ (47) imaging, which works by measuring radiofrequency waves from hydrogen (or other elemental) atoms exposed to a magnetic field. A variant of this procedure, _diffusion_ _tensor_ (48) imaging, measures the movement of water molecules and is useful for identifying brain pathways. Although these techniques produce pictures of the brain, none shows changes over time. Brain activity may be measured by injecting radioactive chemicals such as 2-DG into the bloodstream and then identifying areas of the brain that take up greater amounts of the chemical. This technique is known as _positron_ _emission_ _tomography_ (49), and it allows researchers to determine which brain areas are most involved in specific activities. Another measure of brain activity is the _functional_ (50) MRI procedure (fMRI), which detects differential oxygen

46. (CT) or (CAT)

49. (PET)

increases. Some researchers are concerned about this technique's lower sensitivity and less-than-perfect test-retest reliability.

By comparing the behaviors of related individuals, researchers can determine the extent to which heredity influences traits among related individuals. For example, in a 1981 ___family___ (51) study, researchers discovered that there was a(n) ___correlation___ (52) of about .42 in IQ scores between parents and their children, and a rate of about ___13%___ (53) for schizophrenia in the offspring of a schizophrenic parent as compared to the general population rate of 1%. However, ___adoption___ (54) studies reveal that when children are adopted out, the correlation of their IQ scores with those of their biological parents drops to .22, indicating that some of the similarity between parents and children stems from the environment. One of the best ways of examining the influence of heredity on behavior in humans is through twin studies. ___monozygotic___ (55) twins, who share the same genetic material, are compared to ___dizygotic___ (56) twins; this comparison controls for environment to some extent, although not entirely. Neither twin nor adoption studies eliminate the influence of the ___prenatal___ (57) environment or of the time from birth to adoption. Twin studies reveal correlations of IQ scores in dizygotic twins to be around ___0.60___ (58), whereas correlations in monozygotic twins are about ___0.86___ (59), suggesting a strong genetic component to intelligence. Sometimes researchers use the term ___concordance___ (60) rate to refer to the frequency with which relatives are alike in a characteristic or disorder. Studies show that the rate for schizophrenia in monozygotic twins is about ___three___ (61) times the rate for dizygotic twins.

At present, the experimental manipulation of genes, or genetic ___engineering___ (62), is done mostly with nonhuman animals, particularly mice. One way of changing the genetic makeup of mice is by inserting nonfunctioning genes into mouse embryos and then breeding the offspring, thus creating ___knockout___ (63) mice. The ___antisense___ ___RNA___ (64) procedure is used to alter a gene's activity by blocking the cell's protein-building activity. Gene ___transfer___ (65) is a procedure in which a gene from one species is inserted into the embryonic genome of a different species; when this is done, the resulting organism is referred to as a(n) ___transgenic___ (66) animal. Gene therapy has been used to treat the disorder ___SCID___ (67), experienced by individuals like Ashanthi (described in the chapter introduction), and the gene-editing technique ___CRISPR___ (68) has been used to repair a gene mutation that causes blindness in a patient's stem cells. Future human trials may demonstrate success of CRISPR for treating blindness in a person.

55. (identical)

56. (fraternal)

Short Answer and Essay Questions

Answer the following questions.

4. What is the advantage of autoradiography over Nissl and myelin staining procedures? Give an example of an important discovery that has resulted from the use of autoradiography.

5. How were immunocytochemistry and in situ hybridization used together to identify the likely protein responsible for night-migration in birds? In your answer, be sure to explain how both of these methods work.

6. What are event-related potentials, and how are they obtained? What do they measure?

7. Identify one correlational method that scientists use to study the brain and one experimental method that scientists use to study the brain. Explain what characteristics of each method result in the classification of a study as correlational versus experimental.

8. Why do researchers who want to understand brain damage in humans use ablation and lesioning in animal studies?

9. How do CT and MRI scans work? What does each method reveal about the brain, and what are the limitations of each of these methods?

10. How do PET and fMRI scans work? What does each method reveal about the brain, and what are the limitations of each of these methods?

11. Distinguish between adoption and family studies. Why are adoption studies generally better for studying heredity of traits than family studies?

12. Give some examples of genetic engineering that have been used for research and therapeutic purposes.

Research Ethics

Summary and Guided Review

After studying this section in the text, fill in the blanks of the following summary.

Scientists must adhere to guidelines for ethical conduct. These guidelines cover many aspects of scientists' work, including publishing information and using humans and animals in research. One type of ethical violation involves claiming someone else's ideas as one's own; this is known as __plagiarism__ (69). A more serious violation, in which false or misleading data are published, is __fabrication__ (70). These types of violations are potentially damaging for the scientific community.

Scientists are also obligated to treat their human research participants with dignity and respect and to obtain their informed __consent__ (71) before the individuals participate in the research. This means that participants are fully aware of any potential risks involved in the research. Some behavioral studies, such as the one by Albert Ax in 1953, employ __deception__ (72), which involves withholding information or giving false information at the outset of a study. Some researchers and subjects' rights advocates say its use is never justified.

Many of the recent advances in medicine would not have been possible without animal research. Animals are used as research subjects for a variety of reasons. Many procedures that are potentially dangerous to humans are performed on animals. Animals' genetic makeup and __environment__ (73) can be controlled. Consequently, it is easier to interpret results from studies with animals than those from studies with humans. This preference for using animals in potentially harmful studies, suggesting that the well-being of animals is less important than that of humans, is considered by some to be a dual ethical standard, which they have labeled __speciesism__ (74). Animal rights __activists__ (75), people who work on behalf of the welfare of research animals, may cooperate with animal researchers to improve conditions for research animals, or they may damage or destroy labs to release animals and threaten to harm or actually harm the researchers themselves. Scientists who use animals in research are obligated to treat them humanely. Animals must be well cared for, and discomfort and stress must be __minimized__ (76). In addition, NIH recently withdrew support for biomedical research on __chimpanzies__ (77) (apes most closely related to humans) and relocating the animals to a retirement colony.

Overall, the use of animals in research has fallen by a third, and researchers are increasingly using alternative methods such as tissue ___*cultures*___ (78) and ___*computer*___ (79) simulations.

Perhaps the most controversial area of medical research using humans is in ___*gene*___ ___*therapy*___ (80). Such research involves altering the genetic makeup or genetic activity of individuals in order to treat specific problems. Although this technique resulted in the death of a research participant in 1999, stricter ___*supervision*___ (81) of human studies was one positive outcome from the study. There are other ethical concerns with this type of research as well, including its impact on successive generations of human beings. While CRISPR co-discoverer ___*Jennefer*___ ___*Doudna*___ (82) and colleagues have voiced concerns about editing reproductive cells at this time, scientists in China have already used CRISPR to alter a gene in a human ___*embryo/fetus*___ (83).

The use of human ___*stem*___ (84) cells has also been a controversial area of research. These cells have been used to improve heart functioning, and many researchers expect that they will eventually be used to grow human ___*organs*___ (85) for transplants, and research will provide a better understanding of the development of disease. In the past, most human stem cells came from "extra" embryos from fertility treatments, though new sources are being found in bone marrow, and converting mature cells into embryonic-like induced ___*pluripotent*___ (86) cells. The George W. Bush administration ___*banned*___ (87) federal funding of research with newly developed stem cell lines, and cells from older lines are of little value for human research. However, President ___*Obama*___ (88) reversed this policy in 2009. Because of the complexity of the issue, and the uncertain support from future administrations, it is likely that stem cell research will continue to be controversial.

Short Answer and Essay Questions

Answer the following questions.

13. Describe the study by Albert Ax. Why was this study ethically controversial? Describe the modern ethical protections that may prevent this study from being conducted now.

14. Explain why animals are used as research subjects even in medical research that is done to benefit humans. Provide one or more examples of major discoveries in neuroscience that have required the use of research animals.

15. Discuss the ways that ethical protections for research animals have changed and why those changes have occurred.

16. In what way does the movie *Gattaca* reflect concerns in our society about genetic research and genetic manipulation?

17. What is the major ethical controversy of human stem cell research?

Post-test

Use these multiple-choice questions to check your understanding of the chapter.

1. A theory is
   a. an established scientific fact.
   b. a prediction that can be tested.

    c. an explanation for our observations.

    d. all of the above

2. Which of the following statements is a behavioral neuroscientist LEAST likely to make?

    a. These results suggest that people who drink heavily may suffer from memory loss.

    b. These results show that some people who drink heavily suffer from memory loss.

    c. These results prove that heavy drinking results in memory loss.

    d. From these results, it appears that memory loss may be a result of heavy drinking.

3. Research involving a single person showing interesting behavior is called

    a. a case study.

    b. an experiment.

    c. a survey.

    d. none of the above

4. A study that allows researchers to determine if a cause-and-effect relationship exists between two variables is a(n)

    a. correlational study.

    b. experimental study.

    c. naturalistic observational study.

    d. none of the above

5. Dr. Joy observes the behavior of mice in large colonies, taking particular note of social interactions but does not interfere with the mice in any way. What type of study is this?

    a. an experiment

    b. a case study

    c. naturalistic observation

    d. a survey

6. Dr. Hagen performs a study in which male participants are given different amounts of alcohol and then are tested in a sexual aggression study. In this study, alcohol is the

    a. dependent variable.

    b. correlational variable.

    c. confounded variable.

    d. independent variable.

7. Research volunteers are given either a placebo pill or a drug containing a small amount of benzodiazepine. Then the volunteers are asked to play a game of chess on a computer. The researchers believe that the benzodiazepine will interfere with the participants' ability to play well. What is the dependent variable in this study?

    a. the computer game

    b. the placebo

    c. the benzodiazepine

    d. performance in the chess game

8. Dr. Milgram informs a participant that he will be administering shocks to an unseen (though nonexistent) partner when that partner cannot remember a series of word pairs, to investigate the effect of shocks on learning. The researcher, however, is actually studying an individual's willingness to inflict harm on another and, therefore, has misinformed the participant as to the purpose of the study. Dr. Milgram is using

    a. plagiarism.

    b. fabrication.

    c. deception.

    d. manipulation.

9. The dopamine theory of schizophrenia
   a. suggests that the disorder is a result of dopamine hyperactivity in the brain.
   b. was developed after some researchers noticed drug users showing signs of schizophrenia.
   c. does not account for all cases of schizophrenia.
   d. all of the above

10. The staining procedure that allowed 19th-century anatomists to study individual neurons was discovered by
    a. Santiago Ramón y Cajal.
    b. Camillo Golgi.
    c. Candace Pert.
    d. Henrik Mouritsen.

11. If researchers want to find a nucleus (collection of cell bodies) in the hypothalamus, they are MOST likely to use which of the following techniques?
    a. Nissl staining
    b. myelin staining
    c. in situ hybridization
    d. immunocytochemistry

12. _____ is a substance that may be injected into one area of the brain and then transferred to other cells.
    a. Fluorogold
    b. Nissl stain
    c. Golgi stain
    d. Myelin stain

13. Which procedure involves the use of radioactive sugar molecules, which are absorbed by active neurons and then detected on photographic film?
    a. immunocytochemistry
    b. Nissl staining
    c. autoradiography
    d. fluorogold staining

14. Using the technique in question 13, brain researchers discovered opiate receptors by injecting which radioactive substance into the brains of rats?
    a. cocaine
    b. naloxone
    c. dopamine
    d. mRNA

15. Immunocytochemistry involves the use of _____, whereas in situ hybridization involves the use of _____.
    a. radioactive DNA; dye-labeled antibodies
    b. dye-labeled antibodies; radioactive DNA
    c. dye-labeled antibodies; radioactive sugar molecules
    d. radioactive sugar molecules; radioactive DNA

16. Cryptochromes are proteins that
    a. bind to opiate receptor sites.
    b. impair the immune system's ability to fight infection.
    c. may be responsible for night-migration in some types of birds.
    d. interfere with messenger RNA.

17. Which type of microscope are researchers MOST LIKELY to use if they need to visualize neural activity on the surface of a rat's brain while it presses a bar?
    a. confocal laser scanning microscope
    b. scanning electron microscope
    c. compound microscope
    d. transmission electron microscope

18. Due to the relatively _____ spatial resolution of EEGs, researchers are likely to use this technique for recording activity from _____.
    a. good; individual brain cells
    b. poor; individual brain cells
    c. good; large brain regions
    d. poor; large brain regions

19. Researchers who use event-related potentials to study brain activity are MOST likely interested in
    a. studying patients who are asleep.
    b. identifying how the brain responds to a brief stimulus.
    c. recording from single neurons.
    d. injecting chemicals in the brain.

20. A stereotaxic instrument may be used to
    a. place a recording electrode in a specific location in the brain.
    b. place a stimulating electrode in a specific location in the brain.
    c. locate a specific area of the brain in which to inject chemicals.
    d. all of the above

21. Dr. Medina plans to activate a subset of visual cells in the brains of rats and simultaneously record the resulting electrical activity in visual system cells. Which stimulation technique would BEST fit her plans?
    a. optogenetics
    b. microelectrode stimulation
    c. microdialysis
    d. event-related potentials

22. Microdialysis is a procedure for
    a. removing brain fluid for analysis.
    b. injecting chemicals into the brain to destroy neurons.
    c. injecting radioactive substances into the brain to measure activity.
    d. removing neurons from the brain for analysis.

23. Jerry is undergoing a procedure in which several electrodes are attached to his scalp, and the activity of neurons under the electrodes is recorded. What is this procedure called?
    a. EEG
    b. PET
    c. MRI
    d. CT

24. Aspiration is BEST thought of as a form of
    a. lesioning.
    b. recording brain activity.
    c. microdialysis.
    d. reversible lesioning.

25. Researchers who want to improve attention of human participants experimentally could use this noninvasive technique for increasing neuron excitability.
    a. PET
    b. event-related potential
    c. transcranial direct current stimulation
    d. reversible lesioning

26. Which of the following brain imaging techniques involves the use of X-rays?
    a. MRI
    b. fMRI
    c. DTI
    d. CT

27. If a brain researcher is interested in studying which brain areas are MOST active during a spatial skills task, the procedure of choice would be
    a. MRI.
    b. PET.
    c. CT.
    d. TMS.

28. The effects of heredity and environment on behavior are MOST confounded in
    a. family studies.
    b. adoption studies.
    c. twin studies.
    d. genetic engineering studies.

29. A correlation of −.75 indicates
    a. a weak relationship between two variables.
    b. a strong relationship between two variables.
    c. no relationship between two variables.
    d. a mistake; correlations cannot be negative.

30. Karen found evidence in family studies that the correlation in personality between parents and children was .31, but she read that adoption studies showed a correlation in personality between biological parents and children that was .15. What should Karen conclude about the role of heredity in personality?
    a. Personality is highly heritable.
    b. Environment has a strong influence on personality.
    c. Adoption studies are poor at estimating heritable influences.
    d. Personality is not at all heritable.

31. Compared to identical twins, fraternal twins show _____ concordance for schizophrenia.
    a. a higher
    b. a lower
    c. the same
    d. no

32. The _____ technique of genetic engineering involves preventing or reducing the expression of a particular gene by occupying the cell's ribonucleic acid with a synthetic strand of DNA.
    a. antisense DNA
    b. transgenic
    c. antisense RNA
    d. knockout

33. People with SCID
    a. may be aided by genetic engineering.
    b. are the subject of transgenic research.
    c. have been cured using stem cells.
    d. suffer from severe mental disorders.

34. Jennifer is a graduate student studying the effects of electrical stimulation on the cingulate gyrus in rats' brains. Her initial results are not what she expected, and because she is worried about finishing her dissertation on time, she changes some of her data so that they fit her hypothesis. Jennifer has engaged in
    a. plagiarism.
    b. deception.
    c. fabrication.
    d. breaking the law.

35. Researchers who use humans as participants
    a. are barred from intentionally deceiving them.
    b. may withhold information from them but may not lie to them.
    c. must fully inform them about all details of a procedure beforehand.
    d. may not withhold information about risks or discomfort that might occur.

36. What percentage of laboratory animals are primates?
    a. more than 90%
    b. about 50%
    c. between 10% and 15%
    d. fewer than 5%

37. Regarding animal research guidelines, which of the following is FALSE?
    a. NIH allows the use of chimpanzees in funded research so long as the research does not involve pain or discomfort.
    b. Stress should be minimized.
    c. Researchers prefer to use animals in studies because their environment can be tightly controlled.
    d. Researchers must provide humane housing and medical care to all animals under their care.

38. The researcher Edward Taub, whose Silver Springs, Maryland, laboratory made national headlines in the 1980s,
    a. is currently serving a prison sentence for animal abuse.
    b. received an award from the American Psychological Society.
    c. was able to complete his research after his grant was reinstated by the National Institutes of Health.
    d. none of the above

39. Which of the following statements regarding gene therapy research is TRUE?
    a. No human has died from gene therapy research.
    b. Some humans have been treated for diseases using gene therapy research.
    c. Gene therapy research with humans is illegal in the United States.
    d. Scientists in the United States uniformly support the use of gene therapies to modify human embryos.

40. Which of the following is a privacy concern regarding gene therapy applications?
    a. the use of gene therapies that could harm patients, as occurred with Jesse
    b. the use of gene therapies to create babies with certain characteristics, such as blue eyes
    c. the use of genetic information to determine if a person should be hired to work for a company
    d. the availability of gene therapies being restricted to only those who can afford them

Answers

Guided Review

1. empiricism
2. changes
3. neurogenesis
4. theories
5. hypotheses
6. dopamine
7. independent
8. dependent
9. extraneous
10. experimental
11. correlational
12. ethical
13. transcranial magnetic stimulation
14. Golgi
15. myelin
16. Nissl
17. fluorogold
18. autoradiography
19. opiate
20. antibodies
21. hybridization
22. dendrites
23. 250,000
24. vesicles
25. scanning
26. confocal laser scanning
27. two-photon
28. electroencephalogram (EEG)
29. temporal
30. event-related
31. stereotaxic
32. atlas
33. microelectrode
34. optogenetics
35. neurotransmitter
36. cannula
37. microdialysis
38. ablation
39. aspiration
40. lesioned
41. reversible
42. transcranial magnetic stimulation (TMS)
43. research
44. transcranial direct current
45. imaging
46. computed tomography (CT or CAT)
47. magnetic resonance
48. diffusion tensor
49. positron emission tomography (PET)
50. functional
51. family
52. correlation
53. 13%
54. adoption
55. Monozygotic/Identical
56. dizygotic/fraternal
57. prenatal
58. .60
59. .86
60. concordance
61. three
62. engineering
63. knockout
64. antisense RNA
65. transfer
66. transgenic
67. SCID
68. CRISPR
69. plagiarism
70. fabrication
71. consent
72. deception
73. environment
74. speciesism

75. activists

76. minimized

77. chimpanzees

78. cultures

79. computer

80. gene therapy

81. supervision

82. Jennifer Doudna

83. embryo or fetus

84. stem

85. organs

86. pluripotent

87. banned

88. Obama

Short Answer and Essay Questions

1. Knowledge, or what we think we know to be true, changes. Many ideas that are currently accepted as fact may someday be shown to be incorrect. Therefore, scientists are usually careful about drawing such conclusions from their research. They prefer to be tentative about their conclusions.

2. Many types of questions cannot be answered using experimental procedures. Researchers are bound by ethical and legal rules that forbid the use of humans for many types of potentially interesting studies. Also, researchers are unable to manipulate many variables, such as age, sex, and other factors that are inherent to individuals.

3. The theory was first developed when some researchers noticed that people using certain drugs that increase dopamine activity in the brain showed symptoms of schizophrenia (but these symptoms disappeared when the drugs wore off). It was suggested that schizophrenia is caused by excess dopamine. One hypothesis used to test this theory was that patients with schizophrenia should improve when given drugs that decrease dopamine activity. However, not all such patients show this expected result; therefore, the dopamine theory is recognized as being an incomplete explanation of schizophrenia.

4. Autoradiography allows researchers to see which cells are active, whereas other staining methods only show neurons and their parts against the background. One discovery that stemmed from this method was that the visual cortex contains a map of the retina and the visual field. Another discovery was the identification of opiate receptors in the brain.

5. Immunocytochemistry (in which fluorescent antibodies are used to locate specific cell components, including proteins) revealed that cryptochromes were present in both night-migrating and nonmigrating birds during the day, but that these proteins were present at night only in the night-migrating birds. This suggested that cryptochromes were responsible for migration guided by magnetic fields. Before they did this study, the researchers used in situ hybridization (in which radioactively labeled DNA is paired with the cells' own mRNA) to determine which of two cryptochromes to focus on, CRY1 or CRY2. Results showed that CRY2 was constructed in the nuclei, while CRY1 was constructed outside the nucleus; because a magneto-receptor would likely function outside the nucleus, the researchers focused on CRY1.

6. Event-related potentials are EEG recordings that are taken over a number of trials, during which target stimuli are present or absent. They represent an average response of the brain to specific stimuli, because by looking at several different trials, researchers can filter the change in brain activity in response to the stimulus (which is only weakly detected by the EEG) out of the rest of the brain's normal activity (background noise).

7. Correlational methods for examining the brain include brain imaging techniques such as CT, MRI, PET, and fMRI. Recording techniques such as EEG and event-related potentials, as

well as staining techniques, are also correlational in nature. Experimental methods include ablation and lesion techniques as well as transcranial magnetic stimulation and transcranial direct current stimulation. Gene therapies are also experimental in nature. The key difference between correlational and experimental methods is that experimental methods involve the researcher manipulating what the subjects experience, thus confounds can be eliminated or controlled for. When scientists experimentally inactivate part of the brain (as in lesions, ablations, transcranial magnetic stimulation, or gene knockouts), or activate part of the brain (as in transcranial direct current stimulation, microelectrode stimulation, or optogenetics), they can control which areas are turned on or off at specific points in time, so the ability to determine the causal role of a part of the brain in a function is high.

8. Researchers often want to know the function of a very specific brain area, and studying humans with brain damage is problematic, because brain damage is rarely limited to the areas of interest. Using animals allows researchers to introduce damage to very specific areas of the brain and to learn about the effects of damage under more controlled conditions.

9. A person receiving a CT scan is injected with a dye, and then X-rays of the intact brain are taken from several different angles; finally, the images are compiled by a computer to show a three-dimensional image. In the past, this procedure has been slow to produce the image, but newer technology allows for faster computing. The image, of course, is a still shot of the brain, and it cannot show activity or change as the brain functions. MRI scans measure the radio waves given off by hydrogen atoms in the brain when exposed to a magnetic field. Images are formed because of the different concentrations of this element in different structures. No substances such as dyes or radioactive materials need to be given. This procedure is reasonably fast, and it is becoming less expensive (due to advances in technology), but it also produces a static image.

10. PET scans require the administration of radioactively labeled glucose, which is then taken up to differing degrees by different brain areas according to how active they are. Imaging the radioactivity provides a measure of each brain area's activity during stimulation or task performance. This is an expensive procedure, and it only detects brain changes of at least 45 seconds in duration. Also, the image of the different amounts of radiation must be superimposed on a scan of the brain, usually from an MRI. Functional MRIs measure differences in brain cells' oxygen consumption. They are relatively safe; the biggest disadvantage of this method is its price.

11. The difference between adoption and family studies is that adoption studies look at children raised in homes by adoptive parents, whereas family studies look at children in intact families. Family studies are inherently confounded, because not only do individuals share genes, but they also share an environment. Therefore, any similarities between them may be due to either factor or to both factors.

12. Some examples of genetic engineering are the knockout technique, the antisense RNA procedure, gene transfer, gene therapy, and creation of transgenic animals.

13. One part of Ax's experiment involved convincing his participants that they were in physical danger (which they were not) in order to induce fear. Many of the participants indeed seemed very afraid during the procedure. There are two major reasons why this was ethically questionable. First, human research participants should be able to give their informed consent before participating in a research project. This means that they are informed ahead of time of any risks inherent in the procedure and that with this knowledge they voluntarily agree to participate. The second, related, problem is that the participants were deceived. Deception is allowed in research, but only when the potential benefits of the study outweigh the costs of

using it. At the time of the study, standards had not been established for deception and informed consent. It is unlikely that such a study would be conducted now, because it involved such an extreme manipulation of fear and because the information divulged while obtaining informed consent would likely make the "threat" unconvincing.

14.   There are many procedures that would be unethical to perform on humans. For this reason, procedures that may eventually be used on humans are tested first on animals. Also, the laboratory animal's environment may be controlled, so it is easier to interpret the results (because many potentially confounding variables can be eliminated). One example of a discovery that required the use of research animals is Edward Taub's research into brain reorganization following limb injury, which involved cutting the sensory nerve in the arms of monkeys. Such surgical procedures cannot be performed on humans but can provide much insight into ways to treat human injuries and/or illnesses. Another example is Eric Kandel's research into the brain changes that occur during learning. Since scientists cannot examine fine structures in the human brain without doing damage to the tissue or waiting for a person to die, this type of research has to be completed on animals.

15.   Research on animals is much more regulated than it had been in the past. For example, very few studies today are conducted on nonhuman primates (chimpanzees and other apes) and NIH no longer funds chimpanzee studies. Most studies on animals now use rodents and there are fewer animal studies now than in the past, with more researchers using computer simulations or tissue cultures for research than had occurred previously. These changes have occurred as animal rights activists have become more involved in working with scientists to improve animal research conditions, as there have been more attacks against scientists who conduct animal research, and as more noninvasive ways to study the brain have become available.

16.   The 1997 movie *Gattaca* concerns a future society in which genetically "superior" individuals are more privileged than others. Although the movie is science fiction, some people in our society are concerned that genetic engineering of humans could lead to something similar to this, particularly if people are able to select the most desirable traits for their offspring or to engineer those traits in their children.

17.   The primary reason the use of human stem cells in research is controversial is because it destroys the embryo.

Post-test

1. c   2. c   3. a   4. b   5. c   6. d   7. d   8. c   9. d   10. b   11. a   12. a   13. c   14. b
15. b   16. c   17. a   18. d   19. b   20. d   21. a   22. a   23. a   24. a   25. c   26. d
27. b   28. a   29. b   30. b   31. b   32. c   33. a   34. c   35. d   36. d   37. a   38. b
39. b   40. c

Danies
pizza
cake
Donuts soft pretzels
Hashbrowns
quesadilla
Grilled cez
omlette compread

(cook CL)

WSS shakes

5 Drugs, Addiction, and Reward

Chapter Outline

Learning Objectives

After reading this chapter, you will be able to

1. Identify the main classes of drugs

2. Describe the effects of each class of drugs on the nervous system

3. Predict how different drugs will affect behavior, based on the neural systems on which those drugs act

4. Illustrate how the brain changes during addiction

5. Discuss the role of learning in overdose and addiction

6. Explain how pharmacology can be used to treat addiction

7. Contrast the environmental and hereditary influences on addiction

Psychoactive Drugs

Summary and Guided Review

After studying this section in the text, fill in the blanks of the following summary.

Drugs can affect the brain by acting as ___agonists___ (1) (mimicking the effects of neurotransmitters) or ___antagonists___ (2) (blocking or reducing the effects of neurotransmitters). Individuals who become obsessed with obtaining a drug or who use it compulsively are showing signs of ___addiction___ (3). When a person stops taking a drug, she or he may experience symptoms of ___withdrawal___ (4), which are usually opposite to the effects of the drug. With repeated use, the brain may develop ___tolerance___ (5) to a drug, a result of a reduction in quantity or sensitivity of receptors.

Opiates are drugs that come from opium poppies; these drugs produce euphoria as well as ___analgesic/hypnotic___ (6) and ___hypnotic/analgesic___ (7) psychoactive effects. Morphine has been used clinically for treating the pain of surgery, battle wounds, and ___cancers___ (8). Another opiate drug, commonly used as a cough suppressant, is ___codeine___ (9). The most commonly abused opiate is ___heroin___ (10), because of its intense effects on the nervous system. In a long-term study of those addicted to the opiate, the most common cause of death was ___overdose___ (11), yet about half of those surviving were still using heroin at the end of the study. Opiate drugs affect the nervous system because the body produces its own natural opioids called ___endorphins___ (12), which affect the same receptors as opiates.

Drugs that have inhibitory effects on the central nervous system are called ___depressants___ (13). Alcohol, the most commonly abused drug, impairs both motor and ___cognitive___ (14) functions, as well as causing sedation, euphoria, and ___anxiety___ (15)-reducing effects. In the United States and Canada, someone with a blood alcohol concentration (BAC) of ___0.08 %___ % (16) is legally considered too intoxicated to be driving. At BAC concentrations of 0.3%–0.4%, a person may go into a coma or ___die___ (17). Severe withdrawal symptoms include hallucinations, delusions, and seizures, also known as ___delirium___ tremens

_____ (18), that may occur when recovering from prolonged alcohol abuse. Health problems associated with long-term use of alcohol include cirrhosis of the ____liver____ (19) and a form of brain damage called ____Korsakoff____ (20) syndrome. ____Binge____ (21) drinkers are more likely to be impulsive and have learning and memory deficits. Alcohol affects the central nervous system by inhibiting the release of the excitatory neurotransmitter ____glutamate____ (22) and by increasing the release of the inhibitory neurotransmitter ____GABA____ (23). The latter neurotransmitter normally binds to receptors attached to ____chloride____ (24) ion channels. Exposure to alcohol during prenatal development may result in a cluster of symptoms (including mental retardation, irritability, and facial anomalies) called ____fetal____ ____alcohol____ (25) syndrome.

____Barbiturates____ (26) are depressant drugs that have been used to treat insomnia, epileptic seizures, and were the first used to treat ____anxiety____ (27). They typically produce ____tolerance____ (28), resulting in increasing dosages and addiction. Because there is a fine line between therapeutic and toxic levels of these drugs, they have mostly been replaced with much safer ____benziodiazepines____ (29), such as Xanax.

____Stimulants____ (30) are drugs that produce arousal and elevate mood. Cocaine, which is derived from the coca plant, produces euphoria and relieves fatigue. Pure cocaine, or ____freebase____ (31), produces especially rapid, intense effects when smoked. A lower cost, less pure, and faster-acting version of cocaine is called ____crack____ (32). Cocaine blocks the reuptake of ____dopamine____ (33) and serotonin, which results in removal of cortical ____inhibition____ (34) of lower structures. Although in the past cocaine was not considered dangerous, it is now recognized as being quite addictive, especially when injected or ____smoked/inhaled____ (35). Cocaine users have impairments in memory and ____executive____ (36) functions, and have a high rate of ____psychological____ (37) disorders, which makes rehabilitation difficult. In one study where rats could press a lever to self-administer cocaine or heroin, ____90____ % (38) of the cocaine group died as a result of overdose, compared to only 36% in the heroin group. In addition, a controlled adoption study revealed that ____prenatal____ (39) exposure to cocaine is linked to lower IQs and problems with language and attention in children.

Due to their tendency to enhance alertness and reduce fatigue, ____amphetamines____ (40) such as Dexedrine and the much more powerful drug featured on the television show *Breaking Bad*, ____methamph.____ (41), are often used by people who want to stay awake for long periods of time. These drugs cause an increase in the release of dopamine and ____norepinephrine____ (42). Psychotic symptoms from prolonged use include ____hallucination____ (43) and delusions similar to those seen in paranoid schizophrenia.

Nicotine, the addictive psychoactive ingredient in tobacco, has ____stimulating____ (44) effects when taken in short puffs, but depressant effects when inhaled deeply. Most people find that when they quit smoking, the ____withdrawal____ (45) symptoms such as anxiety and headaches are unpleasant, and they return to smoking. The health risks of smoking are high, but they are due to compounds in tobacco ____smoke____ (46), not nicotine. Children exposed prenatally to nicotine are more likely to be underweight as infants and have up to a 56% increased risk of childhood ____mortality____ (47); however, their tendency to display ____conduct____ (48) disorder and criminal behavior later in life appears to be linked to genes and not nicotine. The positive feeling that nicotine use produces is the result of ____dopamine____ (49) receptor activation, while the alertness is produced through activation of acetylcholine receptors. Caffeine, a milder stimulant than cocaine and amphetamine, affects the nervous system by blocking ____adenosine____ (50) receptors, which results in an increase in the release of dopamine and _acetycholine_ (51). Caffeine withdrawal symptoms are mild but common; the most problematic symptom seems to be an increase in _headaches_ (52).

Psychedelic drugs cause _perceptual_ (53) distortions, such as intensification or changes of visual stimuli and cross-modality perceptions. LSD and drugs derived from the *Psilocybe mexicana* mushroom resemble and stimulate the same receptors as the neurotransmitter _serotonin_ (54). _Mescaline_ (55) comes from the peyote cactus and may be used legally for religious practices by some Native Americans. MDMA, also known as _ecstasy_ (56), stimulates the release of serotonin and dopamine; this drug has _psychomotor_ (57) stimulant effects at lower doses and hallucinatory effects at higher doses. Some studies show a decrease in _serotonin_ (58) functioning, with persistent but small effects on _memory_ (59). Phencyclidine (PCP), also known as angel dust or crystal, was initially developed as a(n) _anesthetic_ (60). However, this drug often triggers symptoms similar to _schizophrenia_ (61) and shows indications of being addictive.

The psychoactive ingredient in marijuana and hashish is _THC_ (62), a substance that binds to cannabinoid receptors on axon terminals. Endogenous (internal) cannabinoids such as anandamide are _retrograde_ (63) messengers; they are released by postsynaptic dendrites and bind to presynaptic receptors. Marijuana's effects on cognition and time perception may be due to its effects on the _frontal_ (64) cortex. Long-term heavy use of marijuana has been associated with reduced volume and impaired white matter connectivity in the _hippocampus_ (65) and corpus callosum as well as damage to the amygdala. Longitudinal studies in individuals who smoked five joints a day demonstrated a progressive decline in _IQ_ (66) as well. Prenatal exposure to marijuana is correlational at best, but there does seem to be an increase in _behavioral_ (67) problems, such as impulsivity, hyperactivity, and visual-spatial task performance. Marijuana does have beneficial uses, such as relieving the _nausea_ (68) associated with chemotherapy. While federal laws prohibit any use of marijuana, numerous states have legalized its use for medical purposes and proponents of legalization cite reports that marijuana can be used to manage _pain_ (69) resistant to relief by opiates.

Because withdrawal from marijuana produces very mild symptoms, its compulsive use has often been attributed to _psychological_ _dependence_ (70). However, monkeys will _self_-_administer_ (71) THC when given the opportunity to do so, suggesting that it is indeed an addictive substance.

Short Answer and Essay Questions

Answer the following questions.

1. What is conditioned tolerance? What evidence is there that heroin use may lead to conditioned tolerance?

2. Describe the structure of the GABA$_A$ receptor complex, and compare the mechanisms by which alcohol, barbiturates, and benzodiazepines affect GABA activity.

3. Compare the effects of withdrawal from opiates, alcohol, cocaine, and nicotine. Which drug produces the most serious withdrawal symptoms?

4. Compare the effects of prenatal exposure to the following drugs: alcohol, cocaine, nicotine, and marijuana.

5. Is marijuana addictive? Support your answer with facts from the text and the Internet.

Addiction

Summary and Guided Review

After studying this section in the text, fill in the blanks of the following summary.

In the past, researchers assumed that addiction to drugs is maintained by the addict's desire to avoid __withdrawal__ (72) effects. However, this does not explain what motivates drug taking until addiction develops. Initial drug taking apparently depends on the drug's __rewarding__ (73) effects, which appear to be physiologically independent processes. People and animals tend to engage in behaviors that have previously resulted in reward from objects such as drugs, sexual stimulation, warmth, and __food__ (74). One major brain circuit for reward is the __mesolimbic__ __dopamine__ (75) pathway, named for the "middle" originating neurons of the midbrain structure called the __ventral__ __tegmental__ __area__ (76) and the limbic regions that receive dopamine projections. In particular, microdialysis studies have shown that dopamine increases in the nucleus __accumbens__ (77) after rats experience rewards such as sexual contact. __Electrical__ __stimulation__ (78) of the brain has as strong a reward effect as drugs, resulting in up to sixfold increases in dopamine in the nucleus accumbens than that observed following food intake. Drugs of abuse, like other rewards, increase dopamine activity via the mesolimbic dopamine system. Evidence for this includes reports of study participants who experienced a cocaine "high" when __47__% (79) of nucleus accumbens dopamine reuptake sites were blocked.

Chronic drug use involves the __mesolimbocortical__ (80) dopamine system, which includes the mesolimbic pathway and dopamine projections to the __frontal__ (81) cortex. Brain changes following chronic drug use result in __decreased__ (82) baseline dopamine and reduced activation from exposure to activities and objects that would normally be rewarding (such as sexual activity). However, long-term drug users also demonstrate __sensitization__ (83), which is defined as an increased responsiveness to the drug itself and drug-related objects. Some of the impulsiveness and drug-seeking behavior demonstrated by drug users is related to decreased activity in parts of the frontal lobe, called __hypofrontality__ (84).

Most people agree that while reward is involved in early drug taking, later stages characterized by craving and withdrawal involve lifelong changes in __brain__ (85) functioning. Research on learning has been important in trying to understand drug addiction. One brain change that occurs in response to drug use involves the neurotransmitter __glutamate__ (86), which can include changes to receptors as well as modifications to synapses in the nucleus accumbens and prefrontal cortex. In addicts, the sight of drug paraphernalia evokes __craving__ (87) for the drug, which coincides with changes of activity in brain areas involved in __learning__ (88) and emotion. Drug-induced brain plasticity is shown, for example, in the changes in the synapses between the nucleus accumbens and both the prefrontal cortex and __amygdala__ (89). Initially, receptors are not available in these synapses, but the receptors appear during withdrawal, which leads to increased craving during periods without drug use. This increased level of craving over time is called __incubation__ (90) of craving.

Quitting an addictive substance can be very difficult. The first step is for the body to rid itself of the drug, a process called __detox__ (91). Withdrawal symptoms during this period can be intense, and in the case of alcohol withdrawal it may be necessary to administer __benzodiazepine__ (92) to prevent life-threatening results. Once the withdrawal symptoms have subsided, abstaining from a drug may involve the therapeutic use of other drugs. For example, __methadone__ (93) is an opiate agonist given to __buprenorphine__

heroin users that has milder effects and can be obtained legally. Antagonist treatments like
naloxone ___naltrexone___ (94) are used to block the effects of opiates on receptors. The muscle
relaxant ___baclofen___ (95) dampens the reward system by stimulating GABA
receptors. ___Antabuse___ (96) is an aversive treatment for alcohol addiction; it works
by making the person violently ill if alcohol is consumed. A promising area of research involves
the use of antidrug ___vaccines___ (97), which stimulate the immune system to
produce antibodies for a drug. By reducing activity of ___dopamine___ (98) neurons,
anti-inflammatory treatments may also assist in reducing drug use in those with addiction.

The combination of addiction and other psychological disorders, or
___comorbidity___ (99), makes addiction treatment even more challenging. One of the
most common psychological disorders exhibited by drug users is a(n) ___personality___
(100) disorder, either mental or emotional. However, some observers believe that the use of
pharmacological treatments, such as methadone for opiate abuse, are not okay because replacing
one drug with another continues the ___pleasures___ (101) of drug taking.

Short Answer and Essay Questions

Answer the following questions.

6. Explain what the problems are with explaining addiction as the avoidance of withdrawal symptoms

7. Discuss the role of dopaminergic reward systems in drug use and addiction. Be sure to identify the brain's reward pathways in your answer.

8. How might cocaine-induced brain changes contribute to addiction to the drug?

9. Give an example of each of the following types of treatment for addiction: agonist, antagonist, and aversive. Explain how each works.

10. How might the immune system be manipulated to treat drug addiction? What are the advantages of this approach?

11. Why are pharmacological treatments for drugs controversial? Do you think they should be used? Why or why not?

The Role of Genes in Addiction

Summary and Guided Review

After studying this section in the text, fill in the blanks of the following summary.

Based on results from twin and adoption studies, there appears to be a strong
hereditary ___genetic___ (102) component to alcoholism. The results of Cloninger and
colleagues' comprehensive study of Swedish adoptees suggested that there are two types of
alcoholism. In Type 1 or ___late___-___onset___ (103) alcoholism,
problem drinking usually emerges after age ___25___ (104); people with this
type of alcoholism may alternate between abstinence and ___binge___ (105)
drinking. Those with Type 2, or early-onset alcoholism, may begin drinking in adolescence and
display a host of personality traits characteristic of ___antisocial___ (106) personality
disorder. People with ___early___ (107)-onset alcoholism are more likely to be
hospitalized. The environment seems to have a great impact on the development of alcoholism
only in the offspring of those with ___late___ (108)-onset alcoholism.

The exact role of genetics in addiction is beginning to be understood. Ten different gene alleles linked to decreased dopamine activity can now be used to calculate a(n) _____Genetic_____ _____Addiction_____ _____Risk_____ (109) score. Genes impact levels of neurotransmitters, numbers of receptors, sensitivity to drugs, and how well drugs are processed by the body. In addition, a person's experience of a drug depends on genes, as shown with the allele for the _____CHRNA5_____ (110) acetylcholine receptor gene, which impacts how much pleasure someone experiences from using tobacco. Moderate alcoholics with two specific alleles of the _____GABRA 2 Gene_____ (111), which influences GABA$_A$ receptor functioning, have more symptoms of alcohol dependence and impulsiveness. Furthermore, addicts who are anticipating a reward or loss have higher activity in the _____insular_____ (112) cortex. In addition, a lowered amplitude in the _____P300_____ (113) wave, which is a dip in the EEG event-related potential after an unexpected stimulus, predicts development of drug abuse disorders by the age of 20. This dip in activity has been seen in a variety of disorders characterized by _____behavioral_____ _____disinhibition_____ (114), which is characterized by impulsivity, risk taking, novelty seeking, and poor stress responsiveness.

Drugs also alter how genes function; in smokers _____methylation_____(115) suppresses activity of up to 7,000 genes, some of which are linked to diseases such as _____cancer_____ (116). The genes of a(n) _____Unborn_____ _____fetus_____ (117) can be similarly impacted by a mother's smoking.

[handwritten margin note: ↑ or Cardiovascular disease]

Short Answer and Essay Questions

Answer the following questions.

12. Distinguish between early- and late-onset alcoholism in terms of (1) the developmental pattern of the addiction and (2) the personality characteristics of people with each type. Be sure to address the way that environment interacts with these categories of alcoholism to result in behavioral outcomes.

13. When we think about a genetic component for a disorder, we might get the idea that one gene controls our risk for something such as addiction. However, that is not the case. Explain, using some of the addiction examples in the text, how multiple genes are important in controlling risk for addiction.

14. Describe three ways in which the EEG patterns of people with alcoholism and those at risk for alcoholism differ from the EEG patterns of nonalcoholics. Why might the EEG be a useful tool for determining who is most at risk for alcoholism?

15. Imagine you are a scientist who studies the biological basis of alcoholism. You are in the process of seeking a multimillion-dollar grant to fund additional research in this area. The granting agency wants to know why alcoholism should be studied so intensely when there are many other forms of addiction and "more dangerous" drugs. How would you justify your continued study of alcoholism?

Post-test

Use these multiple-choice questions to check your understanding of the chapter.

1. Which of the following is NOT true of heroin use?
   a. It may lead to an addiction that is difficult to overcome.
   b. It may lead to withdrawal symptoms that are life-threatening.

c. Users experience intense euphoria followed by relaxation.

d. It may lead to conditioned tolerance.

2. Arlene has been smoking marijuana three or four times a week for two years. She often worries about running out and occasionally steals small amounts from her friends who smoke. She recently tried to quit, but she started again after one month of being off the drug. Arlene is experiencing

a. withdrawal.

b. tolerance.

c. addiction.

d. depression.

3. Alcohol is BEST classified as a(n) _____ drug.

a. depressant

b. stimulant

c. opiate

d. psychedelic

4. Jerry, a 55-year-old chronic alcoholic, has recently begun experiencing memory loss and motor problems. His doctor informs him that he may be suffering from _____ as a result of his long-term alcohol abuse.

a. delirium tremens

b. conditioned tolerance

c. Korsakoff syndrome

d. binge drinking

5. Which of the following drugs influence the activity of GABA?

a. alcohol

b. barbiturates

c. benzodiazepines

d. all of the above

6. Which of the following is NOT true regarding the early historical use of cocaine?

a. The freebase form was used by South American Indians for centuries.

b. It was an ingredient in Coca-Cola until 1906.

c. In the 1800s, it was used as a local anesthetic.

d. Sigmund Freud recommended it to his family and friends.

7. Prenatal exposure to cocaine has been linked to which of the following problem(s)?

a. seizure disorders in children

b. poor cognitive development

c. facial abnormalities

d. all of the above

8. The MOST potent form of amphetamine is

a. Benzedrine.

b. Dexedrine.

c. methamphetamine.

d. dextroamphetamine.

9. Smoking, swallowing, or snorting bath salts results in increased energy, sex drive, and sociability similar to which of the following drugs?

a. marijuana

b. methamphetamine

    c. alcohol

    d. barbiturates

10. Which of the following is NOT a health problem associated with cigarette smoking or tobacco use?

    a. Buerger's disease

    b. cancer of the mouth

    c. emphysema

    d. Korsakoff syndrome

11. Which stimulant affects dopamine and acetylcholine levels indirectly through its effects on adenosine?

    a. caffeine

    b. cocaine

    c. nicotine

    d. amphetamine

12. Which of the following psychedelic drugs is found in a cactus?

    a. ecstasy

    b. angel dust

    c. mescaline

    d. psilocybin

13. Which of the following psychedelic drugs is MOST closely related to amphetamines?

    a. ecstasy

    b. angel dust

    c. LSD

    d. mescaline

14. The psychoactive ingredient in marijuana affects the same receptor sites as which of the following ligands?

    a. endorphin

    b. anandamide

    c. dopamine

    d. glutamate

15. The cognitive deficits seen in children exposed to marijuana prenatally seem MOST likely due to impairment of which part of the brain?

    a. hippocampus

    b. basal ganglia

    c. cerebellum

    d. prefrontal cortex

16. The MOST compelling reason to believe that marijuana is an addictive substance is that

    a. some people experience withdrawal symptoms when they stop using it.

    b. many people use it for years.

    c. animals will self-administer it.

    d. it has negative effects on the fetus.

17. Rats will learn to press a lever in order to inject drugs into which of the following brain structures?

    a. medial forebrain bundle

    b. ventral tegmental area

    c. nucleus accumbens

    d. all of the above

18. Addictive drugs may produce euphoric effects by

    a. stimulating the release of dopamine.

    b. blocking postsynaptic dopamine receptors.

    c. eliminating dopamine from the synapse.

    d. inhibiting the release of dopamine.

19. ESB has its greatest effect

    a. on animals missing a specific subtype of dopamine receptor.

    b. when an animal is also given cocaine or amphetamine.

    c. in brain areas where dopaminergic neurons are highly concentrated.

    d. in brain areas where serotonergic neurons are highly concentrated.

20. Which of the following is a TRUE statement about the effects of reward?

    a. A food reward is just as pleasant to experience as a drug reward.

    b. Sexual contact is the most intensely experienced reward.

    c. Natural rewards (such as food) are experienced more intensely than non-natural rewards (such as electrical brain stimulation).

    d. Drugs and electrical brain stimulation produce stronger effects than natural rewards (such as food).

21. Opiates are implicated in the rewarding effects of which drug?

    a. alcohol

    b. cocaine

    c. amphetamine

    d. nicotine

22. PCP inhibits the effects of

    a. dopamine.

    b. glutamate.

    c. serotonin.

    d. endorphins.

23. Which of the following is NOT part of the mesolimbocortical system that scientists have linked to drug addiction?

    a. nucleus accumbens

    b. ventral tegmental area

    c. medulla oblongata

    d. frontal lobe

24. Cocaine addicts' compulsive drug-using behavior may be a result of

    a. damage to the hippocampus.

    b. damage to the prefrontal cortex.

    c. damage to the ventral tegmental area.

    d. all of the above

25. When a rat that has learned to press a lever in order to receive a drug reward no longer receives the reward, it will stop pressing the lever. However, electrical stimulation of the _____ reinstates the lever pressing.

    a. nucleus accumbens

    b. ventral tegmental area

c. hippocampus
d. lateral hypothalamus

26. Freud suffered from lifelong addiction to
   a. cocaine.
   b. alcohol.
   c. heroin.
   d. nicotine.

27. Sharon was recently admitted to the hospital because she was suffering severe with-drawal symptoms, including seizures. She was given a benzodiazepine to reduce the severity of her symptoms. Which of the following drugs is Sharon MOST likely addicted to?
   a. alcohol
   b. heroin
   c. nicotine
   d. cocaine

28. Nicotine gum is an example of an _____ treatment for drug addiction.
   a. antagonist
   b. aversive
   c. agonist
   d. antidrug

29. Naltrexone may be used to block opiate receptors in people who abuse
   a. nicotine.
   b. cocaine.
   c. amphetamines.
   d. alcohol.

30. Methadone was developed as an analgesic during World War II when _____ was in short supply.
   a. morphine
   b. heroin
   c. codeine
   d. endorphin

31. Which of the following statements is NOT true of antidrug vaccines?
   a. They lead to the destruction of drug molecules before they can reach the brain.
   b. They are more effective than other pharmacological treatments in humans.
   c. They result in fewer side effects than other pharmacological treatments.
   d. Their effects may be longer lasting than other pharmacological treatments.

32. For heroin addicts,
   a. methadone treatment alone is the most effective treatment option.
   b. counseling alone has a high rate of success.
   c. no treatment method has more than a 50% success rate.
   d. methadone plus counseling is quite effective.

33. The heritability for addiction is
   a. 5%–10%.
   b. 20%–30%.
   c. 50%–60%.
   d. 80%–90%.

34. Bill has been drinking alcohol since he was a teenager. He is a risk-taker and frequently drives while intoxicated. Even after being in fights while drunk, Bill does not feel guilty about his alcohol consumption. Which of the following is probably true about Bill?
    a. Bill has Type 1 alcoholism.
    b. Bill has Type 2 alcoholism.
    c. Bill has late-onset alcoholism.
    d. Bill has a weak genetic influence on his alcoholism.

35. Which of the following is a characteristic of Type 1 alcoholism?
    a. problems with alcohol beginning in adolescence
    b. a tendency to behave aggressively when drinking
    c. cautious behavior when drinking
    d. all of the above

36. Cloninger's study of early- and late-onset alcoholism indicates that
    a. exposure to alcoholism in the home has more of an impact on the children of parents with late-onset alcoholism than on the children of those with early-onset alcoholism.
    b. exposure to alcoholism in the home has more of an impact on the children of parents with early-onset alcoholism than on the children of those with late-onset alcoholism.
    c. exposure to alcoholism in the home has about the same effect on the children of parents with early- and late-onset alcoholism.
    d. people with late-onset alcoholism are most likely to have children who have early-onset alcoholism.

37. Genes for which of the following transmitters have been implicated in drug abuse?
    a. dopamine
    b. endogenous opioids
    c. acetylcholine
    d. all of the above

38. Mari smokes 10–20 cigarettes a day and is generally impulsive in her decisions. Which of the following would you also expect to be true of Mari?
    a. White matter connections in the prefrontal cortex will be abnormal.
    b. Her hippocampus will be smaller than normal.
    c. Her ventral tegmental area will not be connected to the nucleus accumbens.
    d. Her frontal lobe will be larger than expected.

39. The P300 wave
    a. shows promise for diagnosing those at risk for alcoholism.
    b. occurs in response to a novel or unexpected stimulus.
    c. occurs in similar ways among genetically related individuals.
    d. all of the above

40. Which of the following is a mechanism by which a mother's smoking can influence the smoking-related cancer risk of her unborn baby?
    a. P300 wave
    b. reduced dopamine receptors in the baby's nucleus accumbens
    c. methylation of some genes
    d. hypofrontality in the infant

Answers

Guided Review

1. agonists
2. antagonists
3. addiction
4. withdrawal
5. tolerance
6. Analgesic or hypnotic
7. hypnotic or analgesic
8. cancer
9. codeine
10. heroin
11. overdose
12. endorphins
13. depressants
14. cognitive
15. anxiety
16. 0.08
17. die
18. delirium tremens
19. liver
20. Korsakoff
21. Binge
22. glutamate
23. GABA
24. chloride
25. fetal alcohol
26. Barbiturates
27. anxiety
28. tolerance
29. benzodiazepines
30. Stimulants
31. freebase
32. crack
33. dopamine
34. inhibition
35. smoked or inhaled
36. executive
37. psychological
38. 90
39. prenatal
40. amphetamines
41. methamphetamine
42. norepinephrine
43. hallucinations
44. stimulating
45. withdrawal
46. smoke
47. mortality or death
48. conduct
49. dopamine
50. adenosine
51. acetylcholine
52. headaches
53. perceptual
54. serotonin
55. Mescaline
56. ecstasy
57. psychomotor
58. serotonin
59. memory
60. anesthetic
61. schizophrenia
62. tetrahydrocannabinol (THC)
63. retrograde
64. frontal
65. hippocampus
66. IQ
67. behavioral
68. nausea
69. pain
70. psychological dependence
71. self-administer
72. withdrawal
73. rewarding
74. food

75. mesolimbic dopamine
76. ventral tegmental area
77. accumbens
78. Electrical stimulation
79. 47
80. mesolimbocortical
81. frontal
82. decreased
83. sensitization
84. hypofrontality
85. brain
86. glutamate
87. craving
88. learning
89. amygdala
90. incubation
91. Detoxification or detox
92. benzodiazepines
93. methadone or buprenorphine
94. Naltrexone or naloxone
95. baclofen
96. Antabuse

97. vaccines
98. dopamine
99. comorbidity
100. personality
101. pleasures
102. genetic or hereditary
103. late-onset
104. 25
105. binge
106. antisocial
107. early
108. late
109. Genetic Addiction Risk
110. *CHRNA5*
111. *GABRA$_2$* gene
112. insular
113. P300
114. behavioral disinhibition
115. methylation
116. cancer or cardiovascular disease
117. unborn fetus

Short Answer and Essay Questions

1. Conditioned tolerance is a learned tolerance that is specific to the setting where it developed; as a result, the individual shows tolerance to a drug in one context but not in another. Rats are more likely to die of overdose when given a large dose in a novel environment (64% versus 32% of rats in each group died). Likewise, human heroin addicts may be more likely to overdose when they take the same amount of drug in a novel setting. When in a different environment, those cues that trigger the tolerance response are no longer present, and the same dose may have a more powerful effect.

2. The GABA$_A$ receptor complex has at least five different receptor sites, only one of which responds to the neurotransmitter GABA. When GABA binds to its receptor, chloride channels open and the neuron is inhibited. The other receptor types are affected by various drugs. Alcohol fits a different receptor in the complex, and it enhances GABA binding, which produces a stronger inhibitory response. Barbiturates fit yet another receptor in the GABA$_A$ complex, also enhancing the effectiveness of GABA, but at high doses they can actually open chloride channels without GABA. Benzodiazepines also act at the GABA$_A$ receptor complex in the limbic system, brain stem, hippocampus, and cortex.

3. Opiate withdrawal is like having the flu. Alcohol produces the most serious withdrawal symptoms, including delirium tremens, convulsions, and even death. Less severe withdrawal symptoms of alcohol include anxiety and mood changes. Cocaine produces mild withdrawal symptoms, including anxiety and loss of motivation and pleasure. Nicotine withdrawal includes anxiety, sleepiness, and headaches.

4. Prenatal exposure to alcohol may result in fetal alcohol syndrome, a cluster of symptoms including facial abnormalities, mental retardation, and irritability. Exposure to cocaine prenatally has been linked to impaired IQ and language development as well as attention problems. Prenatal exposure to nicotine is linked to low birth weight. Marijuana exposure before birth may contribute to behavioral and cognitive deficiencies, but these may not be apparent until after four years of age.

5. There is evidence that marijuana is addictive, although it produces only mild withdrawal symptoms. Compulsive use in humans has been documented, and monkeys will self-administer THC, which is usually taken as evidence of addiction.

6. One problem is that withdrawal symptoms occur later, so avoidance of withdrawal cannot be the mechanism that maintains early drug use. Second, addicts intentionally go through withdrawal to adjust their tolerance level. Third, many addicts start using a drug again after having quit for a long period of time and are presumably no longer experiencing withdrawal. Finally, the power of addiction of a drug is not related to the severity of withdrawal. For example, alcohol can cause severe withdrawal symptoms, but heroin or stimulants may not.

7. The mesolimbocortical dopamine system is a brain reward system that seems to be highly involved in drug use. Various rewards, including drugs of abuse, food, and sexual contact all activate dopaminergic neurons in the ventral tegmental area, which then send signals to limbic brain areas including the nucleus accumbens, amygdala, and hippocampus. This is the mesolimbic dopamine pathway. Drugs of abuse also activate dopaminergic projections to the frontal cortex. These dopamine pathways are important to addiction because activation of the limbic system dopamine neurons leads to positive feelings following drug use, as shown in studies where rats will self-administer electrical brain stimulation to dopamine cells in the nucleus accumbens as many as 1,000 times per hour. In addition, the plasticity in the dopamine system results in reduced activation of the frontal lobe, which promotes impulsivity and drug-seeking behaviors.

8. Learning is associated with synaptic increases in the prefrontal cortex and nucleus accumbens. In addition, the prefrontal cortex also undergoes pathological alterations in dendrites, reduction in dopamine activity, prefrontal deactivation, and reduced behavioral inhibition. As a result of learning, hippocampal stimulation produces a high level of dopamine release and a return to drug-seeking behavior; brain changes from learning are considered to be the reason drugs have a lifelong effect.

9. Agonist treatments, such as methadone for heroin addiction, involve the replacement of a more harmful substance with a less harmful one that basically has the same effect on the nervous system. Antagonistic treatment involves administration of a drug that blocks the effects of the undesirable drug. For example, baclofen seems to block dopamine activity normally stimulated by several addictive substances. Aversive treatments produce an undesirable reaction when the harmful drug is taken. Antabuse, for example, produces nausea and vomiting when alcohol is consumed, because it inhibits the metabolism of acetaldehyde.

10. Antidrug vaccines induce the body to produce antibodies to destroy the drug. They appear to be quite effective and may soon be available for use with humans. The advantages of these drugs are that they do not result in the side effects common to drugs that interfere with neurotransmitters, and their effects may be quite long lasting.

11. Pharmacological treatments are controversial because they involve treating drug addiction by giving a person another drug. In the case of methadone, this means substituting a less problematic addiction for a more problematic one. Other drug treatments (such as treatment with Antabuse and possibly with baclofen) interfere with drug use without leading to addiction. (The argument for these treatments is that they are generally effective, but some people believe

that addiction should be overcome by sheer willpower, and that relying on other drugs to do it is taking the easy way out.)

12.   People with early-onset (Type 2) alcoholism usually begin drinking prior to the age of 25, many of them in their teens. They are more likely to be male, and they often display impulsive, aggressive, and reckless behavior while being socially and emotionally detached from others. This pattern of characteristics is associated with antisocial personality disorder. Those with late-onset (Type 1) alcoholism usually begin having problems with alcohol after the age of 25, following a period of social drinking. They tend to binge drink, which results in guilt feelings; they may abstain from alcohol for long periods. They tend to be cautious and emotionally dependent. Early-onset alcoholism seems to be more strongly related to genetics than late-onset alcoholism, as children of people with late-onset alcoholism were at an increased risk for alcoholism only if their family environment included alcohol abuse.

13.   Addiction involves a variety of behaviors and responses, including a person initially taking a drug, the psychological effect the drug has upon consumption, the long-term effects of drug consumption, and the other activities a person engages in. Genes impact all of these, with different genes impacting short-term and long-term responses to drugs as well as the personality types that might leave someone vulnerable to initial drug experimentation. Examples include the *Met158* allele of the *COMT* gene, which is linked to cautious behavior, predisposing European Caucasian men to late-onset alcoholism, but protecting against alcoholism in American Indians and alleles of the *CHRNA5* and *OPRMI* genes, which influence how much pleasure someone experiences after consuming a drug. Genes involved in addiction have been identified for addiction to coffee, alcohol, and tobacco.

14.   First, when not under the influence of alcohol, male alcoholics and their children show more high-frequency waves than nonalcoholics. Also, alcoholics and their children, who are probably at risk for alcoholism, show a reduced "dip" in the P300 waves in response to novel stimuli, and the P300 wave is also delayed. The EEG may be useful for determining who is most at risk for alcoholism, because children of alcoholics who are not alcoholics themselves often show the same pattern of responses as their parents.

15.   Alcoholism is a good model for studying drug addiction. Many of the addictive drugs have very similar effects in the brain, mostly through their effects on the dopamine reward system. Therefore, any discoveries made about the genetic and neurological bases of alcohol addiction may be applicable to other forms of addiction. Furthermore, alcoholism is the most problematic addiction in our society. Its use is linked to violence, traffic accidents, and other serious behavioral problems. Because it is a legal drug, there are more alcoholics than people addicted to other drugs. Consequently, it makes sense to attempt to understand and perhaps control or even eradicate it. In doing so, it may be possible to treat other forms of addiction as well.

Post-test

1. b   2. c   3. a   4. c   5. d   6. a   7. b   8. c   9. b   10. d   11. a   12. c   13. a   14. b
15. d   16. c   17. d   18. a   19. c   20. d   21. a   22. b   23. c   24. b   25. c   26. d
27. a   28. c   29. d   30. a   31. b   32. d   33. c   34. b   35. c   36. a   37. d   38. a
39. d   40. c

6 Motivation and the Regulation of Internal States

CONCEPT CHECK

In Perspective

Chapter Summary

Study Resources

Learning Objectives

After reading this chapter, you will be able to

1. Summarize the psychological theories of motivation

2. Describe how temperature regulation and thirst reflect the concept of homeostasis

3. Explain the role of taste in choices of food

4. Identify the brain signals that control when we begin and end eating

5. Compare the roles of environment and heredity in risk for obesity

6. Examine how the environment and genetics impact risk for disordered eating

7. Discuss the role of neurotransmitters in eating disorders

Motivation and Homeostasis

Summary and Guided Review

After studying this section in the text, fill in the blanks of the following summary.

_____Motivation_____ (1) refers to factors that initiate, sustain, and direct behaviors; there are several theories of motivation. Ancient Greeks, as well as some early 20th-century psychologists, proposed that many human behaviors are ___instictively___ (2) motivated; a more precisely defined concept continues to be used with animal behavior, but most contemporary psychologists believe instincts have little influence on human behavior. Another explanation for motivation is _____drive_____ (3) theory, which proposes that the body attempts to maintain ___homeostasis___ (4), or balance. Although this theory helps explain some behaviors, it does not explain behaviors that do not satisfy bodily needs, such as seeking fame or academic excellence. ___Incentive___ (5) theory accounts for the fact that people are often motivated by external stimuli, such as money. Another theory, ___arousal___ (6) theory, suggests that people are also motivated to maintain a preferred level of stimulation, although this level varies from person to person. Perhaps the best way to think about drives is to assume that they represent _____brain_____ ___states___ (7) rather than conditions of the body. This is supported by the fact that many stimuli can motivate a behavior, even in the absence of ___tissue___ (8) needs, such as suddenly feeling hungry when smelling food, even after a meal.

A useful way of representing homeostasis and the preferred state of a control system is the ___set___ (9) point; when conditions deviate too far from this point, the nervous system becomes operative to restore it. For example, all animals must maintain their body ___temp.___ (10) within a particular range, or they will die.

In mammals, body temperature is controlled by the ___preoptic___ (11) area of the hypothalamus. Here, warmth- and ___cold___-___sensitive___ (12) cells respond to the temperature of the blood and to temperature receptors in other parts of the body by initiating physiological activities, such as sweating if the organism is too hot, or ___shivering___ (13) if the organism is too cold.

Another drive that nicely fits the homeostatic model is ___thirst___ (14). Water is essential for the proper function of the bodily systems, but it is continually lost through urination, defecation, and ___evaporation___ (15). There are two types of thirst: ___osmotic___ (16) thirst is a result of low intracellular fluid, whereas ___hypovolemic___ (17) thirst occurs when blood volume drops. The first type is regulated by cells in the ___OVLT___ (18), along the third ventricle, that detect low levels of intracellular fluid and communicate the deficit to the ___median___ ___preoptic___ ___nucleus___ (19) of the hypothalamus, which initiates drinking. The second type of thirst is detected by pressure receptors in the atrium of the heart that signal the brain via the ___vagus___ (20) nerve to the ___NST___ (21) in the medulla. The kidneys also respond to low blood volume by releasing renin; this increases the level of ___angiotensin___ (22) II, which is detected by the ___subfornical___ (23) organ and induces drinking via the median preoptic nucleus. Homeostasis is not achieved immediately after ingesting water; rather the SFO also responds to water intake so that ___satiety___ (24), satisfaction of appetite for water, can be met.

Short Answer and Essay Questions

Answer the following questions.

1. Explain why drive theory alone is insufficient to account for motivation. Include in your answer the ways that other motivational theories address the shortcomings of drive theory.

2. Compare and contrast temperature regulation and thirst as motivated processes. How are set point and homeostasis important in understanding both of these processes?

Hunger: A Complex Drive

Summary and Guided Review

After studying this section in the text, fill in the blanks of the following summary.

As a drive, hunger is more complicated than temperature and thirst, because the ___set___ (25) point can undergo dramatic changes and because there are so many different types of ___nutrients___ (26) that the body needs.

Humans eat a variety of plant, animal, and other foods, meaning that we are ___omnivores___ (27); to remain healthy, we need to eat a varied diet and at the same time carefully select foods that are not toxic or spoiled. The sense of ___taste___ (28) helps us select nutritious, safe foods and avoid nonnutritious, dangerous ones. We have at least ___five___ (29) primary taste sensations, each of which seems to indicate different qualities of food. Foods that taste ___sweet___ (30), such as fruits, and those that taste salty are highly preferred. These types of food typically provide nutrients necessary for survival. The other qualities, ___sour___ (31) and ___bitter___ (32), often indicate that food

NST- nucleus of the solitary tract

is spoiled or toxic, respectively, and should therefore be avoided. A recently discovered taste, ___umami___ (33), has been described as "meaty" or "savory"; some researchers believe it could be important in our selection of ___proteins___ (34). Sensory information about taste is transmitted from the taste buds located on the surface of tongue ___papillae___ (35), through the nucleus of the ___solitary___ ___tract___ (36) in the medulla, and via the thalamus to the ___insula___ (37), which is the primary gustatory cortex. Information from different taste receptors travels to the cortex via separate pathways to distinct areas; this is referred to as ___labelled___ ___line___ (38) coding of stimuli.

A food particularly becomes less appealing as we eat more of it, a phenomenon known as ___sensory___-___specific___ (39) satiety, which is an important mechanism for ensuring that we eat a variety of foods. This form of satiety seems to be controlled by the ___NST___ (40). Taste is an important cue for learning which foods may be harmful; experiments with rats have shown that if a certain taste becomes associated with illness, they will ___avoid___ (41) items with that taste in the future. Humans also demonstrate these ___learned___ ___taste___ (42) aversions, although the bouts of sickness are often not caused by the foods they become associated with, as in the case of children undergoing ___chemotherapy___ (43) who learned to avoid a particular flavor of ice cream presented just prior to treatment. There is even some evidence that rats will form an aversion to foods ___deficient___ (44) /cues in thiamine. Taste is also an important cue for learning which foods to eat even when the nutrients themselves may not be detected; for example, rats deprived of a specific nutrient/vitamin/chemical (45) learned to eat a food enriched with it that was flavored with anise (licorice). Finally, there is a difference between food taste, the sensation gained from the receptors in the mouth, and ___flavor___ (46), which is a combination of both taste and smell.

___Digestion___ (47) begins in the mouth, where ___saliva___ (48) is added to food. In the stomach, pepsin and ___hydrochloric___ (49) acid are added to food to break it down. If food contains toxins that irritate the stomach too much, or if toxins reach the area postrema via the blood, ___vomiting___ (50) occurs. The first segment of the small intestine, the ___duodenum___ (51), is where most food is digested. Here, carbohydrates are broken down into simple sugars (52) such as glucose, and proteins are broken down into ___amino___ ___acids___ (53). Fats are converted to fatty acids and ___glycerol___ (54) in the intestines. These basic nutrients are then absorbed into the bloodstream and taken to the ___liver___ (55) by the ___hepatic___ ___portal___ (56) vein. Any remaining excess water is reabsorbed in the ___large___ (57) intestine. Digestion is controlled by the parasympathetic (58) part of the autonomic nervous system and can be disrupted by arousal, which may lead to vomiting, nausea, constipation, or ___diarrhea___ (59).

For the first few hours after a meal, during the ___absorptive___ (60) phase of the feeding cycle, recently ingested nutrients provide fuel for the body. This is managed by the parasympathetic nervous system, which is activated by ___high___ (61) levels of glucose. Insulin is secreted by the ___pancreas___ (62), allowing glucose to be used by the cells. ___Diabetes___ (63) is a result of not producing enough insulin or being less responsive to it. Glucose is also converted to ___glycogen___ (64) for short-term storage in the muscles and liver. Excess glucose and proteins are converted to ___fats___ (65) and stored in ___adipose___ (66) tissue. When glucose levels in the blood decline, the body enters the ___fasting___ (67) phase of the feeding cycle. Parasympathetic activity is replaced by ___sympathetic___ (68) activity, resulting in the secretion of ___glucagon___ (69) from the pancreas.

This substance is instrumental in the conversion of glycogen to ___glucose___ (70) and of fat into fatty acids and ___glycerol___ (71), the latter of which is converted into glucose for the brain by the ___liver___ (72). Eating and metabolism are governed by the lateral ___hypothalamus___ (73) and the ___PVN___ (74).

There are three major signals of hunger; ___glucoprivic___ (75) hunger tells the brain that there is a low level of glucose, ___lipoprivic___ (76) hunger indicates a deficit in fatty acids, and the third signals low levels of nutrients in the ___stomach___ (77). Blood levels of glucose and fatty acids are monitored by the liver; when these levels are low, a message is carried to the medulla via the ___vagus___ (78) nerve. Glucose levels in the brain are monitored directly by the ___NST___ (79) in the medulla. Next, the message is carried to the ___arcuate___ (80) nucleus, which in turn sends signals to the PVN and ___lateral___ (81) hypothalamus. As the stomach empties during fasting, the peptide ___ghrelin___ (82) is released and stimulates the arcuate nucleus to encourage eating. Excess ghrelin may be involved in the uncontrollable appetite of people with ___Prader___-___Willi___ (83) syndrome. All three of the hunger signals exert their influence through NPY/AgRP neurons in the arcuate nucleus, which releases ___NPY___ (84) and ___agouti-related___ (85) protein. Both substances excite the PVN and lateral hypothalamus to encourage eating and slow down ___metabolism___ (86).

There are a number of satiety signals, including those from ___volume___ (87) ~~Stretch~~ receptors in the stomach that become active when it is full. The stomach and intestines also release a number of ___peptides___ (88) that trigger digestive enzyme release and also signal the brain. For example, the duodenal hormone ___CCK___ (89) detects fats and triggers the release of bile from the ___gallbladder___ (90) and initiates a signal in the vagus nerve to the NST and hypothalamus to stop eating. ___PYY___ (91) is another peptide hormone released from the intestines that inhibits NPY release in the ___arcuate___ (92) nucleus, which decreases caloric intake over several hours. Rats with lesions in the ___ventromedial___ (93) hypothalamus overeat in part because insulin production is increased, which results in nutrients being stored rather than utilized. In ___parabiotic___ (94) rats with joined circulation, in which one was lesioned and one was not, the normal rat reduced its eating in response to a satiety signal to which the lesioned rat was insensitive. The satiety signal turned out to be the hormone ___leptin___ (95); obese individuals have ___higher___ (96) blood levels of this hormone. Leptin and insulin decrease eating by inhibiting the NPY/AgRP neurons, but also activating ___POMC___ (97) cells. In turn, these cells reduce feeding by inhibiting the ___PVN___ (98) and the lateral hypothalamus.

Short Answer and Essay Questions

Answer the following questions.

3. Contrast hunger with the drives of thirst and temperature regulation. In your answer, explain what makes hunger a more complex drive.

4. Why is it advantageous for us to prefer sweet and salty foods and to dislike sour and bitter foods?

5. Explain the role of learning in a person's food choices. What sort of experiences result in someone learning to like or avoid specific foods?

6. Describe the signals from the body and the brain areas that are involved in initiating eating.

7. Explain the signals that end a meal, including the neural pathways between the body and brain areas, as well as the hormones involved.

Obesity

Summary and Guided Review

After studying this section in the text, fill in the blanks of the following summary.

There are currently more overweight than underweight people in the world, and more than a third of adults in the United States qualify as _____ (99). Worldwide, the rate of this quality has doubled in men and _____ (100) in women since 1974, in part because of the availability of high-calorie junk food. Overweight and obese individuals are more at risk for many health problems; for example, in a Swedish study, the more overweight a woman was, the more likely she was to have shrinkage in her _____ (101) lobes. Obesity is also expensive for society; possible costing as much as $305 _____ (102) per year in the United States. In contrast, dietary restrictions may prolong life. In elderly subjects who reduced their total number of calories by 30%, they saw improvements in blood pressure, heart health, and even _____ (103) memory.

Obesity seems to be most directly linked to eating high-calorie foods and not getting enough _____ (104). Research has not supported the popular opinion that obesity is completely under _____ (105) control, is the result of a maladaptive eating style, or is the inability to delay _____ (106).

If obesity runs in families, it is more likely due to _____ (107) than environment, as evidenced by the fact that the correlation of BMI scores in identical twins raised apart is _____ (108), only slightly lower than the .74 correlation for those raised together. However, the role of inheritance is complicated, as several genes are involved, such as the _____ (109) gene on chromosome 6 and the _____ (110) gene on chromosome 4. Coleman used the parabiotic technique described earlier to experimentally study the effects of recessive genes on food intake and weight in mice. The *db/db* mice produced a signal to stop eating but were insensitive to it, whereas the _____ (111) mice were sensitive to the signal but did not produce it. It was not until later that researchers discovered that the signaling substance was _____ (112). The *ob* and *db* genes are rare and account for few cases of obesity. On the other hand, individuals with a particular allele (A) of the _____ (113) gene have a 30% greater risk of obesity, which increases to 70% if they are homozygous (AA). And four variants of the _____ (114) gene may account for 6% of cases of severe obesity, presumably by interfering with a receptor involved in regulating appetite. _____ (115) characteristics are inheritable traits that result from modifications of gene expression rather than changes in the individual's DNA sequence. One form of this occurs if mothers have low levels of carbohydrates while pregnant; this causes _____ (116) of the *RXRA* gene, which accounts for more than 25% of weight variation in childhood.

A person's basal _____ (117) rate (BMR) largely determines how much food is needed to maintain weight, and someone with a higher BMR needs to take in _____ (118) calories than someone with a lower BMR. When a person loses weight, the BMR usually _____ (119), making additional weight loss difficult. The increase in metabolism is variable among people, partly due to nonexercise forms of spontaneous _____ (120), such as fidgeting; these individuals expend more energy and gain less weight than others. Another factor that may make weight loss difficult is that after a person gains weight, she or he may develop a new _____ _____ (121).

Exercise seems to be an important part of losing weight, more because of its effects on one's _____ _____ (122) than because of the calories expended during the exercise itself. Some medications have been used to treat obesity, but frequently they have side effects that can sometimes be serious. _____ (123) remains on the market despite rare reports of liver damage, and many other medications are no longer considered safe enough for use. In some people, whose weight gain is linked to high carbohydrate consumption, drugs that prevent the reuptake of _____ (124) can assist in weight loss. Treatment with the hormone _____ (125) has been shown to be effective in increasing metabolism and reducing fat while sparing lean mass, but it works only in the 5%–10% of obese individuals who lack it.

A new approach to understanding and treating obesity is to view overeating as an addictive behavior. One neurotransmitter that plays a key role in both compulsive overeating and addiction is _____ (126). The drug _____ (127) is a combination of two anti-addiction drugs, has been more effective than placebo, and is in the final stages of FDA approval. Because drugs and lifestyle changes are frequently not effective with the morbidly obese, bariatric surgical procedures such as _____ _____ (128) and lap band may be required to save lives. The former procedure works by limiting meal size and nutrient absorption in the digestive tract, while the latter places a restrictive band around the stomach without surgically altering it. Bariatric surgery not only reduces weight through decreased stomach size, but also increases PPY and decreases ghrelin after eating, and improves _____ (129) balance in the intestine. However, because these surgeries have many risks and are expensive, they are often a last resort for weight management.

Short Answer and Essay Questions

Answer the following questions.

8. Explain why it is easier to gain than lose weight.

9. Identify and describe the roles of four genes that have been linked to obesity.

10. Discuss how the environment an individual lives in can affect their risk for obesity. In your answer, be sure to address the influence of diet on metabolism and the role of epigenetics.

Anorexia, Bulimia, and Binge Eating Disorder

Summary and Guided Review

After studying this section in the text, fill in the blanks of the following summary.

Though men are overrepresented among obese Americans, women are three times as likely to be diagnosed with anorexia nervosa or _____ (130) and are _____ (131) times as likely to suffer from binge eating disorder. _____ (132) nervosa is characterized by maintaining weight at an unhealthy low level, which can lead to serious health problems and even death. Individuals who binge eat and control their weight by vomiting or using _____ (133) are called _____-_____ (134), whereas _____ (135) are those who simply eat very little food. Health risks associated with this disorder include heart damage, loss of bone density, and death. This disorder is not due to a lack of hunger; they have elevated _____ (136) and _____ (137), and leptin levels are diminished, suggesting that they are experiencing hunger. Brain imaging studies have shown increased activation of the _____ _____ (138) in anorexics, likely related to high food control behaviors. Weight in individuals with _____ (139) nervosa is usually normal. Their _____ (140) levels are a third higher than those of controls, and remain higher than those of controls following a meal. People with _____ _____ (141) disorder eat large amounts of food in a short time, and cannot control how much they eat. They are usually obese and feel shame about their eating. This disorder involves _____ (142) pathway disruptions similar to those observed in substance abuse and other impulsive and compulsive disorders. There are other eating disorders as well: night eating disorder, _____ (143) (eating non-food objects), rumination disorder, and avoidant/restrictive food intake disorder.

   The social environment plays a role in eating disorders, including exposure to thin models in the media. After satellite TV became available in _____ (144) in 1995, 74% of the teenage girls there considered themselves too fat, and the number of those who admitted to vomiting to control their weight rose from 3% to _____ (145). Genetic inheritance also appears to play a role; the concordance rate of anorexia among identical twins is _____ (146) times greater than in fraternal twins. Surprisingly, environment exerts a strong effect on eating disorders in adolescent girls; hormonal changes, stress, and dieting produce _____ (147) changes in the genes that play a role in anorexia and bulimia. In addition, eating disorders typically are accompanied by _____ (148) psychological disorders such as depression, anxiety, and obsessive-compulsive disorders.

   Antidepressants that increase the levels of the neurotransmitter _____ (149) reduce bingeing and purging in bulimics and also decrease relapses in anorexics. Anorexics have lower levels, but only when they are underweight, apparently due to malnutrition. Evidence also points to a dysfunctional _____ (150) system in anorexia. Administering amphetamine to control subjects produced euphoria, but it increased _____ (151) in those who were recovering from anorexia. In addition, patients with anorexia and bulimia have more _____ (152) receptors in the insula, which contribute to the rewarding effects of food.

Short Answer and Essay Questions

Answer the following question.

11. Compare and contrast the impacts of environment and biology on disordered eating. In your answer, be sure to include at least one piece of evidence showing the role of each in eating disorders.

Post-test

Use these multiple-choice questions to check your understanding of the chapter.

1. Christopher, the person described in the introduction to the chapter, exhibited all of the following EXCEPT
   a. poor impulse control.
   b. short stature.
   c. mental disability.
   d. violent outbursts.

2. Which of the following statements regarding motivation is TRUE?
   a. Motivation is controlled by the thalamus.
   b. Motivations are best thought of as instinctive drives.
   c. Motivation refers to bodily states of need.
   d. Motivation is sometimes confused with emotion.

3. The fact that some people need higher levels of excitement than others is BEST explained by _____ theory.
   a. incentive
   b. arousal
   c. drive
   d. instinct

4. Which of the following animals is ectothermic?
   a. elephant
   b. chicken
   c. cow
   d. snake

5. Endothermic animals can reduce their body temperature by
   a. burrowing into the ground.
   b. finding shade.
   c. sweating.
   d. all of the above

6. Warmth-sensitive and cold-sensitive cells that help mammals regulate their body temperature are found in the _____ of the hypothalamus.
   a. preoptic area
   b. area postrema
   c. ventromedial nucleus
   d. nucleus of the solitary tract

7. Jason has just eaten an entire bag of potato chips and suddenly feels thirsty. What type of thirst is he experiencing?
   a. hypovolemic
   b. osmotic
   c. hypervolemic
   d. endothermic

8. Which of the following does NOT result in loss of extracellular water?
   a. exercise
   b. blood loss
   c. ingesting a lot of salt
   d. vomiting

9. Osmotic thirst
    a. results from activation of baroreceptors in the heart.
    b. results from the release of renin by the kidneys.
    c. is controlled by the subfornical organ.
    d. is disrupted when the OVLT is lesioned.

10. Which of the following statements is TRUE?
    a. The set point for temperature is less variable than the set point for hunger.
    b. The set point for thirst is more variable than the set point for hunger.
    c. The set point for temperature is more variable than the set point for hunger.
    d. Once we reach adulthood, the set point for hunger becomes stable.

11. A species of animal that eats only berries and leaves is a(n)
    a. carnivore.
    b. omnivore.
    c. herbivore.
    d. endovore.

12. Of all of the primary taste qualities, _____ is the MOST recently discovered.
    a. umami
    b. sour
    c. bitter
    d. salty

13. Foods that provide the ions necessary for neural transmission are MOST likely to taste
    a. sweet.
    b. salty.
    c. bitter.
    d. sour.

14. Foods that contain toxins tend to taste
    a. sweet.
    b. sour.
    c. salty.
    d. bitter.

15. The taste buds send signals to the _____ area of the cortex.
    a. olfactory
    b. auditory
    c. gustatory
    d. somatosensory

16. Learned taste aversion accounts for all of the following EXCEPT
    a. bait shyness in rats.
    b. coyotes' refusal to eat lamb after consuming a tainted carcass.
    c. rats' decreased responsiveness to glucose placed on the tongue after receiving a glucose injection.
    d. children avoiding certain flavors of ice cream eaten while undergoing chemotherapy.

17. Which of the following statements regarding taste preferences is TRUE?
    a. Rats are better at "listening to what their bodies need" than humans.
    b. Rats deprived of a vitamin can develop a preference for a food high in that vitamin.
    c. Rats' behavior does not change when their diet is missing critical nutrients.
    d. Rats find the taste of cinnamon aversive.

18. Which of the following is released by the stomach as an aid to digestion?
    a. pepsin
    b. leptin
    c. insulin
    d. cholecystokinin

19. Most of digestion occurs in the
    a. large intestine.
    b. small intestine.
    c. liver.
    d. stomach.

20. Glycerol is a product of the transformation of
    a. fats.
    b. proteins.
    c. carbohydrates.
    d. all of the above

21. After nutrients are absorbed into the bloodstream, they are transported to the
    _____ by the hepatic portal vein.
    a. kidneys
    b. liver
    c. brain
    d. large intestine

22. During the absorptive phase of the feeding cycle,
    a. recently eaten food may be stored.
    b. recently eaten food is used for energy.
    c. the parasympathetic nervous system is activated.
    d. all of the above

23. Which of the following statements regarding insulin is TRUE?
    a. Brain cells can import glucose without it.
    b. All body cells can import glucose without it.
    c. Diabetics produce too much of it.
    d. Its production is activated by the sympathetic nervous system.

24. Which of the following contributes to adipose tissue?
    a. excess protein
    b. excess glucose
    c. fat
    d. all of the above

25. Which of the following statements regarding glucagon is FALSE?
    a. It is secreted by the pancreas.
    b. It transforms proteins to fatty acids.
    c. It transforms glycogen to glucose.
    d. It converts stored fat to glycerol.

26. A rabbit injected with 2-deoxyglucose into its hepatic portal vein will
    a. start eating but will eat only a small amount.
    b. not eat for several hours.
    c. start eating and eat more than usual.
    d. enter a diabetic coma.

27. Which of the following statements regarding neuropeptide Y is FALSE?
    a. It is released by the preoptic area of the hypothalamus.
    b. It stimulates eating.
    c. It is released in response to low glucose.
    d. It may help an animal conserve energy.

28. Satiety may be signaled by
    a. stretch receptors in the stomach.
    b. the release of cholecystokinin.
    c. the presence of nutrients in the liver.
    d. all of the above

29. Rats injected with CCK over several days will
    a. gain a lot of weight.
    b. lose a lot of weight.
    c. stay at the same weight.
    d. lose a little bit of weight but then gain it back when the injections are withheld.

30. In Hervey's parabiotic rats, the rat without a lesion lost weight because
    a. the lesioned rat was digesting all of the food that both rats consumed.
    b. the lesioned rat continually produced a satiety signal that inhibited eating only in the nonlesioned rat.
    c. the nonlesioned rat became insensitive to hunger cues.
    d. the lesioned rat refused to eat.

31. As leptin _____, neuropeptide Y _____.
    a. increases; increases
    b. increases; decreases
    c. decreases; decreases
    d. increases; remains the same

32. Which of the following is NOT a health risk associated with obesity?
    a. loss of bone density
    b. colon cancer
    c. Alzheimer's disease
    d. heart disease

33. Which of the following influences obesity risk?
    a. time spent sedentary
    b. hours spent sleeping per night
    c. viral infections such as adenovirus-36
    d. all of the above

34. Correlations for BMI are HIGHEST for
    a. identical twins raised together.
    b. identical twins raised apart.
    c. fraternal twins raised together.
    d. fraternal twins raised apart.

35. A rat of normal weight is MOST likely to starve to death when biotically paired with a(n) _____ rat.
    a. *db/db*
    b. *ob/ob*
    c. *db/db* or *ob/ob*
    d. normal

36. Basal metabolism accounts for energy used to fuel the brain and other organs and for
    a. exercise.
    b. digestion.
    c. maintaining body temperature.
    d. physical activity.

37. Mavis, who does not exercise, has reduced her calorie intake by 25% and expects to lose a lot of weight. What is likely to happen?
    a. She will lose as much weight as she wants.
    b. Her metabolism will increase.
    c. Her metabolism will decrease.
    d. It is impossible to predict.

38. Someone who responds to increased caloric consumption by fidgeting a lot
    a. will probably gain a lot of weight.
    b. may gain little or no weight.
    c. will probably lose weight.
    d. may develop other nervous habits.

39. In some obese people, carbohydrate consumption
    a. elevates mood.
    b. leads to depression.
    c. reduces serotonin levels.
    d. a and c

40. Which of the following drugs blocks the absorption of fat?
    a. leptin
    b. sibutramine
    c. PYY
    d. orlistat

41. Serotonin-enhancing drugs are LEAST likely to be useful for treating
    a. obesity.
    b. bulimia.
    c. purging anorexia.
    d. restrictive anorexia.

42. Leptin seems to
    a. increase appetite.
    b. increase metabolism.
    c. decrease appetite.
    d. b and c

43. Based on recent research, the neurotransmitters most involved in anorexia and bulimia are
    a. dopamine and norepinephrine.
    b. serotonin and norepinephrine.
    c. serotonin and dopamine.
    d. dopamine, norepinephrine, and serotonin.

44. The difference between bulimics and purging anorexics is that
    a. bulimics are usually of normal weight.
    b. purging anorexics purge by using laxatives, whereas bulimics rely on vomiting.
    c. purging anorexics are usually male.
    d. bulimics, but not purging anorexics, tend to be impulsive.

Answers

Guided Review

1. Motivation
2. instinctively
3. drive
4. homeostasis
5. Incentive
6. arousal
7. brain states
8. tissue
9. set
10. temperature
11. preoptic
12. cold-sensitive
13. shivering
14. thirst
15. evaporation
16. osmotic
17. hypovolemic
18. OVLT (organum vascolosum lamina terminalis)
19. median preoptic nucleus
20. vagus
21. NST (nucleus of the solitary tract)
22. angiotensin
23. subfornical
24. satiety
25. set
26. nutrients
27. omnivores
28. taste
29. five
30. sweet
31. sour
32. bitter
33. umami
34. proteins
35. papillae
36. solitary tract
37. insula
38. labeled line
39. sensory-specific
40. NST (nucleus of the solitary tract)
41. avoid
42. learned taste
43. chemotherapy
44. deficient or low
45. nutrient or vitamin or chemical
46. flavor
47. Digestion
48. saliva
49. hydrochloric (HCl)
50. vomiting
51. duodenum
52. (simple) sugars
53. amino acids
54. glycerol
55. liver
56. hepatic portal
57. large
58. parasympathetic
59. diarrhea
60. absorptive
61. high
62. pancreas
63. Diabetes
64. glycogen
65. fat(s)
66. adipose
67. fasting
68. sympathetic
69. glucagon
70. glucose
71. glycerol
72. liver
73. hypothalamus

74. PVN (paraventricular nucleus)
75. glucoprivic
76. lipoprivic
77. stomach
78. vagus
79. NST (nucleus of the solitary tract)
80. arcuate
81. lateral
82. ghrelin
83. Prader-Willi
84. NPY (neuropeptide Y)
85. agouti-related
86. metabolism
87. volume or stretch
88. peptides
89. CCK (cholecystokinin)
90. gallbladder
91. PYY (peptide YY_{3-36})
92. arcuate
93. ventromedial
94. parabiotic
95. leptin
96. higher
97. POMC
98. PVN (paraventricular nucleus)
99. obese
100. tripled
101. temporal
102. billion
103. verbal
104. exercise
105. voluntary
106. gratification
107. genetics or heredity
108. .62
109. obesity (*ob*)
110. diabetes (*db*)
111. *ob/ob*
112. leptin
113. *FTO* (fat mass and obesity-associated)
114. *Mrap2*
115. Epigenetic
116. methylation
117. metabolic
118. more
119. decreases
120. activity
121. set point
122. basal metabolism or basal metabolic rate (BMR)
123. Orlistat
124. serotonin
125. leptin
126. dopamine
127. Contrave
128. gastric bypass
129. microbial
130. bulimia
131. two
132. Anorexia
133. laxatives
134. binge-purgers
135. restrictors
136. NPY (neuropeptide Y) or ghrelin
137. ghrelin or NPY (neuropeptide Y)
138. dorsal striatum
139. bulimia
140. ghrelin
141. binge eating
142. dopamine
143. pica
144. Fiji
145. 11%
146. three
147. epigenetic
148. comorbid
149. serotonin
150. dopamine
151. anxiety
152. cannabinoid

Short Answer and Essay Questions

1. Drive theory explains behaviors resulting from tissue deficits, such as eating and drinking, but not other forms of behavior such as sex, striving for achievement, thrill seeking, and even eating when we are not hungry. Incentive theory suggests that behaviors such as eating occur in order to obtain some external reward or incentive. This theory addresses the idea that behaviors can be motivated by things external to an animal. Arousal theory addresses the idea that people can be motivated to increase their arousal rather than just to fulfill a tissue deficit, which helps to explain thrill seeking and sexual behavior. Most researchers conceptualize motivation in terms of brain states, which can account for all of these forms of motivation.

2. Animals function best within a limited range of body temperatures, which is their set point. Ectothermic animals try to maintain a temperature homeostasis by adjusting their behavior—seeking cooler or warmer locations, whereas endothermic animals can also adjust their body temperature use internal mechanisms such as sweating and shivering. Temperature control involves the preoptic area of the hypothalamus. Thirst is another drive that helps animals achieve homeostasis for fluid levels, and part of the hypothalamus (the median preoptic nucleus) is involved in this drive. Thirst can be initiated by drops in blood volume in the body (hypovolemic thirst) or by low intracellular fluid (osmotic thirst). Maintaining a set point of the correct fluid levels is critical to survival, so the SFO participates both in the motivation to begin drinking and in ending thirst in order to avoid water intoxication.

3. First of all, the set point for hunger fluctuates to a greater extent than the set point for thirst or temperature regulation. Since eating provides energy that is needed for so many other processes, it is important that an organism can alter its eating to address new energy demands such as growth or repair from injury. The second difference has to do with the fact that thirst is satiated by water, whereas satiation of hunger requires a variety of nutrients. Parts of the hypothalamus are involved in initiation of thirst and eating, as well in signaling that it is time to end drinking or eating. However, as shown by the fact that no one universal gene is responsible for obesity, eating behavior is controlled by multiple brain and body systems.

4. Naturally sweet foods are generally nutritious, and those that are salty contain salt, which is converted to ions that we need. Sour foods are often rotten or spoiled, and bitter foods may contain toxins. In both cases, we could become sick from eating them.

5. Learning plays an important role in our eating behavior. Most of us have probably had the experience of eating a food shortly before becoming ill from a virus. Just one experience being ill after eating a food can be sufficient to develop a learned taste aversion. Through learning, a food item can become repulsive. Learned taste preferences are also possible, as in the study by Scott and Verney (1947), in which rats became conditioned to eat vitamin-rich food that tasted of anise.

6. The three major signals for hunger are low levels of glucose (glucoprivic hunger), low levels of fats (lipoprivic hunger), and the release of ghrelin synthesized in the stomach (low levels of stomach nutrients). Signals about low glucose and fat levels in the blood are then sent to the nucleus of the solitary tract (NST) in the medulla via the vagus nerve. The arcuate nucleus of the hypothalamus receives hunger signals from the NST, and NPY/AgRP cells in the arcuate nucleus then communicate with the lateral hypothalamus and PVN of the hypothalamus to adjust eating and metabolism.

7. All of the following play a role in satiety: stretch or volume receptors in the stomach, release of CCK in response to food in the duodenum, PYY released in the intestine, leptin secreted by fat cells, and insulin released by the pancreas. Stretch or volume signals in the stomach result in signaling of the NST via the vagus nerve. The vagus nerve also sends signals

to the brain about peptides that mark fullness, including CCK. PYY signals travel to the arcuate nucleus via the bloodstream, so this signal is important to adjusting food intake over a day rather than impacting one meal. Leptin and insulin signals inhibit NPY/AgRP cells in the arcuate nucleus and activate POMC neurons, which results in inhibition of cells in the PVN and lateral hypothalamus, stopping eating.

8. The body seems to be programmed to hold on to weight. Under survival conditions this is adaptive, because in times of deprivation the body conserves fat. Although the body for the most part maintains weight around a set point, it is less likely to inhibit weight gain than weight loss.

9. The *ob* gene promotes weight gain due to a lack of leptin production in recessive individuals, whereas the *db* gene promotes weight gain due to a lack of leptin sensitivity in recessive individuals. Variants of the *FTO* and *MC4R* genes lead to increased calorie intake, which prompts obesity. The *Mrap2* gene impacts obesity risk by affecting appetite and energy expenditure.

10. Environment can contribute to both diet and activity level. Although our modern environment provides less opportunities for daily activity than in the past, spontaneous activity such as casual walking, fidgeting, and posture maintenance may contribute to an increase in energy expenditure. Because altering diet can affect metabolism, people who have reduced their calorie intake may have a reduced basal metabolic rate. Reduced sleep and viruses such as the human adenovirus have also been associated with obesity. The bacteria that colonize your gut can also influence obesity risk. Finally, the prenatal environment (such as low maternal carbohydrate intake during pregnancy) can result in methylation of genes that impact obesity risk in offspring.

11. Eating disorders are more common in cultures where the media tend to portray thin people as beautiful, reflecting the role of environment in eating disorders. For example, in Fiji, when television was introduced in the 1990s, the rates of anorexia and bulimia rose quickly among adolescent girls, supposedly in response to seeing thin Western actresses. The serotonin system appears dysfunctional in individuals with eating disorders. Both purging anorexics and bulimics are more likely to display impulsive behavior, and they also have low levels of serotonin. Restrictive anorexics, by contrast, are in some ways more like people with obsessive-compulsive disorder. Following weight gain, they have higher levels of serotonin than purgers or bulimics; starvation may be a means of reducing serotonin and reducing obsessive concerns. Imaging studies have also shown that both anorexics and bulimics have increased serotonin binding at the $5HT_{1A}$ receptor and decreased serotonin binding at the $5HT_{2A}$ receptor. Individuals with anorexia also have lower dopamine levels in their cerebrospinal fluid, again suggesting that starvation may be a means of controlling anxiety by influencing dopamine and serotonin.

Post-test

1. c   2. d   3. b   4. d   5. d   6. a   7. b   8. c   9. d   10. a   11. c   12. a   13. b   14. d
15. c   16. c   17. b   18. a   19. b   20. a   21. b   22. d   23. a   24. d   25. b   26. c
27. a   28. d   29. c   30. b   31. b   32. a   33. d   34. a   35. a   36. c   37. c   38. b
39. a   40. d   41. d   42. d   43. c   44. a

7 The Biology of Sex and Gender

Chapter Outline

Parental Influences on Brain Structure and Function

Social Implications of the Biological Model

CONCEPT CHECK

In Perspective

Chapter Summary

Study Resources

Learning Objectives

After reading this chapter, you will be able to

1. Contrast sex with other motivated behaviors

2. Demonstrate the role of hormones and brain structures in sexual behavior

3. Identify hormonal and brain differences between females and males

4. Describe how behavioral differences between males and females are influenced by biology and environment

5. Explain the role of biological influences on gender identity

6. Assess the impact of biological influences on sexual orientation

Sex as a Form of Motivation

Summary and Guided Review

After studying this section in the text, fill in the blanks of the following summary.

Sex shares some similarities with other forms of motivation, such as cycles of arousal and _____ (1), and regulation by hormones and specific brain areas. But unlike hunger and thirst, there is no homeostatic _____ (2) need for sex.

The cycle of sexual arousal and satiation in humans was studied extensively by the researchers _____ and _____ (3) in the 1960s. They described four phases: _____ (4), during which physiological arousal increases sharply; _____ (5), during which arousal levels off; _____ (6), marked by intense pleasure, vaginal contractions in females, and ejaculation in males; and _____ (7), during which the body returns to its resting state. Whereas _____ (8) can reenter the excitement phase immediately after orgasm, men have a(n) _____ (9) phase during which time they cannot be aroused or have another orgasm. Among some animals, a male will return to arousal more quickly if he is exposed to a novel female rather than the one with which he has most recently mated; this phenomenon is known as the _____ (10) effect.

The role of hormones in sexual behavior is often studied in nonhuman animals, in part because hormones control their behavior to a(n) _____ (11) extent than in humans. The method of _____ (12) involves removing the gonads, the major source of sex hormones; this is done to determine the hormonal effects on behavior. Occasionally humans undergo castration, and those who do often experience a(n) _____ (13) in sexual interest and behavior (although there is a great deal of variability). Some male criminals have volunteered to undergo physical or chemical castration, which reduces _____ (14), a class of hormones responsible for a number of male characteristics and functions, in order to curb their violent or sexual behavior. The primary compound in that class, which serves as the major sex hormone in male humans, is _____ (15). Apparently, in human males just a small amount of testosterone is needed to maintain sexual interest and behavior.

In many animal species, females will mate only while they are in _____ (16), when they are ovulating and estrogen levels are high. Human females will engage in sex throughout the reproductive cycle, although they are more likely to initiate sex around the time of _____ (17), which corresponds with peaks in _____ (18) and, possibly more important, testosterone. Postmenopausal women's sexual behavior seems to be most closely tied to _____ (19) levels.

Research with animals has revealed several brain areas involved in sexual behavior that probably work in conjunction with one another. The _____ (20) of the hypothalamus is active during copulation in both male and female rats, and studies with monkeys indicate that it is more involved in sexual _____ (21) than motivation. Lesioned monkeys would masturbate but not _____ (22). The _____ (23) amygdala is responsive to sexual stimuli and is also active during copulation in both sexes. In male rats, when the _____ (24) of the MPOA (which is three to four times larger in males) is lesioned, the result is reduced sexual activity. In female rats, when the _____ (25) hypothalamus is lesioned, they are less likely to respond to a male's advances.

Several chemical signals are involved in sexual functioning. _____ (26) activity in the MPOA contributes to sexual motivation in both males and females. In males, as dopamine levels rise, they initially stimulate D_1 receptors, activating the parasympathetic response increasing motivation and a(n) _____ (27) in males; later, _____ (28) receptors are activated, leading to ejaculation under _____ (29) control. Low dopamine levels in the nucleus _____ (30) may also be responsible for the Coolidge effect, during which a recently mated male presented with a new female will show an increase in dopamine levels in that area. The hormones testosterone, oxytocin, and _____ (31) also play an important role in intimate behavior. As stated in the _____ (32) theory of social bonds, low vasopressin is seen in cases of social _____ (33) while _____ (34) aggression is observed with high levels of vasopressin. Oxytocin levels interact with testosterone levels such that high oxytocin levels are associated with sexual intimacy when testosterone levels are _____ (35) and with _____ (36) when testosterone levels are low. The refractory period in males appears to be influenced by the neurotransmitter _____ (37); individuals taking reuptake inhibitors (increasing levels) frequently report an inability to have orgasms.

External factors are also involved in sexual motivation and behavior and are particularly sensitive to _____ (38)—so much so that the nose is considered a sex organ in many species. Airborne odorous materials are detected by receptors in the _____ (39) cavity. Axons from the olfactory receptors pass through openings in the base of the skull and enter the _____ _____ (40) above this cavity. The information then travels to the olfactory cortex in the temporal lobes. The nasal cavity also contains the _____ (41) organ, which is used to detect _____ (42)—airborne chemicals released by an animal that have physiological or behavioral effects on another animal of the same species. This organ sends messages to the _____ (43) and the ventromedial hypothalamus, as well as to the emotion center, the _____ (44). While some researchers believe that this organ is no longer functional in humans, studies indicate that pheromones may be involved in _____ (45) synchrony in women living together in dorms, but these findings have been difficult to replicate. In another study, men exhibited a preference for the scent of T-shirts worn by women who were _____ (46) over ones who were not. However, some scientists believe that our ability to detect _____ (47), rather than pheromones, accounts for these findings.

Genetics may also play a role. Mating in prairie voles begins with the release of the neurotransmitter _____ (48) in reward areas. Prairie voles are monogamous and mate for life due to their increased preference for females they have mated with. In both prairie voles and humans, the neuropeptide _____ (49) facilitates bonding and plays a role in muscle contractions in lactation and _____ (50). The hormone also contributes to social _____ (51) and attractiveness, which is necessary for developing mate preferences.

Short Answer and Essay Questions

Answer the following questions.

1. Compare hunger and sex as forms of motivation. Point out their similarities and differences.

2. What role does testosterone play in sexual motivation in men and women? Discuss the research that indicates this hormone's importance for sexual arousal and for behavior in men and in women.

3. Identify the brain areas most important for sexual behavior in males and females based on animal studies.

The Biological Determination of Sex

Summary and Guided Review

After studying this section in the text, fill in the blanks of the following summary.

The term *sex,* which refers to the biological characteristics that distinguish males and females, should not be confused with _____ (52), which refers to the behavioral characteristics associated with being male or female, or gender _____ (53), which is the sex an individual identifies herself or himself. Although in many individuals these three qualities are the same, in other individuals they may be quite different.

The first step in the determination of sex occurs during _____ (54), when a sperm cell fuses with an egg cell. The egg and sperm cells each contain a single chromosome from each of the 23 pairs of chromosomes present in other cells. The sex of the fetus is determined by the combination of the two sex chromosomes. The mother always contributes a(n) _____ (55) chromosome. If the sperm cell also contains an X chromosome, the fetus will be a _____ (56), and if it contains a Y chromosome, the fetus will be a _____ (57). Fetuses of both sexes initially possess identical sexual tissue that will later differentiate into male or female sex organs. In XX fetuses, the primitive (indifferent) gonads become _____ (58), the uterus develops from the _____ (59) ducts, the _____ (60) ducts are absorbed, and the external structures form the _____ (61), part of the vagina, and the labia. In XY fetuses, the _____ (62) gene on the Y chromosome transforms the gonads to become _____ (63). These produce _____-_____ (64) hormone, which causes the ducts to degenerate, and _____ (65), which transforms the Wolffian ducts into the _____ (66) vesicles and vas deferens. The hormone _____ (67) causes the external structures to form into a penis and the testes-containing _____ (68). The permanent effects of male hormones are called _____ (69) effects, because they occur early in development and produce changes that will last throughout the life span. Hormones also have temporary _____ (70) effects, which are reversible changes that can come and go as hormone levels change. In humans, sexual maturation is completed during _____ (71), when gonadal hormones are again released in large amounts. Puberty is accompanied by organizing effects, such as maturation of the _____ (72). It also has activating effects, such as breast and muscle development, the release of _____ (73) in females, and production of sperm cells in males.

In many species, sex hormones are largely responsible for sexual behavior. There are periods during development when exposure to a particular hormone alters the brain and thus influences future behavior. In rats, for example, a newborn male that is castrated will be more likely to engage in _____ (74) (presenting its hindquarters for mounting) as an adult. A young female rat exposed to _____ (75) will perform male-typical mounting more often as an adult than females with normal hormone levels. The hormone _____ (76) is critical both for feminizing female brains and for masculinizing male brains (through aromatization of testosterone).

Behavioral sex differences in humans are less clear than they are in other animals, in part because of the limitations of research in this area. However, _____ and _____ (77) in a 1974 review of the research literature found consistent differences between males and females. In cognitive performance, girls tended to be better at _____ (78) tasks, whereas boys tended to be better at visual-spatial tasks and _____ (79). Boys were also found to be more _____ (80) than girls. These findings have been controversial because there is considerable _____ (81) between males and females in these characteristics.

The source of male-female differences has been debated. There is evidence that experience contributes to them, in that the differences have been decreasing over the past few decades, particularly in the area of _____ (82). The dramatic differences in aggression rates in countries suggest that there is a strong _____ (83) influence on aggression. However, there is evidence that biological factors contribute to some of the differences. Most researchers attribute the gender differences to hormonal exposure during _____ (84). Males who produce low levels of testosterone during the developmental years have lower _____ (85) ability later in life. Men who identify as women and who take estrogen gain in _____ performance (86) but decrease in _____ (87) performance. The opposite is true for females who identify as men and are taking _____ (88).

Although elevated testosterone is associated with aggression, it is unclear whether the hormone is the cause or result of the behavior. For example, winning at sports _____ (89) testosterone, and losing decreases it.

Some researchers explain gender differences in traits by referring to brain anatomy and organization. One explanation for women's superiority on verbal tasks is that they use both _____ (90) of the brain during the tasks, not just the language-based one (usually the left). In terms of spatial rotation tasks, women rely more on _____ (91) areas, whereas men use _____ (92) areas. Males are also more likely to experience disorders like _____ (93), Tourette syndrome, and attention-deficit/hyperactivity disorder. Females are more likely to suffer from _____ (94) and Alzheimer's disease.

Short Answer and Essay Questions

Answer the following questions.

4. Which of the sex organs and structures in females and males develop from the same primitive tissue? What factors are responsible for transforming these primitive structures into the male-typical structures? Be sure to include both internal and external structures.

5. Distinguish between organizing and activating effects of hormones, and give an example of each.

6. What evidence is there that differences in estrogen levels may be partly responsible for the gender differences seen in verbal abilities?

Gender-Related Behavioral and Cognitive Differences

Summary and Guided Review

After studying this section in the text, fill in the blanks of the following summary.

For decades, gender identity has been assumed to be a combination of genital appearance and parenting. For example, many of the physical differences between males and females are clearly the result of the effects of hormones and genes on development. However, some individuals believe they have been born into the wrong sex and are called _____ (95). The distress that these people may feel due to the perception that sex and gender are mismatched is called gender _____ (96). Males in this category have been studied more extensively than females, and there are striking parallels in the brains of these two groups. The brain areas _____ (97) and _____ (98), both in the hypothalamus, are larger in males than females or male-to-female transgender individuals. These differences were independent of sexual preference. However, more studies are needed as this type of research has limited numbers of participants and the participants are often undergoing _____ (99) treatments.

If there is a physical difference between the sex chromosomes and genitalia, these individuals have a DSD, meaning a _____ in _____ _____ (100). One cause of 46 XY DSD is the lack of the enzyme 17α-_____ (101) that converts testosterone into dihydrotestosterone; males with this condition appear female at birth but undergo some _____ (102) at puberty due to a surge of testosterone from the internal, undescended testicles. A similar condition, caused by the lack of 5α-reductase, has a genetic basis; researchers studied 18 girls with this genetic defect in the _____ _____ (103). In all of the cases, the individuals were reared as girls, but they began questioning their gender during late childhood. When masculine characteristics developed in puberty, all but one adopted a male gender identity. Although this suggests that hormones are largely responsible for our sense of gender, the fact that males are more valued in this society indicates that _____ (104) may play a role as well. A third condition that produces 46 XY DSD individuals is _____ _____ (105) syndrome (AIS) such as that seen in Eden Atwood; due to a genetic mutation, these individuals lack male hormone receptors and therefore develop the physical characteristics of females, although they have undescended and usually normal functioning _____ (106). They undergo further feminization at puberty due to estrogen from the gonads as well as the adrenal glands, developing strong female secondary sex characteristics that include well-developed _____ (107), flawless complexion, and long slender legs. For these reasons, individuals with AIS can frequently outcompete women for modeling jobs.

46 XX DSD typically results from exposure to high levels of _____ (108) such as testosterone during fetal development. These individuals have internal female gonads, but externally they resemble males. The clitoris is enlarged and resembles a(n) _____ (109), and the _____ (110) may be partially or completely fused. One cause of 46 XX DSD is _____ _____ _____ (111), or CAH, which involves excessive androgen production by the adrenal glands. Parents may decide to raise the baby as a boy or a girl; reconstructive surgery may be performed to alter the appearance of the genitals to match the baby's assigned sex. Some researchers believe that we need to recognize more than two categories for sex, including _____ (112) for individuals who are in the gray areas between maleness and femaleness. This ambiguity was recently highlighted in the case of athlete Caster Semenya (detailed in one of the Applications in the chapter). Following suspicions over her strong performance and masculine physique, Semenya underwent extensive _____ (113) testing. Despite rumors that Semenya had two testicles and triple the normal amount of _____ (114) for a woman, she was cleared to compete again. One major result of this case is the realization that the International Olympic Committee does not have a good definition of what are _____ (115) levels of male hormone, and as of 2017 has been unable to provide sufficient evidence demonstrating how elevated levels of testosterone affect female performance to satisfy the courts.

There are cognitive and behavioral effects of sex hormones as well. These hormones strongly influence brain development both within the womb and in early life. For example, androgen-insensitive males are more like females in terms of their higher _____ (116) ability and lower spatial ability, and they are also decidedly _____ (117) in sexual orientation. Although 95% of XY males with CAH who are reared as girls accept a(n) _____ (118) gender identity, they are somewhat more likely to display masculine characteristics and define their sexual orientation as _____ (119) or _____ (120). Furthermore, women who were exposed to the anti-miscarriage drug DES (diethylstilbestrol) before they were born reported increased _____ (121) behavior and fantasies.

But what about gender identity in individuals without hormonal anomalies? The debate between "neutral-at-birth" and "_____ (122)-at-birth" theorists is played out in the case of an eight-month-old boy whose penis was accidentally destroyed during _____ (123). The researcher Money (who followed his case) believed the theory that sexuality is not established until a "critical period" ends after the first several years of life. His evidence was that the child underwent sexual reassignment surgery and was reared as a girl after this period and that "Brenda" became a well-adjusted, feminine child. However, when "Brenda" discovered the truth at the age of 14 after several years of feeling like a male, she reverted to her original biological sex, took the name David, married, and adopted a typically masculine role. In addition to cases of ablatio penis, there have been hundreds of cases of infants born with genitalia that were missing or underdeveloped, but whose hormonal exposures were as expected for their sex. Of male infants with underdeveloped or missing penises who were raised as boys, all but one were satisfied with their gender whereas _____% (124) of the 77 raised as girls later transitioned to males and _____% (125) showed signs of gender dysphoria. Therefore, sexuality may be established at birth (or earlier), regardless of later hormonal or social influences. It is important to keep in mind that these are case studies, and we must be careful about any conclusions we draw from them.

Short Answer and Essay Questions

Answer the following questions.

7. Explain why androgen-insensitive males perform more poorly on tests of spatial skills than their sisters and other females.

8. Describe how the case of Caster Semenya demonstrates the difficulties with gender determination. In your answer, indicate the practical implications of organizations such as the International Olympic Committee applying unclear definitions of gender to decisions about a person's career.

9. Describe why researchers must be careful in drawing conclusions about the influence of biology and experience on gender from the ablatio penis studies.

Sexual Orientation

Summary and Guided Review

After studying this section in the text, fill in the blanks of the following summary.

Identifying the basis of sexual orientation is difficult. However, if we can understand why some people are not attracted exclusively to members of the opposite sex, this may help to identify the aspects of each sex that trigger sexual attraction. It is important to understand that many more people have homosexual experiences than are considered homosexuals. The rate of homosexuality in the population is difficult to determine, but in a recent literature review, the average rate in the United States was approximately _____ (126). Although equally prevalent in men and women, there was a much stronger tendency for males to be exclusively _____ (127) than females. Furthermore, an estimated 1% expresses no interest in sex at all, referred to as _____ (128).

There is evidence that homosexuality develops early in life, but the strength of parental figures or seduction from someone of the same sex has no effect on future sexual orientation. _____ (129) learning and experience have been implicated in the formation of _____ (130) behaviors. Adult homosexuals are more likely to have displayed gender _____ (131) earlier in life, preferring companions, mannerisms, dress, and activities typical of the opposite sex. However, Bell and colleagues interpreted these behaviors as early signs of preexisting sexual orientation rather than as causes.

There is strong evidence for a genetic component in homosexuality. For example, early research on identical twins reported a(n) _____ (132) rate of 50%, but the actual figures may be lower due to the "volunteer effect." One researcher, Hamer, claims to have found an area of DNA on the _____ (133) chromosome that contributes to homosexuality in males. Hamer's study group included pairs of gay brothers with gay relatives on the _____ (134) side of the family, and _____% (135) of the brother pairs had identical genotypes in the region in question.

The idea that homosexuality is a heritable trait runs counter to _____ (136) theory, which argues that traits that promote survival and reproduction are the ones more likely to be passed on. However, researchers have found a correlation between genes on the X chromosome to both higher birth rates, as well as increased attraction to _____ (137) in both men and women. Additionally, recent evidence indicates that male homosexuality may be related to an epigenetic process known as _____ (138) that involves selective inhibition of one of the mother's X chromosomes rather than inheritance of "gay genes." Another possible epigenetic influence is if _____ (139) to testosterone is heritable, which could have significant effects on the sexual and gender development of the children. Methylation in five DNA regions predicted homosexual orientation with _____ (140) accuracy in a recent study, although researchers are uncertain how these results will generalize.

In animal studies, experimental manipulation of hormone levels can produce homosexual preferences and behaviors. Critics argue that these animals display homosexuality only when isolated from members of the other sex, not as a permanent state of sexuality. But numerous studies have demonstrated homosexual behaviors in mixed-sex groups occurring spontaneously in many different animal species, such as in 10% of _____ (141), and a small number of female gulls remain in stable homosexual pairs for multiple years. The evidence for hormonal influences in humans is weak, but there is compelling evidence that hormonal factors may alter brain _____ (142) during gestation, which in turn may contribute to differences in sexual orientation.

Differences in brain structure between homosexual and heterosexual people have been documented. Lesbians and heterosexual men have a larger _____ _____ (143) whereas heterosexual women and homosexual _____ (144) have cerebral hemispheres of equal size. In another study, the _____ (145) (SCN) nucleus was comparable in size in gay men and lesbians. Whether these differences contribute directly to sexual behavior in humans is unclear. Though not a brain difference, lesbians resemble men of all sexual orientations in their _____ to _____ (146) finger ratios, which indicate _____ (147) exposure in the womb. It may be that the timing of exposure results in masculinization of mechanisms for sexual orientation. There are comparably few replicated studies of sexual orientation focusing on _____ (148) homosexuality, suggesting a need for more research.

These differences in the brain and body suggest that the social implications of the _____ (149) model of sexuality are important. If sexual preference is a voluntary _____ (150), then those who display homosexuality are not eligible for civil rights protection since a minority group is defined as one with clearly defined, inborn, and unalterable characteristics. However, if sexual preference has a clear biological basis, as many homosexuals claim, then their status as a minority group should be protected. Although the majority of homosexuals believe that they are "born that way," some are opposed to this model because of its association with a disease explanation, and fear of efforts to eliminate the "problem" through _____ (151) manipulation or abortion. Other homosexuals embrace the biological model, because they think it will make homosexuality more _____ (152) in society. The increases in legal same-sex marriage and benefits seen across the nation and across the world lend this argument strong empirical support.

Short Answer and Essay Questions

Answer the following questions.

10. Describe how studying homosexuality tell us about heterosexuality.

11. What evidence is presented for the social learning hypothesis of homosexuality? What are the problems with interpreting this evidence?

12. Why is homosexuality difficult to explain from an evolutionary standpoint? What evidence is there that homosexuality may be the result of epigenetic processes?

13. Why are some members of the homosexual community opposed to the biological model of homosexuality? What benefits could be gained if this model is accepted?

Post-test

Use these multiple-choice questions to check your understanding of the chapter.

1. As forms of motivation, how are hunger and sex different?
   a. Sex, but not hunger, involves arousal and satiation.
   b. Hunger, but not sex, is under the influence of hormones.
   c. Hunger, but not sex, represents a homeostatic tissue need.
   d. Sex, but not hunger, is entirely under the control of external stimuli.

2. Penile and clitoral erection first occur in the _____ phase of the sexual response.
   a. excitement
   b. plateau
   c. orgasm
   d. resolution

3. Which of the following statements regarding the refractory phase of the sexual response is TRUE?
   a. Females have a shorter refractory phase than males.
   b. During the refractory phase, orgasm cannot occur.
   c. Males typically have a refractory phase of 3–5 hours.
   d. all of the above

4. Anti-androgen drugs
   a. may block the production of testosterone.
   b. may reduce deviant sexual behaviors.
   c. may reduce sexual fantasies.
   d. all of the above

5. Which of the following statements regarding sexual activity in females is TRUE?
   a. Only female humans will engage in sexual activity when they are not ovulating.
   b. Women on birth control pills are less likely to initiate sex midcycle than at other times.
   c. In women, the increased likelihood of initiating sex corresponds with an increase in sex hormone levels.
   d. Women are less likely to engage in sexual intercourse during ovulation than at other times of the cycle.

6. Which of the following brain areas is active during copulation in female, but not male, rats?
   a. medial preoptic area
   b. medial amygdala
   c. sexually dimorphic nucleus
   d. ventromedial nucleus

7. Which of the following is predicted by the steroid/peptide theory of social bonds?
   a. males caring for young while sexually aroused
   b. males defending territory when vasopressin is high
   c. females caring for young while not sexually aroused
   d. females engaging in sex when testosterone is low

8. Which of the following neurotransmitters increases in the nucleus accumbens during sexual activity?
   a. dopamine
   b. serotonin
   c. norepinephrine
   d. endorphin

9. Which of the following statements regarding olfactory receptors is TRUE?
   a. Humans can distinguish approximately 1,000 odors.
   b. Humans have more genes for them than mice.
   c. Humans have 400–600 genes for odor receptors.
   d. There are as many different odor receptors as odors that can be detected.

10. Receptors in the VNO project to which TWO of the four areas of the hypothalamus listed below?
    a. lateral geniculate nucleus (LGN)
    b. sexually dimorphic nucleus (SDN)
    c. medial preoptic area (MPOA)
    d. ventromedial nucleus of the hypothalamus (VMH)

11. Which of the following statements regarding pheromones in humans is FALSE?
    a. Women's menstrual cycles may be synchronized by pheromones.
    b. Men wearing pheromones are more likely to engage in intercourse than controls.
    c. Pheromones have been linked to sexual behavior, but not nonsexual behaviors like aggression.
    d. Women wearing pheromones are more likely to engage in intercourse than controls.

12. Oxytocin
    a. plays a role in bonding.
    b. is important in social recognition.
    c. causes muscle contractions involved in lactation and orgasm.
    d. all of the above

13. Which of the following statements regarding egg cells is TRUE?
    a. They contain both X and Y chromosomes.
    b. They contain only Y chromosomes.
    c. They contain only X chromosomes.
    d. They contain either an X or a Y chromosome.

14. Which of the following internal structures must be actively inhibited in order for the normal pattern of male genitalia to form?
    a. Müllerian ducts
    b. Wolffian ducts

    c. ovaries

    d. testes

15. The penis in males and the _____ in females develop from the same embryonic tissue.

    a. vagina

    b. labia

    c. uterus

    d. clitoris

16. What hormone(s) is (are) responsible for masculinization of the external genitalia in males?

    a. testosterone

    b. dihydrotestosterone

    c. Müllerian-inhibiting hormone

    d. a and b

17. Which of the following represents an activating effect of a hormone?

    a. maturation of the genitals at puberty

    b. the enlargement of the SDN in male rats

    c. production of a mature egg cell during ovulation

    d. masculinization of the genitals during prenatal development

18. Which of the following statements regarding sexual behavior in rats is TRUE?

    a. Among male rats, castration does not affect sexual behavior because it occurs after birth.

    b. Androgenized females will mount other rats but do not display lordosis.

    c. Castrated males do not display lordosis.

    d. Normal females occasionally mount other females.

19. Which is NOT true of the hormone estradiol?

    a. It is critical for masculinization of the male brain.

    b. It is critical for feminization of the female brain.

    c. It can be converted by the aromatization of testosterone.

    d. It is found only in females.

20. Which of the following gender differences has NOT been found in the research literature?

    a. Females are more emotional than males.

    b. Females tend to score better on verbal tasks than males.

    c. Males tend to score better on spatial tasks than females.

    d. Males tend to be more aggressive than females.

21. Which of the following is NOT a sex difference reported in the literature?

    a. Males are more susceptible to autism.

    b. Women are more affected by stress than males.

    c. Females are genetically more resistant to pain than males.

    d. Attention-deficit/hyperactivity disorder is more common in males.

22. Which hormone may be linked to enhanced verbal fluency?

    a. testosterone

    b. estrogen

    c. progesterone

    d. dihydrotestosterone

23. Which hormone may be linked to enhanced spatial skills?
    a. testosterone
    b. estrogen
    c. progesterone
    d. dihydrotestosterone

24. Which of the following statements regarding sex differences in aggression is FALSE?
    a. The cultural influence on aggression is weak compared to other factors.
    b. Studies indicate that males are much more likely than females to kill another person.
    c. Studies indicate that aggression is moderately heritable.
    d. Studies indicate that testosterone is related to aggression.

25. Steve believes he should have been born into a woman's body, and he wishes to get gender reassignment surgery to fix the apparent "mistake." However, he is still sexually attracted to women. If Steve's doctor were to examine his brain, what area would be smaller in size than it is in his homosexual and heterosexual male friends?
    a. central bed nucleus of the stria terminalis (BSTc)
    b. medial amygdala
    c. ventromedial hypothalamus (vmH)
    d. medial preoptic area (MPOA)

26. Which of the following will NOT result in 46 XY DSD?
    a. 17α-hydroxysteroid deficiency
    b. androgen insensitivity syndrome
    c. 5α-reductase deficiency
    d. congenital adrenal hyperplasia

27. Which of the following statements regarding 46 XX DSD individuals is TRUE?
    a. They are always raised as girls.
    b. They have ovaries.
    c. The external genitalia are clearly male in appearance.
    d. They lack testosterone receptors.

28. Which of the following groups tends to score the LOWEST on spatial tasks?
    a. CAH females
    b. 46 XX DSD individuals
    c. normal females
    d. normal males

29. Regarding the case of "Bruce-Brenda-David," which of the following is TRUE?
    a. Brenda wanted to become a boy before she knew her true sex.
    b. Brenda was comfortable with her feminine role until adolescence.
    c. Brenda's identical twin brother also exhibited many feminine characteristics.
    d. This case clearly demonstrated that the "neutral-at-birth" position is incorrect.

30. The study of 46 XY DSD in the Dominican Republic found that
    a. the source of the condition was androgen insensitivity.
    b. most individuals developed a sexual preference for male partners.
    c. although raised as girls, most of the individuals adopted male gender identities.
    d. all of the above

31. An early study indicated that, compared to other females, CAH females
    a. were more oriented toward male-typical occupations.
    b. were less likely to engage in same-sex erotic contact.

    c. were more feminine as children.

    d. were more likely to want to have children.

32. Which of the following statements regarding sexual orientation is TRUE?

    a. Gay men are more likely than lesbians to be bisexual.

    b. Lesbians make up a larger proportion of the population than do gay men.

    c. Gay men and lesbians are usually bisexual to a certain degree.

    d. Many more people engage in homosexual behavior than are considered homosexual.

33. Which of the following statements is TRUE about sex, gender, and sports?

    a. Sports organizations have successfully established a definition for gender.

    b. Physical examination and chromosome testing are currently acceptable measures for determining gender.

    c. Sports organizations can conduct gender tests on women with strong athletic performance and a male physique to verify their eligibility for female sporting events.

    d. Sports organizations currently require physical exams for all athletes to verify gender.

34. Gender nonconformity includes

    a. early heterosexual experiences.

    b. a childhood preference for friends of the other sex.

    c. a preference for activities usually associated with the other sex.

    d. b and c

35. Which of the following is evidence for a biological basis of sexual orientation?

    a. shared genetic material in region Xq28 of homosexual brothers

    b. volunteer bias in family studies of homosexuality

    c. childhood preference for friends of the other sex

    d. seduction by older males in youth

36. Epigenetic influences on sexual orientation, such as methylation of an X chromosome, indicate that

    a. genes are critical to determining sexual orientation.

    b. prenatal environment can influence sexual orientation.

    c. early childhood experiences shape sexual orientation.

    d. experiences during adolescence determine sexual orientation.

37. Homosexuality in other species

    a. occurs only under controlled laboratory conditions.

    b. results only from the manipulation of hormones during development.

    c. sometimes resembles heterosexuality (e.g., pair bonding, parenting).

    d. is never observed.

38. LeVay's study of brain anatomy showed that the INAH3 is similar in which two groups?

    a. heterosexual males and homosexual males

    b. homosexual males and females

    c. heterosexual females and heterosexual males

    d. homosexual females and homosexual males

39. According to the text, why aren't there many studies of homosexual females?
    a. Bisexuality is more common in females than in males, which makes female sexuality harder to categorize.
    b. There is not enough money to study males and females.
    c. Females are much more likely than males to be heterosexual.
    d. There is greater stigma for homosexuality in females, so they do not elect to participate in studies.

40. Which statement about the causes of homosexuality is most accurate?
    a. Homosexuality is caused by radically different events than heterosexuality.
    b. Homosexuality is caused by one specific gene.
    c. Experience early in life is the most important cause of sexual orientation.
    d. Heredity, hormones, brain structures, and experiences all seem to play a role in determining sexual orientation.

Answers

Guided Review

1. satiation
2. tissue
3. Masters and Johnson
4. excitement
5. plateau
6. orgasm
7. resolution
8. females
9. refractory
10. Coolidge
11. greater
12. castration
13. decline
14. androgens
15. testosterone
16. estrus or heat
17. ovulation
18. estrogen
19. testosterone
20. MPOA (medial preoptic area)
21. performance or behavior
22. copulate
23. medial
24. SDN (sexually dimorphic nucleus)
25. ventromedial
26. Dopamine
27. erection
28. D_2
29. sympathetic
30. accumbens
31. vasopressin
32. steroid/peptide
33. dominance
34. protective
35. high
36. nurturing
37. serotonin
38. odors
39. nasal
40. olfactory bulb
41. vomeronasal
42. pheromones
43. MPOA (medial preoptic area)
44. amygdala
45. menstrual
46. ovulating
47. odors
48. dopamine
49. oxytocin
50. orgasm
51. recognition
52. gender
53. identity
54. fertilization
55. X
56. female or girl
57. male or boy
58. ovaries
59. Müllerian
60. Wolffian
61. clitoris
62. *SRY* (sex-determining region Y)
63. testes
64. Müllerian-inhibiting
65. testosterone
66. seminal
67. dihydrotestosterone
68. scrotum
69. organizing
70. activating
71. puberty
72. Genitals or gonads
73. ova/eggs
74. lordosis

75. testosterone
76. estradiol
77. Maccoby and Jacklin
78. verbal
79. Mathematics
80. aggressive
81. overlap or narrowing
82. mathematics or cognitive abilities
83. cultural
84. gestation or pregnancy
85. spatial
86. verbal
87. spatial
88. testosterone
89. increases
90. hemispheres
91. frontal
92. parietal
93. autism
94. depression
95. transgender
96. dysphoria
97. BSTc (bed nucleus of the stria terminalis) or INAH3 (third interstitial nucleus of the anterior hypothalamus)
98. INAH3 (third interstitial nucleus of the anterior hypothalamus) or BSTc (bed nucleus of the stria terminalis)
99. hormone
100. difference in sexual development
101. hydroxysteroid
102. masculinization
103. Dominican Republic
104. culture or environment
105. androgen insensitivity
106. testes or testicles
107. breasts
108. androgens
109. penis
110. labia
111. congenital adrenal hyperplasia
112. intersexes
113. gender
114. testosterone
115. normal
116. verbal
117. female
118. female
119. homosexual/bisexual
120. bisexual/homosexual
121. homosexual
122. sexuality
123. circumcision
124. 22
125. 13
126. 3.5%
127. homosexual
128. asexuality or asexual
129. Social
130. sexual
131. nonconformity
132. concordance
133. X
134. mother's
135. 64
136. Darwinian
137. men
138. methylation
139. sensitivity
140. 70%
141. sheep
142. development
143. right hemisphere
144. men
145. suprachiasmatic
146. index to ring
147. androgen
148. female
149. biological
150. choice
151. genetic
152. acceptable

Short Answer and Essay Questions

1. Sex and hunger are similar in that they are under the regulation of the brain and hormones, and they both involve arousal and satiation. However, there are important differences. Usually, we eat to reduce hunger, but we seek out stimuli that will increase sexual arousal. Hunger is also more controlled by internal conditions, including tissue needs, whereas sexual arousal is relatively more responsive to external conditions.

2. Testosterone seems to be required for sexual motivation in both men and women, although only a low level appears to be necessary. However, sexual activity also increases testosterone levels, so the picture is somewhat complicated. In both men and women, castration leads to a reduction of sexual functioning. Men who are voluntarily castrated or are given testosterone-blocking drugs show reduced aggression and sexual tendencies. In women, testosterone levels are correlated with initiating sexual activity. When given testosterone, women show more sexual responsiveness.

3. For females and males, the important brain areas are the MPOA and the medial amygdala. For males, the paraventricular nucleus and the sexually dimorphic nucleus (SDN, in the MPOA) are also involved. In females, the ventromedial hypothalamus plays a role in sexual behavior.

4. Internally, the primitive gonads develop into either ovaries or testes; development of testes is dependent on the presence of the *SRY* gene on the Y chromosome. Without the presence of dihydrotestosterone, the external genitalia will become a clitoris, outer segment of the vagina, and labia, which is typical for females. If dihydrotestosterone is present, as it is in males, then the external structures become a penis and scrotum.

5. Organizing effects typically occur when the developing individual is first exposed to the hormone, either before or shortly after birth. This exposure leads to permanent changes in bodily structures. One example is how dihydrotestosterone changes the primitive external genital structures into a penis and scrotum, but there are many other examples in the book. Activating effects can occur any time in the life span after the initial exposure when hormone levels change, and they are reversible. An example is the development of breast tissue in females during puberty, but there are other examples in the book as well.

6. The book cites a study by Miles et al. that showed transgender women taking estrogen supplements scored higher on verbal tasks than those not taking estrogen.

7. They are insensitive to the effects of masculinizing hormones. Even females outperform them on spatial tasks because their brains are not capable of responding to the small amount of androgens their bodies produce. This is another piece of evidence that suggests hormones influence cognitive functioning.

8. After Semenya won the gold medal in a key track event, some people became suspicious about her gender due to her strong performance and masculine appearance. Her sports participation remained in jeopardy for a year while the International Association of Athletic Federations evaluated the results of her gender testing. These tests include chromosome testing, which treats androgen-insensitive XY individuals as males despite testosterone providing them no athletic benefit and treats XXY males as females, even though they do benefit from the effects of testosterone. Eventually, she was cleared to participate as a woman, but the IOC has not clarified how they are defining females or what "normal" testing levels are for females. Instead, the IOC has stated that anyone who has male levels of androgens and responds to androgens will not be permitted to compete in female athletic events.

9. Each case involves only a single individual, so generalizing to others is very difficult. Another problem is that these were not experiments, and there was virtually no control over the many factors influencing gender.

10. Studying individuals with different sexual and gender identity from the majority of humans, and in particular the differences in brain function, can help us discover the determinants of sexual orientation. Doing so will tell us not only why some people exhibit homosexual behaviors but also why others are heterosexual, bisexual, or gender-neutral.

11. The social learning hypothesis suggests that people who have early homosexual experiences will be more likely to become homosexual later. There is evidence for this; for example, individuals who reported having other-sex friends, masturbating in the presence of or being masturbated by a same-sex partner, and having homosexual contact prior to age 18 were more likely to be homosexual as adults. But an alternative interpretation is that these experiences are early manifestations of an underlying homosexual tendency rather than the origin of homosexuality.

12. It seems unlikely that natural selection would favor a trait such as homosexuality that reduces the likelihood of reproduction. However, Italian researchers have found higher female birth rates in the mother's side of the family of male homosexuals, suggesting that homosexuality may not reduce overall birth rates. Homosexuality may result from an epigenetic process, rather than inheritance of "genes for homosexuality."

13. They are concerned that if a biological basis to homosexuality is discovered, it will be understood in terms of a physical abnormality that can be corrected medically to "cure" homosexuality or genetically to prevent it. One potential benefit is that any minority groups that are created by biological differences are protected under U.S. civil rights laws. In addition, polls show that people who believe that homosexuality is biologically determined also hold more positive views of homosexuality.

Post-test

1. c 2. a 3. b 4. d 5. c 6. d 7. c 8. a 9. c 10. c & d 11. c 12. d 13. c
14. a 15. d 16. b 17. c 18. d 19. d 20. a 21. c 22. b 23. a 24. a 25. a
26. d 27. b 28. c 29. a 30. c 31. a 32. d 33. c 34. d 35. a 36. b 37. c
38. b 39. a 40. d

8 Emotion and Health

Learning Objectives

After reading this chapter, you will be able to

1. Describe the brain structures and neurotransmitters involved in emotion

2. Explain how the body and the peripheral nervous system contribute to the experience of emotion

3. Identify the adaptive and maladaptive components of the stress response

4. Discuss the contributions of genetics and environment to stress responses

5. Compare the affective and sensory components of pain

6. Examine the brain structures and chemical systems involved in aggression

Emotion and the Nervous System

Summary and Guided Review

After studying this section in the text, fill in the blanks of the following summary.

Emotions enrich our lives and _____ (1) our behavior. For example, anger intensifies _____ (2) behavior and accelerates flight, whereas happiness encourages the behavior that produces it. Emotions make experiences more _____ (3), so we are likely to repeat behaviors that bring joy and avoid those that produce pain. As Damasio would have said about Jane's case in the introduction, reason without emotion is inadequate for making the decisions that guide our lives.

Emotions involve subjective "feelings," expressions, and behavior, all of which are rooted in the nervous system. For example, the autonomic nervous system is intimately involved in emotional responding; activation of the _____ (4) branch produces arousal, and the _____ (5) branch helps to reduce activity and restore bodily resources. _____ (6) is an important hormone released from the adrenal glands in times of stress, due to activation of the sympathetic nervous system.

In the late 1900s an American psychologist and a Danish physiologist independently proposed what has become known as the _____-_____ (7) theory of emotion, which states that emotional experience results from the physiological arousal that precedes it. In an experiment in which subjects were made angry or frightened, the two emotions were accompanied by _____ (8) patterns of physiological activity. Years later, Schacter and Singer interpreted these results based on _____ (9) theory, stating that the _____ (10) of the emotion is based on cognitive assessment of the situation, and physiological arousal only determines the emotion's _____ (11). This theory is supported by the finding that similar patterns of arousal can be interpreted differently, based on the _____ (12) context. More recently, studies of facial expression in emotion have added support for the James-Lange theory. Ekman found that posed facial expressions could actually produce the _____ (13) of the intended emotion. When a woman's facial muscles are paralyzed with injections of _____ (14), it affects the ability not only to produce facial expressions of emotion but to experience them as well; this has been verified by fMRI evidence of reduced activation of the amygdala while trying to imitate angry expressions. Feedback from emotional expressions may also help us _____ (15) other people's emotions, which is critical to social communication. Special cells in the brain called _____ (16) neurons may be involved in our ability to show _____ (17) for others, based on the finding that observation of other people's emotions activate our own "emotional brain" pathways. People with _____ (18) have difficulty understanding the emotions of others; they can imitate expressions, but the mimicry is delayed.

There are several brain structures that play important roles in emotions. Many of these areas are located in the _____ (19) system, which also contributes to learning, memory, and motivation. In humans undergoing brain surgery, Heath found that electrical stimulation of the _____ (20) elicited autonomic arousal, and patients reported feeling different emotions, depending on the placement of the electrode. Sexual interest seems to be at least in part a result of stimulation of the _____ (21) area. Recent brain imaging studies indicate that the _____ (22) cortex and _____ _____ (23) are involved in disgust. Because it combines emotional, attentional, and bodily information, the anterior _____ (24) cortex is believed to be important for cognitive processing of emotion. This structure is also larger on the right side in people who manifest _____ (25) avoidance, which involves worry about possible problems, fearfulness, and shyness. Although research has linked emotions to particular brain areas, it is important to remember that no emotion can be linked to a(n) _____ (26) part of the brain.

Patients with damage to the prefrontal cortex have difficulty making rational _____ (27). When damage includes the _____ (28) cortex, people show a lack of responsiveness to a gambling task; their skin _____ (29) response (SCR) is not affected by risk, and they do not learn to avoid making risky choices. In _____ (30) takers, brain scans have found strong connections in a loop involving the nucleus accumbens, amygdala, and the right prefrontal cortex. The amygdala and _____ _____ (31) appear to increase risky behavior, whereas the prefrontal cortex decreases the chances of risk taking. Studies also identified another part of the brain that participates in evaluating risk, the posterior _____ (32) cortex. As discussed in the Application, _____ (33) dependent individuals have the strongest connections between the striatum and the _____ (34) areas, suggesting evaluation of the risks when deciding whether to perform a behavior.

The prefrontal areas receive most of their inputs from the _____ (35), a limbic structure that is especially involved in the negative emotions of fear and _____ (36). Rats with damage to the amygdala display no _____ (37) of cats, and humans with a damaged amygdala are very trusting of others. Furthermore, they seem incapable of learning to recognize harmful situations or experiencing emotional responses to rewards and _____ (38).

There are hemispheric differences in emotion; the left frontal area seems to be more involved in _____ (39) emotions, whereas the right frontal area is more involved in _____ (40) emotions. Right hemisphere damage has been linked to impairment of emotional responses and perception of emotions in others, perhaps because people with such damage have diminished _____ (41) response. People with right hemisphere damage often speak in an unemotional _____ (42) and have trouble recognizing emotion from a person's speech.

Short Answer and Essay Questions

Answer the following questions.

1. Assess the adaptive value of emotions for humans and other animals. In your answer, address the potential for emotions to promote effective decision making.

2. Compare the James-Lange and cognitive theories of emotion.

3. Identify key brain areas involved in emotion. How do the right and left hemispheres differ in the roles they play in emotion?

Stress, Immunity, and Health

Summary and Guided Review

After studying this section in the text, fill in the blanks of the following summary.

The term _____ (43) is used to refer to external events that challenge an organism as well as internal responses to the challenge. The internal experience of stress is highly variable; not everyone feels stress under the same conditions.

Usually, the internal changes associated with stress are positive and _____ (44). These include activation of the _____-_____-_____ (45) (HPA) axis, a mechanism responsible for the release of stress _____ (46) that prepare the body for "fight or flight" via their effects on circulation and energy availability. For example, the stress hormone _____ (47) converts proteins to glucose and increases both fat availability and _____ (48); this provides more energy for a longer period of time than the _____ (49) nervous system does, for prolonged stressful situations. Changes also occur in the _____ (50) system, which protects the body against foreign substances that could be introduced during injury. There are several types of _____ (51), including macrophages, T cells, and antibody-producing _____ (52). Another type of immune cell, _____ _____ (53) cells, destroy cancer and viral-infected cells. The final type of immune cell, the _____ (54), acts in a similar fashion as a macrophage, protecting the central nervous system from invaders that penetrate the blood-brain barrier. In _____ (55) disorders, such as multiple sclerosis and AIDS, the immune system improperly attacks the body's own cells.

If the stress response continues over a long period of time, considerable harm can occur, including memory _____ (56), motivational changes, mood changes, and immune system impairment. People in the vicinity of the Three Mile Island nuclear accident continued to experience reduced _____ (57) functioning as long as six years after the event. In another study, volunteers exposed to cold viruses were more likely to develop _____ (58) if they had experienced stress for longer than a month. Increased vulnerability to stress may produce cardiovascular disease, as evidenced by the fact that children who were more reactive to having their hands placed in _____ _____ (59) were more likely to have high blood pressure as adults. There is even evidence that acute stress can lead to sudden _____ _____ (60). For example, on the day of the 1994 earthquake in Southern California, the number of deaths due to _____ _____ (61) was five times higher than average. Stress may also contribute to brain damage in victims of torture or abuse, particularly in the _____ (62), perhaps due to prolonged exposure or greater sensitivity to cortisol. Combat veterans as well as victims of childhood trauma have reduced brain volume in this area, and are frequently diagnosed with _____ _____ _____ (63) disorder (PTSD). The hormone cortisol may cause hippocampal damage, possibly through increased number or _____ (64) of _____ (65) receptors during times of prolonged stress. Removing stress and improving social support, by contrast, can improve health.

Social, _____ (66), and genetic factors are linked to stress-related health problems as well. For example, people who are _____ (67) are more likely to suffer from heart disease, and among _____ (68) patients, those who lose hope or accept their disease have a lower survival rate than those who display a fighting spirit. Individuals with greater left prefrontal activity (associated with positive emotion) developed more antibodies following _____ (69) vaccination. Introverted HIV-positive men had _____ (70) viral loads than extroverts, presumably because of elevated neurotransmitter levels. However, these studies are correlational, so personality may not be the sole reason for immune response differences. Vulnerability to stress is heritable, and researchers have implicated two genes in the stress response: Individuals with a low-functioning version of _____ (71) reported more negative emotions when anticipating unpleasant events. Methylation of the _____ _____ (72) gene *OXTR* has also been linked to oxytocin's responses to stress. Stress may trigger _____ (73) changes to these genes, which could be inherited by offspring.

Like stress, _____ (74) is in many ways an adaptive response. People with congenital _____ (75) to pain have difficulty learning to avoid injuries and may die from untreated injuries. Pain can be considered a(n) _____ (76) response as well as a sensation. How people experience pain varies on an individual and cultural basis. For example, in the United States _____ (77) is considered more painful than it is in some other cultures. A study of World War II soldiers wounded in combat revealed that 68% refused morphine, compared with only 17% of civilian patients receiving similar _____ (78) procedures. Although the soldiers still felt pain, they were better able to cope with it since it was a signal that they were still alive.

Pathways that carry pain messages connect to the _____ (79) area, the cortex dealing with body sensations, and the _____ _____ (80) cortex, which is involved in the emotional component of pain. The _____ (81) cortex is also involved in emotional responses to pain; it is presumably where pain is evaluated and a response to it is planned. People who underwent a _____ (82) of this area reported that they could still experience pain, but were not bothered by it.

Short Answer and Essay Questions

Answer the following questions.

4. Discuss the role of personality factors in cancer survival. Why is it difficult to determine if factors such as introversion are directly responsible for reduced immune functioning?

5. Why is pain considered to be adaptive? What would your life be like if you could not feel, or were not bothered by, pain?

6. Discuss the role of the anterior cingulate cortex in pain. How do researchers know that it is involved in the emotional response to, but not the sensation of, pain?

Biological Origins of Aggression

Summary and Guided Review

After studying this section in the text, fill in the blanks of the following summary.

_____ (83) is defined as a behavior intended to do harm. It is sometimes, but not always, an adaptive response, involving both motivation and _____ (84). There are several different forms of aggression. The cold, emotionless form is _____ (85) aggression, when an animal attacks and kills prey, or when a person commits a premeditated, unprovoked attack on another individual. Another form is _____ (86) aggression, which is characterized by its impulsiveness and emotional arousal. In humans, emotionless acts that are done to gain something from a victim are categorized as acts of _____ (87) aggression, whereas _____ (88) aggression involves heightened emotionality and is prompted by a perceived threat.

Studies of humans and other animals have identified several brain structures that are involved in these types of aggression. Cats, rats, and monkeys display aggression when the _____ (89) is stimulated. Optogenetic stimulation has further identified the medial, ventromedial, and _____ (90) hypothalamic areas as critical to aggressive behavior. Although the amygdala is important to aggression, people who show disorders of impulsive aggression (such as borderline personality disorder) have _____ (91) activity here, and reduced amygdala activity is hypothesized to correlate with _____ (92) aggression. Similarly, people who commit impulsive crimes demonstrated reduced activity in the _____ _____ (93), but this was not true of people who had committed acts of instrumental aggression.

The sex hormone _____ (94) has been linked to aggression in rats, monkeys, and humans. However, the causal relationship between hormones and aggression is not clear, because it has been shown that testosterone _____ (95) while watching one's team win a sports event, and even after receiving a college degree. In addition, the effects of high testosterone depend on the activity of serotonin and _____ (96). People who exhibit aggression show persistently reduced binding of _____ (97) at receptors in the prefrontal cortex and amygdala. Furthermore, drugs that inhibit reuptake at the synapse, such as _____ (98), reduce aggressiveness and increase prefrontal cortex activity. In a study performed on monkeys, those with high _____ (99) levels and low serotonin levels were most likely to be impulsive and aggressive to others. In humans, a similar relationship is seen, particularly in violent offenders when _____ (100) is involved. In boys and girls, high testosterone and low levels of the stress hormone _____ (101) have been correlated with aggression; cortisol seems important in _____ (102) aggression. The inhibitory neurotransmitter _____ (103) and dopamine have also been associated with aggression, but their roles are less clearly understood.

Although there is a genetic basis for aggression—_____% (104) of the variation among people in aggression is genetic—the environment also plays a role. Most of the genes that have been linked to aggression involve transmission of the neurotransmitters serotonin and _____ (105). For example, the dopamine transporter gene _____ (106) and the serotonin transporter gene _____ (107) have been associated with aggression. The *MAOA-L* _____ (108) of the *MAOA* gene, sometimes called the "warrior gene," results in low levels of the enzyme

_____ _____ (109) and has been found in people who show impulsive aggression. Environmental influences on aggression include family adversity and _____ (110) status. Several studies suggest that genes and environment interact. The interaction of genes and environment in aggression is demonstrated by the finding that the *MAOA-L* allele produced violence only in males who had been subjected to _____ _____ (111) in childhood.

Short Answer and Essay Questions

Answer the following questions.

7. Contrast instrumental and impulsive aggression, including the behavioral and brain characteristics of each aggression type. Give an example of each.

8. Critique the causal relationship between testosterone levels and aggression. Be sure to address the support for a causal relationship as well as reasons why a causal relationship is controversial.

9. Explain how serotonin, cortisol, and testosterone interact in contributing to aggression.

10. Describe some environmental influences in aggression, including ways that environment and genes might interact to influence aggression.

Post-test

Use these multiple-choice questions to check your understanding of the chapter.

1. Sympathetic arousal involves all of the following EXCEPT
   a. increased heart rate.
   b. increased blood pressure.
   c. increased respiration.
   d. increased digestion.

2. According to the James-Lange theory, emotional experiences occur in which order?
   a. stimulus-arousal-emotion
   b. stimulus-emotion-arousal
   c. stimulus-appraisal-emotion
   d. stimulus-arousal/appraisal-emotion

3. Which of the following is NOT true about mirror neurons?
   a. They respond both when we engage in a specific act and when we observe the same act in others.
   b. They show increased activity in autism.
   c. They most likely play a role in the emotion of empathy.
   d. They were discovered when researchers noted that the same neurons responded when monkeys reached for food and when they saw the researcher pick up food.

4. Facial expressions
   a. are probably less important in emotional feedback than autonomic arousal.
   b. are all learned from one's family.
   c. can evoke emotions consistent with the expression.
   d. none of the above

5. Which of the following provides support for the James-Lange theory of emotion?
   a. Following Botox treatments to the facial muscles, women experience less negative emotions.
   b. People with autism do not understand the facial expressions of others.
   c. Amygdala damage results in rats not fearing cats.
   d. Stimulating the hypothalamus results in fear in epilepsy patients.

6. Which of the following structures is NOT considered part of the limbic system?
   a. amygdala
   b. cingulate gyrus
   c. hippocampus
   d. medulla

7. In the gambling task described in this chapter, individuals with ventromedial prefrontal damage
   a. produced a strong skin conductance response to the risky piles but did not learn to avoid choosing from the risky card piles.
   b. did not produce a strong skin conductance response to any pile but learned to avoid choosing from the risky card piles anyway.
   c. did not produce a strong skin conductance response to any pile and did not learn to avoid choosing from the risky card piles.
   d. produced a strong skin conductance response to the risk piles and learned to avoid choosing from the risky card piles.

8. In an early study by Heath with humans, stimulation of the septal area evoked
   a. pleasure.
   b. fear.
   c. anxiety.
   d. sadness.

9. In an MRI study, investigators found that the right _____ was larger in people with high scores on _____ avoidance.
   a. hippocampus; pain
   b. amygdala; predator
   c. anterior cingulate; harm
   d. prefrontal cortex; alcohol

10. Someone with heightened activity in the amygdala would be MOST likely to experience
    a. pleasure.
    b. anxiety.
    c. anger.
    d. sadness.

11. People with damage to the amygdala
    a. are completely fearless.
    b. often exhibit fits of rage.
    c. have difficulty learning to avoid harmful situations.
    d. suffer from antisocial personality disorder.

12. People with prefrontal damage can probably do all of the following EXCEPT
    a. experience any emotion at all.
    b. learn to avoid venomous snakes.
    c. experience negative emotions.
    d. learn to avoid risky investments.

13. People with right hemisphere damage have difficulty with all of the following EXCEPT
    a. recognizing facial expressions in others.
    b. recognizing emotion in others' voices.
    c. understanding verbal expressions of emotion.
    d. displaying nonverbal signs of emotion.

14. Cortisol is released by the
    a. hypothalamus.
    b. pituitary gland.
    c. adrenal glands.
    d. all of the above

15. Cortisol is responsible for all of the following EXCEPT
    a. increased oxygen transport to muscle cells.
    b. conversion of protein to glucose.
    c. increase in fat availability.
    d. increase in metabolism.

16. Immune system cells that work by ingesting foreign substances and then displaying their antigens are called
    a. T cells.
    b. B cells.
    c. macrophages.
    d. natural killer cells.

17. Which of the following is not a leukocyte?
    a. T cells
    b. B cells
    c. macrophages
    d. natural killer cells

18. Following the Three Mile Island accident, nearby residents displayed
    a. a reduced number of immune cells.
    b. a higher cancer rate.
    c. a reduced ability to concentrate.
    d. a and c

19. Children who showed the greatest amount of reactivity (in terms of blood pressure increase) when placing their hands in ice water were MORE likely to develop
    a. cancer as children.
    b. cancer as adults.
    c. high blood pressure as children.
    d. high blood pressure as adults.

20. Sudden cardiac death may be linked to
    a. stress.
    b. earthquakes.
    c. sports.
    d. all of the above

21. Which of the following structures is not one of the ones that helps the body cope with stress?
    a. hypothalamus
    b. hippocampus
    c. pituitary gland
    d. adrenal glands

22. Brain damage in posttraumatic stress may be due to increased sensitivity to
    a. cortisol.
    b. norepinephrine.
    c. epinephrine.
    d. all of the above

23. The personality factor of hostility is MOST strongly associated with
    a. cancer.
    b. heart disease.
    c. ulcers.
    d. reduced immune functioning.

24. Greater prefrontal right hemisphere activity is associated with
    a. greater antibody production following vaccination.
    b. greater T-cell levels among AIDS patients.
    c. lower antibody production following vaccination.
    d. lower T-cell levels among AIDS patients.

25. Introversion is associated with
    a. increased natural killer cell activity.
    b. higher levels of HIV.
    c. higher cancer rates.
    d. a and b

26. Which of the following statements regarding pain is FALSE?
    a. It is both a sensation and an emotion.
    b. Situational factors may influence how strongly it is felt.
    c. The ability to experience pain is not adaptive.
    d. Some people are unable to experience pain.

27. The emotional component of pain is MOST directly linked to activity in the
    a. somatosensory cortex.
    b. anterior cingulate cortex.
    c. prefrontal cortex.
    d. insular cortex.

28. People who underwent prefrontal lobotomy for pain that failed to respond to other treatments
    a. no longer experienced pain.
    b. were no longer bothered by the pain.
    c. experienced more pain than before the procedure.
    d. were often paralyzed as well as rendered insensitive to pain.

29. Which of the following is an example of impulsive aggression?
    a. teen stealing candy from a convenience store
    b. a cheetah chasing down and killing an antelope
    c. a woman killing an attacker in self-defense
    d. a man hunting deer for meat

30. Which of the following brain structures has NOT been linked to aggression?
    a. amygdala
    b. hypothalamus

    c. prefrontal cortex

    d. thalamus

31. Which of the following individuals is most likely to have reduced amygdala activity?

    a. Carol, who has borderline personality disorder

    b. Ian, who has intermittent explosive disorder

    c. Susan, who has frontal lobe damage

    d. John, who played violent video games for 10 years as a teenager

32. Among prisoners, testosterone would probably be LOWEST in those convicted of which of the following crimes?

    a. drug offenses

    b. rape

    c. murder

    d. armed robbery

33. Which of the following statements regarding hormones and aggression in humans is FALSE?

    a. Testosterone, serotonin, and cortisol are all linked to aggression.

    b. Winning a sporting event increases testosterone.

    c. High testosterone is linked to aggression in men but not women.

    d. Their peers rate male prisoners with higher testosterone as tougher.

34. Antidepressants reduce all of the following EXCEPT

    a. alcohol cravings.

    b. serotonin levels.

    c. aggression.

    d. none of the above

35. Monkeys who are impulsive, reckless, and prone to aggressive behavior probably have high _____ and low _____ levels.

    a. serotonin; testosterone

    b. testosterone; serotonin

    c. estrogen; testosterone

    d. serotonin; dopamine

36. Males who commit violent crimes most likely have high _____ and low _____ levels.

    a. serotonin; testosterone

    b. dopamine; serotonin

    c. cortisol; GABA

    d. testosterone; cortisol

37. Which of the following neurotransmitters has NOT been linked to aggression?

    a. acetylcholine

    b. dopamine

    c. serotonin

    d. GABA

38. Heredity accounts for about _____% of the variability in aggression.

    a. 50

    b. 75

c. 25

d. 15

39. Which of the following are known as the "warrior genes" for their link to impulsive aggression?

a. alleles of the androgen receptor gene

b. *5HTT*

c. alleles of the *MAOA* gene

d. *DAT1*

40. Which of the following has been associated with increased risk for aggressive behavior in people?

a. family history of abuse in childhood

b. high parental education

c. high family income

d. parental age under 30 at the time of a child's birth

Answers

Guided Review

1. motivate
2. defensive
3. memorable
4. sympathetic
5. parasympathetic
6. Cortisol
7. James-Lange
8. different
9. cognitive
10. identity
11. intensity
12. environmental
13. experience
14. Botox or botulinum toxin
15. recognize or understand
16. mirror
17. empathy
18. autism
19. limbic
20. hypothalamus
21. septal
22. insular
23. basal ganglia
24. cingulate
25. harm
26. single or specific
27. judgments
28. ventromedial
29. conductance
30. risk
31. nucleus accumbens
32. parietal
33. reward
34. prefrontal
35. amygdala
36. anxiety
37. fear
38. punishments
39. positive
40. negative
41. autonomic
42. monotone
43. stress
44. adaptive
45. hypothalamus-pituitary-adrenal
46. hormones
47. cortisol
48. metabolism
49. sympathetic
50. immune
51. leukocytes
52. B cells
53. natural killer
54. microglia
55. autoimmune
56. impairment or loss
57. immune
58. infections
59. ice water
60. cardiac death
61. heart attacks
62. hippocampus
63. posttraumatic stress disorder
64. sensitivity
65. glucocorticoid
66. personality
67. hostile
68. cancer
69. influenza (flu)
70. higher
71. *NPY*
72. oxytocin receptor
73. epigenetic
74. pain

75. insensitivity
76. emotional
77. childbirth
78. surgical
79. somatosensory
80. anterior cingulate
81. prefrontal
82. lobotomy
83. Aggression
84. emotion
85. predatory
86. affective
87. instrumental
88. impulsive
89. hypothalamus
90. anterior
91. enhanced or increased
92. instrumental
93. prefrontal cortex

94. testosterone
95. increases
96. cortisol
97. serotonin
98. antidepressants
99. testosterone
100. alcohol
101. cortisol
102. inhibiting
103. GABA (gamma aminobutyric acid)
104. 50
105. dopamine
106. *DAT1*
107. *5HTT*
108. allele
109. monoamine oxidase
110. socioeconomic
111. physical abuse

Short Answer and Essay Questions

1. There are many possible answers, but a correct response should refer to the role of emotions in decision making, communication, preparation or motivation for a response, and/or learning. In particular, the studies of people whose emotional capacities are impaired suggest that without emotion, we would not make very good decisions. For example, people with prefrontal damage seem to be unable to learn from the emotions that normally accompany rewards and punishment, and so their behavior is often impulsive.

2. The James-Lange theory states that emotional experience results from the physiological arousal that precedes it, and different emotions are the result of different patterns of arousal. The cognitive theory of emotion stated that the identity of the emotion is based on the cognitive assessment of the situation, and physiological arousal contributes only to the emotion's intensity.

3. The important systems are the parts of the limbic system, including the hypothalamus, septal area, insula, anterior cingulate cortex, amygdala, and prefrontal cortex. The right hemisphere seems more important in negative emotions, whereas the left hemisphere is more active during positive emotions.

4. Cancer survival is higher among patients with a fighting spirit and lower among those who are depressed. However, this research is correlational, which makes cause and effect difficult to determine. A good example comes from the association between introversion and HIV levels in AIDS. Introverted patients had high levels of sympathetic activity. Increased sympathetic activity is caused by epinephrine and norepinephrine, both of which are high in introverted individuals, and norepinephrine increases HIV virus multiplication in the laboratory. Thus, norepinephrine may be responsible for both the introversion and the HIV virus proliferation in the subjects; personality characteristics and emotional states may be more of a marker for physiological activity that results in the health condition rather than a causal influence.

5. Pain is adaptive because it lets us know when we have done something that is harmful, and therefore we can learn to avoid such behaviors. People who are insensitive to or are not bothered by pain do not respond to the warning signals of pain and are subject to greater injury; lacking the emotional deterrent, they have difficulty learning to avoid behaviors that can lead to injury.

6. The anterior cingulate cortex appears to mediate the emotional aspect of pain. When a painful stimulus is presented several times and participants feel increasing unpleasantness (but the stimulus remains the same), there are changes in the anterior cingulate cortex, but not the somatosensory cortex. Also, when participants under hypnosis are instructed that a painful stimulus is becoming more unpleasant (again, without any change in the stimulus), the same result occurs.

7. Instrumental aggression involves a premeditated, unprovoked attack on another individual, such as when a CEO embezzles money from his or her company. This type of aggression generally lacks the emotional components seen in the other forms of aggression. Impulsive aggression involves a response to a threat or attack and is motivated by fear. An example of this is when someone murders his or her spouse for having an adulterous relationship. This form is usually impulsive and motivated by emotion, typically fear or anger. Instrumental aggression is linked to reduced amygdala activity, as seen in antisocial personality and psychopathy. High serotonin and enhanced activity in the prefrontal cortex may occur with this type of aggression and accounts for the lack of emotionality displayed by criminals who engage in instrumental aggressive behaviors. Impulsive aggression has been associated with enhanced activity in the amygdala, as seen in borderline personality disorder or intermittent explosive disorder, and reduced activity in the prefrontal cortex. Low serotonin activity, including reduced binding of serotonin in the prefrontal cortex and amygdala, are characteristic of this type of aggression, which has also been linked to the *MAOA-L* gene.

8. Support for a causal link between high testosterone and high aggression comes primarily from studies of rats where castration reduces aggression and testosterone implants increase aggression. Human studies are mostly correlational and show that high testosterone levels in male and female prisoners are associated with more violent crimes. One argument against testosterone causing aggression is that testosterone levels have been shown to increase following arousing events such as winning a sporting event, suggesting that aggression could cause an increase in testosterone. In addition, the impacts of testosterone on aggression depend on the levels of both serotonin and cortisol.

9. Aggression is most likely to occur in individuals who have both high testosterone and low cortisol levels. In some cases, high serotonin levels can reduce aggressive behavior by increasing prefrontal cortex activity and thus inhibiting amygdala and hypothalamus activity. In other cases, high serotonin levels are associated with instrumental aggression. Low serotonin levels are linked to impulsive aggression.

10. Environmental factors associated with increased aggression include inadequate parenting, abuse in childhood, and low family income/education. Environment seems to interact with genes in risk for aggression. For example, the *MAOA-L* gene was associated with aggression only in people with a history of childhood abuse.

Post-test

1. d 2. a 3. b 4. c 5. a 6. d 7. c 8. a 9. c 10. b 11. c 12. d 13. c 14. c 15. a 16. c 17. c 18. d 19. d 20. d 21. b 22. a 23. b 24. c 25. b 26. c 27. b 28. b 29. c 30. d 31. d 32. a 33. c 34. b 35. b 36. d 37. a 38. a 39. c 40. a

9 Hearing and Language

Learning Objectives

After reading this chapter, you will be able to

1. Summarize how the nervous system processes sound stimuli

2. Identify the brain structures involved in hearing

3. Describe the role of specific brain structures in language ability

4. Explain how lateralization is important to the brain organization of language processing

5. Predict the brain regions that are impaired in specific language disorders

6. Contrast the communication abilities of other animals with human language

Hearing

Summary and Guided Review

After studying this section in the text, fill in the blanks of the following summary.

When we encounter environmental stimuli, our ___receptors___ (1), often specialized neurons, respond to specific types of stimuli and convert sensory information such as light or sound into neural signals. These cells pick up a very specific form of environmental energy, called a(n) ___adequate___ ___stimulus___ (2), and nothing else. ___sensation___ (3) is the first step in information processing that allows us to interact with the external environment. Then the sensory information is interpreted through a process known as ___perception___ (4). It is the amplitude and timing, or ___pattern___ (5), of the neural impulses that makes sensory information meaningful. For hearing, the process of sensation occurs in the ___cochlea___ (6) of the inner ear.

Our sense of hearing is highly complex. The auditory stimulus is the vibration of molecules in a(n) ___conducting___ ___medium___ (7), which may be air, water, and even the skull. These vibrations can be represented graphically as number of cycles or ___waves/compressions___ (8) per second, with their frequency expressed in ___hertz (Hz)___ (9). ___Pitch___ (10) is our psychological experience of the sound frequency. The range of frequencies that humans are most sensitive to is ___1000___ – ___4000___ Hz (11). A sound with a single frequency is a(n) ___pure___ ___tone___ (12). Most sounds are complex, because they contain many frequencies. The sound ___amplitude___ (13), or height of the signal measured in millivolts, represents the physical intensity of sound, which we experience as ___loudness___ (14), measured in dB.

To hear, we must get information about the sound; this involves sound reception, ___amplification___ (15), and conversion of sound waves into neural impulses. The ___pinna___ (16), or outer ear, filters sound waves and amplifies them by directing them into the smaller auditory canal. Then sound waves reach the ___tympanic___ (17) membrane or eardrum, which separates the outer and middle ear. Its vibration transmits the sound energy to the second part of the middle ear, the ___ossicles___ (18), which are the hammer, anvil, and stirrup bones. The stirrup rests against the oval window, which is the point of entry into the small coiled ___cochlea___ (19) in the inner ear (which is about 35 millimeters long in humans).

This structure contains three fluid-filled canals. The vestibular canal connects with the **tympanic** (20) canal at the far end of the cochlea (called the helicotrema). Fluid movement in these canals creates vibration in the cochlear canal, where the auditory **receptors** (21) are located. Conversion of sound waves to neural impulses occurs when vibrations reach the organ of Corti, which is part of the **basilar** (22) membrane. The organ of Corti consists of four rows of **hair** (23) cells, their supporting cells, and the shelf-like **tectorial** (24) membrane into which the hairs are embedded. Vibration of the basilar membrane causes the hair cells to bend, which opens **potassium (K)** (25) and calcium channels, depolarizing the hair cell membrane, which stimulates the connected **auditory** (26) neurons. The inner hair cells, less numerous than the **outer** (27) hair cells, are apparently responsible for encoding what we hear, as is evidenced by the observation that mice lacking inner hair cells due to a mutant gene are **deaf** (28). The other hair cells are involved in sharpening frequency tuning at the point of peak vibration.

Cochlear neurons project to the primary auditory cortex in the **temporal** (29) lobe via the auditory nerves, passing through the brain stem, inferior colliculi, and the **medial geniculate** (30) nucleus of the thalamus. Most, but not all, of the fibers from the auditory nerves cross over to the opposite hemisphere. Some of the functions of the auditory cortex of each hemisphere are specialized: **language** (31) in the left, and aspects of music identification in the right. The auditory cortex is also **tonotopically** (32) organized, as neurons from adjacent sites on the basilar membrane project to adjacent points on the cortex and encode similar frequency sounds. Sound information is conveyed to areas beyond the primary auditory cortex; the **dorsal** (33) stream flows through the parietal lobe and processes information about where a sound is coming from, while the **ventral** (34) stream processes information about identifying the sound.

In converting sound waves into neural impulses at the cochlea, the auditory system codes for both the intensity and frequency of stimuli. One group of ideas for how this conversion occurs are called **frequency** (35) theories, because the rate of generated action potentials matches the rate of sound waves per second. The earliest idea for this mechanism was a 19th-century theory of coding advanced by Rutherford, called the **telephone** (36) theory, which postulated that auditory neurons fire at the same rate as the sound that stimulates them. This idea was tested by Wever and Bray (1930), who found evidence to support it. But they recorded from the auditory **nerve** (37) rather than a single neuron or axon, and Wever later hypothesized that several neurons cooperatively encoded frequencies, and this pattern was called **volleying** (38). However, even this cooperation can only reproduce frequencies below about 5200 Hz; some other mechanism must be responsible for encoding higher frequencies.

The 19th-century scientist Helmholtz proposed a(n) **place** (39) theory of frequency coding that suggested that vibration of the **basilar** (40) membrane varies along its length with the frequency of the sound; frequency is encoded according to the place of maximal vibration. This selective responsiveness helps explain why structures from the cochlea to the cortex contains a(n) **tonotopic** (41) map corresponding with different points along the basilar membrane, and why one can hear through **bone** (42) conduction. In the auditory cortex, neurons have very selective **tuning curves** (43), where individual neurons are selective to a very small range of frequencies and are sharpened through lateral inhibition. Since place theory falls apart at low frequencies (below 200 Hz), and frequency theory falls apart at high frequency (due to the refractory period), most researchers believe that the combined ___*frequency - place*___ (44) theory is the most accurate account of auditory frequency processing across the entire spectrum of sound we hear.

Intensity coding is simpler. With low-frequency sounds, more intense stimuli produce responses in more neurons; for higher-frequency sounds, intensity is coded by the ___*rate/frequency*___ (45) of neural impulses.

Restoring hearing effectively depends on the cause of the hearing impairment, as different parts of the auditory system can be involved in hearing loss. Since ___*90*___ % (46) of hearing impairment cases are caused by hair cell loss, hearing aids are not usually effective. Instead, neurons in the ___*basilar*___ (47) membrane can be activated via electrodes using a device called a ___*cochlear implant*___ (48).

Most of the sounds that we hear are complex, containing multiple frequencies. Research suggests that the ear performs a(n) ___*Fourier*___ (49) analysis of complex sounds, in which the sound is analyzed by breaking it down into individual frequency bands. The basilar membrane carries out this analysis by responding ___*simultaneously*___ (50) along its length to these individual sound frequencies. We must also explain why we are capable of identifying and following a single auditory object among multiple competing sound sources, such as when we attend to a particular conversation among many different conversations at a social gathering. This is known as the ___*cocktail party*___ (51) effect. Such selective attention involves both attending to parts of the auditory environment, and ___*suppressing*___ (52) irrelevant background information. Sound localization also helps us distinguish among auditory objects. Recognizing different environmental sounds requires frontal and ___*posterior*___ (53) temporal areas, whereas recognizing individual voices involves the secondary auditory cortex in the ___*superior*___ (54) temporal area. For the most part, recognizing a sound involves the "___*what*___" (55) pathway of hearing.

Much of our ability to locate sounds involves automatic processing of sounds within the nervous system. Animals with two ears use three different ___*binaural*___ (56) cues to locate sounds: phase differences, ___*intensity*___ (57) differences, and timing differences at the two ears. The farther apart the ears are, the easier it is to locate sounds. Phase differences, which help us locate sounds below ___*1500*___ (58) Hz, and intensity differences, which help us locate sounds above ___*2000*___ (59) Hz, are detected by cells in the ___*medial superior olivary*___ (60) nucleus. Timing cues have been studied extensively in the barn owl. Neurons called ___*coincidence*___ (61) detectors, which are located in the avian nucleus laminaris (a structure analogous to the lateral superior olivary nucleus), fire maximally when they receive input from both ears at the same time. The most amazing form of sound localization based on timing and phase cues is found in the bat: These animals use ___*echolocation*___ (62) to find food in total darkness by emitting ultra-high frequencies of sounds and interpreting the echoes bouncing off of objects. Aquatic mammals, some birds, and even blind humans can also use sound to see.

Short Answer and Essay Questions

Answer the following questions.

1. Why do we need different terms for the physical properties of sound (frequency, intensity) and for the experience of sound (pitch, loudness)?

2. Describe Rutherford's telephone theory of frequency analysis. How did Wever and Bray test this theory? What was wrong with their procedure?

3. How do frequency theory and place theory account for our ability to process low-frequency and high-frequency sounds, respectively? Why is neither theory sufficient to explain all frequency analysis?

4. How does the organization of neural input from auditory neurons to coincidence detectors account for the ability to locate sounds based on timing cues?

Language

Summary and Guided Review

After studying this section in the text, fill in the blanks of the following summary.

__Language__ (63), which includes spoken, written, and gestural communication, is of central importance in human behavior. Many brain areas are involved in language, and damage to each impairs different language functions. For example, in the 19th century Broca and Wernicke identified different forms of language impairment, or __aphasia__ (64), resulting from damage to different areas of the __left__ (65) hemisphere of the brain.

Broca's aphasia, also referred to as __expressive__ (66) aphasia, is the result of damage to Broca's area, which is located on the __frontal__ (67) lobe anterior to the motor cortex. People with Broca's aphasia have difficulty expressing themselves. They often display __nonfluent__ (68) (halting) speech, __anomia__ (69) (difficulty finding the right word), difficulty with articulation, and __agrammatic__ (70) speech (lacking function words). They also have problems with reading, writing, and comprehension of language.

Wernicke's aphasia, sometimes referred to as __receptive__ (71) aphasia, is the result of damage to Wernicke's area, located on the left posterior __temporal__ (72) lobe. People with Wernicke's aphasia can articulate words, but their utterances, described as __word salad__ (73), have little meaning. As the term _receptive aphasia_ implies, they also have difficulty understanding all forms of language.

According to the Wernicke-Geschwind model, language processing (answering a verbal question) occurs along a pathway from the auditory cortex to Wernicke's area to __Broca's area__ (74) and then to the facial area of the __motor cortex__ (75) (for a spoken response), or to the __angular gyrus__ (76) (for a written response). When a person reads aloud, the route is from visual areas to the angular gyrus, then to __Wernicke's area__ (77) (for converting the visual symbols into language), then to Broca's area for speech production. However, damage to areas outside this pathway, including other areas of the cortex and subcortical structures such as the basal ganglia and __thalamus__ (78), also results in language impairment, indicating the wide distribution of language processing. However, there does seem to be an association between the location for storing __tool__ (79) names and the brain structures that would produce the motor actions to use them. Electrical stimulation and brain damage studies have shown that language functions are scattered throughout the four lobes, but the Wernicke-Geschwind model is essentially correct in that temporal areas are most important for comprehension, and frontal areas are most important for __articulation__ (80).

Damage to the __angular__ (81) gyrus, which connects the visual projection area with auditory and visual association areas, can result in _____alexia_____ (82) (the inability to read) and __agraphia__ (83) (the inability to write). _____ (84), the most common type of learning disorder, also involves reading and listening difficulties. This disorder can be acquired through damage, but for most individuals it is of __Developmental__ (85) origin. The public is most familiar with the __visual__ - __perceptual__ (86) symptoms of dyslexia, in which words are read backward, letters are confused, and words seem to move around on the page. The __phonological__ (87) hypothesis argues that difficulty with processing similar-sounding phonemes (the sound phrases inside words) underlies dyslexia. One area of the brain that appears to be different in dyslexics is the __planum__ __temporale__ (88): The right side is larger than normal, and the left lacks the usual orderly arrangement. This disorganization suggests that those neurons have __migrated__ (89) past their normal destination during development. There is also a cultural effect of language on dyslexia: Countries with phonologically complex languages (such as multiple pronunciations for the same syllable such as in *dough* and *tough*) have __higher__ (90) incidences of dyslexia than ones with simpler languages.

Recovery from aphasia following brain injury is possible, but generally someone affected by __Broca's__ (91) aphasia has a greater recovery than someone with the other type. Recovery is due in part to a decrease in __swelling__ (92) that occurs around the area of focal injury. Reorganization of the brain is also involved but is age dependent. For example, evidence indicates that if the left hemisphere is damaged before the age of __five__ (93), the right hemisphere can take over language functions. For left hemisphere damage occurring later in life, language control can shift into the neighboring __parietal__ (94) lobe. The right hemisphere is important in processing __prosody__ (95) (intonation, emphasis, and rhythm) to convey meaning in speech, as well as understanding the __figurative__ (96) rather than the literal meaning of words.

Because language is readily learned by almost all children, including those born deaf who are exposed to sign language, some theorists believe that the brain contains a language __acquisition__ (97) device: brain areas whose sole functions are to acquire language. Regardless of the form of language children learn, they all show the same stages of language development, including early __babbling__ (98) through either speech or gestures. Most people show left hemisphere dominance for language, and several left hemisphere structures, including Broca's area, the __lateral__ (99) fissure, and the planum temporale are larger than their counterparts in the right hemisphere. Prenatal and early postnatal differences in structure and function of the left hemisphere have been observed, suggesting that the left hemisphere in most people is designed to support language. In newborns, speech activates the same left hemisphere language areas as in adults, and sentence __melody__ (100) activates the right hemisphere. Even though it is a visual language, __sign__ (101) language activates left hemisphere structures similar to those used in spoken language. People who have learned two languages early in life show overlapping activation of the same areas for both languages, whereas those who acquired a(n) __second__ (102) language after childhood show activation in adjacent areas, but still within Broca's and Wernicke's areas. Although language involves specific structures, it is not clear if these structures evolved specifically for language or if they originally served a more general purpose and were later taken over by language.

Studying language abilities in other species allows us to speculate on the evolutionary basis of language in humans, although the results of such studies must be interpreted with caution. Language abilities in ___chimpanzees___ (103) and bonobos have been studied the most intensively, although because of limitations to the vocal apparatus, they are unable to speak. The chimpanzee Washoe was exposed to American _____sign_____ _____language_____ (104) from an early age, and she learned _____132_____ (105) signs in four years. Additionally, Washoe's adopted son Loulis learned 47 signs from Washoe and other adults, and the group of chimps would frequently have sign language conversations with each other. The Rumbaughs used a different approach involving symbols on a panel. The bonobo Kanzi first began using the symbols as a(n) ___infant___ (106) when his mother was being trained on it. Savage-Rumbaugh claims that Kanzi's use of symbols is about as sophisticated as that of a(n) ___two___ (107)-year-old child. Remarkable language abilities have also been demonstrated by Alex, an African gray _____parrot_____ (108), who was able to give the name, color, quantity, and shape of objects. Birds, as well as humans, can show regional differences in language, called ___dialects___ (109) and can learn ___grammatical___ (110) patterns.

There is also evidence that the brains of some species are lateralized in ways similar to humans. The lateral fissure and planum ___temporale___ (111) are larger in the left hemisphere in chimpanzees. Japanese macaques show a(n) ___left___ (112) hemisphere dominance for responding to the calls of other Japanese macaques but not to those of other monkey species. Dolphins and chimpanzees demonstrate faster learning of symbols when the symbols are presented to the left hemisphere. ___Canaries___ (113) and zebra finches with lesions to the dominant side of the brain area HVC (analogous to Wernicke's area) are unable to sing normally. Humans and primates also have similar hand and face ___gestures___ (114), such as waving someone away. Researchers believe that prelanguage communication in humans also relied more on these hand and face movements to communicate, which supported the expansion of our emerging language areas. ___Mirror___ (115) neurons, which are found in language areas in humans and animals, may be important in the ability to imitate the movements and sounds of others. One gene that has been implicated in language is ___FoxP2___ (116). In humans, this gene differs slightly from its counterpart in chimpanzees, and people with a mutated form of the gene show several language-related deficits. Our human version, which is also found in ___Neanderthals___ (117), may have contributed to our increased abilities in reading, writing, and speaking.

Short Answer and Essay Questions

Answer the following questions.

5. Compare the language limitations observed in people with Broca's and Wernicke's aphasias.

6. Explain how the Wernicke-Geschwind model accounts for your ability to write a response to an oral question and read aloud.

7. Compare and contrast American Sign Language and spoken language in both the ways they are acquired and the involved brain mechanisms.

8. Identify the criticisms of the claims that chimpanzees and bonobos like Washoe were capable of language. Explain how subsequent work has addressed some of these criticisms.

Post-test

Use these multiple-choice questions to check your understanding of the chapter.

1. If you see a particular pattern of dots on a wall but do not realize that the pattern is that of a dog, you have experienced a
    a. perception.
    b. sensation.
    c. conversion.
    d. translation.

2. The range of human hearing is about
    a. 20–200,000 Hz.
    b. 2–20,000 Hz.
    c. 20–20,000 Hz.   15-20,000 Hz
    d. 200–2000 Hz.

3. Sound may be conducted through
    a. air.
    b. water.
    c. bone.
    d. all of the above

4. We experience the frequency of a sound as
    a. pitch.
    b. loudness.
    c. amplitude.
    d. intensity.

5. A pure tone is MOST likely to be produced by a(n)
    a. clarinet.
    b. tuning fork.
    c. air conditioner.
    d. flute.

6. Humans are MOST sensitive to sounds with frequencies in the range of
    a. 1000–3000 Hz.
    b. 200–400 Hz.
    c. 2000–20,000 Hz.
    d. 1000–4000 Hz.

7. The ossicles (middle ear bones) amplify sound approximately
    a. 30-fold.
    b. 4-fold.
    c. 100-fold.
    d. 1,000-fold.

8. If you go up to 30,000 feet in an airplane, and your ears start hurting, what problem do you need to alleviate?
    a. You need to open the oval windows.
    b. You need to open your Eustachian tubes.
    c. You need to activate your middle ear bones.
    d. Your tympanic membranes have ruptured.

9. Which of the following canals is NOT found in the cochlea?
   a. vestibular canal
   b. tympanic canal
   c. cochlear canal
   d. semicircular canal

10. Vibrations are initiated in the cochlea by movement of the _____ against the oval window.
    a. stapes/stirrup
    b. malleus/hammer
    c. incus/anvil
    d. helicotrema

11. Hair cells complete which function in hearing?
    a. amplification
    b. conduction
    c. vibration
    d. reception

12. Hair cells rest within the _____, and their hairs are embedded in the _____
    a. helicotrema; basilar membrane.
    b. tectorial membrane; basilar membrane.
    c. basilar membrane; tectorial membrane.
    d. tympanic membrane; helicotrema.

13. When hair cells bend, _____ channels open, causing depolarization.
    a. sodium and chloride
    b. potassium and calcium
    c. calcium and sodium
    d. chloride and calcium

14. The primary auditory cortex is located in the _____ lobe.
    a. temporal
    b. frontal
    c. parietal
    d. occipital

15. Neurons from the left ear project
    a. exclusively to the right hemisphere.
    b. exclusively to the left hemisphere.
    c. mostly to the right hemisphere.
    d. mostly to the left hemisphere.

16. At low frequencies, sound intensity is coded by
    a. the number of neurons responding.
    b. the volley pattern of neurons.
    c. the point on the basilar membrane responding.
    d. none of the above

17. The volley theory was proposed by
    a. Rutherford.
    b. Helmholtz.
    c. Békésy.
    d. Wever.

18. Békésy discovered that the basilar membrane is stiffer at one end than at the other, and not a series of piano strings as earlier envisioned by Helmholtz. This discovery led directly to the _____ theory of pitch perception.
    a. frequency
    b. telephone
    c. place
    d. volley

19. What physiological limitation prevents a single auditory neuron from reliably tracking a high-frequency tone (such as one at 10,000 Hz)?
    a. glucose availability
    b. refractory period
    c. basilar membrane stiffness
    d. temporal harmonics

20. A 15,000-Hz tone will produce the greatest vibrations at which point along the basilar membrane?
    a. near the base
    b. at the apex
    c. near the apex
    d. in the middle

21. Which sound frequency does NOT seem to produce maximal vibration at a specific point on the basilar membrane?
    a. 20,000 Hz
    b. 10,400 Hz
    c. 8200 Hz
    d. 20 Hz

22. Which structure helps to screen out background noises and focus on relevant sounds?
    a. medial geniculate nucleus
    b. frontal lobe
    c. parietal lobe
    d. superior olivary nucleus

23. Which of the following animals probably would you expect to have the MOST difficulty localizing sounds using binaural cues?
    a. elephant
    b. alligator
    c. mouse
    d. owl

24. A sound with a frequency of 50 Hz is located by which of the following cues?
    a. phase difference
    b. intensity difference
    c. timing difference
    d. a and c

25. In humans, binaural cues for localizing sound are processed by cells in the
    a. planum temporale.
    b. nucleus laminaris.
    c. medial superior olivary nucleus.
    d. medial geniculate nucleus.

26. Differences in timing are processed using _____, which fire only when sounds from both ears reach it at the same time.
    a. sound shadows
    b. coincidence detectors
    c. reflector plates
    d. binaural cells

27. Broca's area lies anterior and adjacent to the
    a. motor cortex.
    b. auditory cortex.
    c. somatosensory cortex.
    d. visual cortex.

28. In MOST people, Wernicke's area is found on the _____ lobe.
    a. left frontal
    b. right frontal
    c. left temporal
    d. right temporal

29. Which of the following is NOT a characteristic of Broca's aphasia?
    a. impairment in writing
    b. word salad
    c. agrammatic speech
    d. difficulty with articulation

30. People with Wernicke's aphasia
    a. have difficulty saying words.
    b. have difficulty understanding others.
    c. produce utterances that have no meaning.
    d. b and c

31. Frank had a mini-stroke while driving home, but he did not realize it until later that afternoon when he found he couldn't write a shopping list. He also was surprised that he couldn't read the newspaper. Since he could still hear and speak normally, what part of his brain was affected by the stroke?
    a. planum temporale
    b. Broca's area
    c. Wernicke's area
    d. angular gyrus

32. The angular gyrus connects the visual projection area with the
    a. auditory association areas.
    b. visual association areas.
    c. motor cortex.
    d. a and b

33. According to the Wernicke-Geschwind model, when we give a spoken response to an oral question, what is the sequence of brain activation?
    a. auditory cortex to Broca's area to Wernicke's area
    b. Broca's area to Wernicke's area to auditory cortex
    c. auditory cortex to Wernicke's area to Broca's area
    d. Wernicke's area to Broca's area to auditory cortex

34. The most likely developmental anomaly in the language centers of the brain that give rise to dyslexia is a lateralized difference in the size of the
    a. arcuate fasciculus.
    b. planum temporale.
    c. Wernicke's area.
    d. Broca's area.

35. A phonological symptom of dyslexia is
    a. difficulty distinguishing speech sounds from each other.
    b. confusing mirror-image letters like b and d.
    c. reading words backward.
    d. difficulty tracking words on a page.

36. Dyslexia has a higher incidence rate in languages
    a. with symbolic, not letter, representation.
    b. with a higher number of possible words in them.
    c. with different pronunciations of the same spelling.
    d. that differ from other languages by only a few sounds.

37. Someone with damage to the premotor cortex would MOST likely have difficulty
    a. naming tools.
    b. using verbs.
    c. imagining hand movements.
    d. all of the above

38. There is evidence that the right hemisphere may assume left hemisphere language functions
    a. in adults who have suffered strokes or other brain injuries.
    b. in adults who learn a second language.
    c. in children under five who suffer brain injury.
    d. in children who acquire two languages simultaneously.

39. Babies exposed only to American Sign Language
    a. will babble in gestures, but only if they are deaf.
    b. babble in gestures, but at a later age than that at which babies exposed to spoken language begin babbling in sounds.
    c. babble in gestures at about the same age as babies exposed to spoken language babble in sounds.
    d. are at a disadvantage for language learning, because sign language is not a true language.

40. Which of the following is TRUE?
    a. Left-handed people are more likely to show left-hemisphere dominance for language than right-hemisphere dominance for language.
    b. All right-handed people show left-hemisphere dominance for language.
    c. Left- and right-handed people are both more likely to show left-hemisphere dominance for language.
    d. The hemisphere dominant for language has no relationship to whether someone is left- or right-handed.

41. Based on information in the text, which language capability in nonhuman animals has the least support?
    a. Using signs and symbols to communicate with humans.
    b. Producing grammatically correct sentences.
    c. Using signs and symbols to communicate with each other.
    d. Teaching their offspring signs and symbols.

42. Which of the following species has NOT demonstrated a possible capacity for language?
    a. dog
    b. African gray parrot
    c. bonobo
    d. dolphin

43. One interesting genetic finding is that humans share the _____ gene with chimpanzees, though the genes differ by two amino acids. However, our version is identical to those found in _____.
    a. *FOXP2*; gorillas
    b. *COMT*; songbirds
    c. *FOXP2*; Neanderthals
    d. *GEN3C*; bonobos

44. Mirror neurons _____; this might explain why we find them in _____.
    a. are found only in humans; the motor cortex
    b. are active only during language use; the angular gyrus
    c. are found only in nonhuman animals; chimpanzees and not humans
    d. are active during observation and imitation; Broca's and Wernicke's areas

Answers

Guided Review

1. receptors
2. adequate stimulus
3. Sensation
4. perception
5. pattern
6. cochlea
7. conducting medium
8. waves or compressions
9. hertz (Hz)
10. Pitch
11. 1000–4000
12. pure tone
13. amplitude
14. loudness
15. amplification
16. pinna
17. tympanic
18. ossicles
19. cochlea
20. tympanic
21. receptors
22. basilar
23. hair
24. tectorial
25. Potassium (K)
26. auditory
27. outer
28. deaf
29. temporal
30. medial geniculate
31. language
32. tonotopically
33. dorsal
34. ventral
35. frequency
36. telephone
37. nerve

38. volleying
39. place
40. basilar
41. tonotopic
42. bone
43. tuning curves
44. frequency-place
45. rate or frequency
46. 90
47. basilar
48. cochlear implant
49. Fourier
50. simultaneously
51. cocktail party
52. suppressing
53. posterior
54. superior
55. what
56. binaural
57. intensity
58. 1500
59. 2000
60. medial superior olivary
61. coincidence
62. echolocation
63. Language
64. aphasia
65. left
66. expressive
67. frontal
68. nonfluent
69. anomia
70. agrammatic
71. receptive
72. temporal
73. word salad
74. Broca's area

75. motor cortex
76. angular gyrus
77. Wernicke's area
78. thalamus
79. tool
80. articulation
81. angular
82. alexia
83. agraphia
84. Dyslexia
85. developmental
86. visual-perceptual
87. phonological
88. planum temporale
89. migrated
90. higher
91. Broca's
92. swelling
93. five
94. parietal
95. prosody
96. figurative
97. acquisition
98. babbling
99. lateral
100. melody
101. sign
102. second
103. chimpanzees
104. Sign Language
105. 132
106. infant
107. two
108. parrot
109. dialects
110. grammatical
111. temporale
112. left
113. Canaries
114. gestures
115. Mirror
116. *FOXP2*
117. Neanderthals

Short Answer and Essay Questions

1. Although pitch varies with frequency and loudness varies with intensity, neither relationship is precise. Our sensitivity is not the same across the range of sounds; for example, we are more sensitive to sounds between 1000 and 4000 Hz, and we can detect smaller changes in amplitude in that range. Thus, a sound of a particular intensity and frequency will not have the same loudness at another frequency, and it will not have the same pitch at a different intensity.

2. Rutherford proposed that auditory neurons fire at the same frequency as sounds that stimulate them, so that the brain received signals that matched or followed the frequency of sounds in the environment. Wever and Bray tested this theory by recording from the auditory nerve of a cat while it was exposed to sounds and amplifying the signal so that it could be heard; the result was very faithful to the original sound. However, this wasn't an adequate test of the theory, because Wever and Bray were not recording from a single neuron. Individual neurons cannot fire fast enough to follow the frequency of most environmental sounds; Wever and Bray found frequency following only because the combined firing of many neurons was able to follow the frequency of the sounds used.

3. Frequency theory accounts for low-frequency sounds, as neurons do fire at the same rate as low-frequency sounds. Place theory accounts for higher-frequency sounds, as different points along the basilar membrane are most responsive to particular frequencies and many auditory neurons are frequency specific. However, neither theory alone is sufficient to account

for all frequency analysis. Frequency theory is limited by the physical property of neurons that prevents them from firing more than a few hundred times per second, and place theory cannot account for processing of low-frequency sounds, because sounds below 200 Hz cause the entire basilar membrane to vibrate equally.

4. Coincidence detectors receive input from neurons from both ears. When a sound occurs, it will reach the closer ear first and the farther ear later, but the two signals will arrive at a particular coincidence detector simultaneously because the length of the neuron from the closer ear compensates for the delay in the sound reaching the distant ear. Which coincidence detector is responding most indicates the sound's location relative to the two ears.

5. In Broca's aphasia, people have difficulty recalling the appropriate words, their speech is halting and impaired in articulation, and function words are missing. Their understanding is also impaired by their inability to process function words. Reading and writing are disrupted as well. People with Wernicke's aphasia, by contrast, often speak fluently, but their utterances make little sense, and they have difficulty understanding what others are saying to them.

6. According to this model, when you write an answer to an oral question, the pattern of activation begins in the auditory cortex, then moves to Wernicke's area, and then to the angular gyrus to elicit the visual pattern. When reading out loud, the visual system sends input through the angular gyrus to Wernicke's area, and then to Broca's area. This model reflects not only the roles of Broca's and Wernicke's areas in language but also connections with other brain areas.

7. Babies exposed to sign language seem to progress in language development along the same lines as babies exposed to speech. Both babble at about the same time, and the babbling seems to have the same function in each case (although it is of a very different form). Furthermore, similar areas of the left hemisphere are involved in both spoken language and sign language.

8. Terrace and colleagues claimed that chimpanzees do not form sentences, that the utterances lacked grammatical structure and were simply strings of words. Loulis acquired signs from Washoe and other chimps and used these signs to communicate with other chimps, suggesting that the signs are being used like language. The Rumbaughs' work with Kanzi indicates that chimpanzees are capable of spontaneously making complex utterances and understanding complex directions. In addition, Japanese macaque monkeys show a left hemisphere advantage for identifying calls from others of their species, suggesting involvement of the left hemisphere as seen in humans.

Post-test

1. b 2. c 3. d 4. a 5. b 6. d 7. a 8. b 9. d 10. a 11. d 12. c 13. b
14. a 15. c 16. a 17. d 18. c 19. b 20. a 21. d 22. d 23. c 24. d 25. c
26. b 27. a 28. c 29. b 30. d 31. d 32. d 33. c 34. b 35. a 36. c 37. d
38. c 39. c 40. c 41. b 42. a 43. c 44. d

10 Vision and Visual Perception

Learning Objectives

After reading this chapter, you will be able to

1. Describe the functions of structures within the eye

2. Illustrate the processing pathways of visual information from the eye up to cortical brain areas

3. Compare the major theories of color processing

4. Contrast the major theories of form processing

5. Discuss how visual information is segregated and reconstructed in the visual system

6. Identify how action potentials and synaptic transmission can produce a variety of visual experiences

7. Predict how damage to specific portions of the visual system will impact a person's visual perceptions

Light and the Visual Apparatus

Summary and Guided Review

After studying this section in the text, fill in the blanks of the following summary.

The adequate stimulus for the visual system is visible light, which makes up a very small portion of the _____ (1) spectrum. Other forms of electromagnetic energy that humans cannot detect without special devices are X-rays, _____ (2) energy (which some animal species use to detect prey at night), and radio and television waves. Light is measured not in terms of frequency like sounds, but in terms of _____ (3), the distance oscillating energy travels before reversing directions; the portion of the electromagnetic spectrum humans are capable of detecting is _____–_____ (4) nanometers. (A nanometer is 1 _____ (5) of a meter.) Within this range, light rays of different wavelengths are perceived as different _____ (6).

The eye is filled with fluid, and with the exception of the transparent _____ (7), its outer covering, or sclera, is opaque. Behind the cornea, the flexible _____ (8) allows us to focus on objects at different distances. The circular _____ (9) is a muscle that partially covers the lens, which changes its size to accommodate different levels of light, and the opening in its center is the _____ (10). The visual receptors are located in the _____ (11) at the back of the eye; these light-sensitive cells are collectively called _____ (12). The different types of receptors, _____ (13) and _____ (14), are specialized for different aspects of vision, because they contain different photopigments and have different neural connections. The more numerous rods contain _____ (15), which is highly sensitive to light; this accounts for our ability to see under low light conditions. Cones, which contain _____ (16), function best in bright light. There are different types of this photopigment, each responding most to different ranges of wavelengths; this is what allows us to see different colors. In the retina, cones are concentrated in the _____ (17) in the center, whereas rods are more numerous in the periphery. Foveal cones show less convergence on the ganglion cells than cones outside the fovea, which accounts for better visual _____ (18) for images falling on the fovea. Many rods converge on a single ganglion cell, which contributes to greater light _____ (19) but not acuity. The _____ (20) fields of foveal cells are smaller than those in the periphery. In the dark, photoreceptors release _____ (21), which inhibits bipolar cells. When stimulated by light, sodium and _____ (22) channels close, thus disinhibiting the bipolar cells and increasing the firing rate in the ganglion cells to which they are connected. Horizontal and _____ (23) cells interconnect the receptor cells and ganglion cells, respectively, producing a complex web of information processing.

The ganglion cells' _____ (24) form the optic nerve and exit the retina at the _____ _____ (25); the optic nerves join for a short distance at the _____ _____ (26), where axons from the nasal sides of each retina cross over to the opposite side of the brain. Neurons from the _____ (27) side of the eyes project to the same side of the brain. Nerves next project to the _____ _____ (28) nuclei of the thalamus and then to the cortex. The partial crossover of information is organized such that, for example, stimuli detected by the right half of each retina, which receives light from the _____ (29) visual field, are projected to the _____ (30) hemisphere. We are able to perceive objects in three-dimensional space due in part to _____ _____ (31), in which each eye receives a slightly different version of a visual scene. The degree of retinal disparity triggers activity in different cells in the cortex. The ViewMaster, a toy from your childhood, uses this disparity to produce an illusion of three dimensions. Three principles are helpful in understanding how the visual system works: _____ (32), which allows for sharpening information beyond what is possible from excitation alone; _____ _____ (33), which means that more basic elements of visual stimuli are processed in lower areas of the nervous system, and this information is then analyzed sequentially by higher areas of the visual system; and _____ (34), which reflects the fact that aspects of visual processing is carried out in discrete brain structures.

Short Answer and Essay Questions

Answer the following questions.

1. Explain how the receptive fields of ganglion cells that receive input from cones in the fovea differ from those receiving input from rods. How do these differences contribute to the visual specializations of each system?

2. Sometimes due to injury or cloudiness, an individual needs to have his or her natural lens replaced with a nonflexible plastic lens. Describe some of the issues one would need to consider when having this procedure, related to being able to focus on objects.

Color Vision

Summary and Guided Review

After studying this section in the text, fill in the blanks of the following summary.

Just as pitch refers to our perceptual experience of the frequency of a sound, color refers to our perceptual experience of the _____ (35) of light but does not correspond perfectly with it. Thus, color is not a property of an object but an experience produced by the brain. The _____ (36) theory of color vision, proposed separately by Young and _____ (37), explained that our ability to see color is due to three different color processes that are sensitive to red, green, and _____ (38) light. All colors are the result of mixing different combinations of these colors of light; this principle is used in the design of televisions and computer displays. The competing _____ _____ (39) theory, proposed by Hering, explained color vision as the result of receptors whose _____ (40) are broken down by one type of light and regenerated by another. This theory is based on the observation of complementary colors, that is, colors that when mixed in equal amounts produce neutral _____ (41) or white. Also, over-stimulating the eye with one color of light increases sensitivity to its complement. This theory explains complementary colors as well as the phenomenon of _____ (42) color aftereffect: When you stare at a green object and then look at a white piece of paper, you will experience the same image in _____ (43). It is important to remember that mixing lights is _____ (44) (leading to white), whereas mixing pigments is subtractive (leading to black). Hering's theory was not well accepted because of his controversial notion that a single photochemical could be affected in opposite ways by different wavelengths of light.

In 1957, Hurvich and Jameson proposed a theory of color vision that included elements of both the trichromatic and opponent process theories; this theory suggests that our ability to see color depends on two different levels of processing in the cells of the _____ (45). The first level of color processing occurs in the _____ (46), which contain one of three different photopigments, each of which is maximally sensitive to different wavelengths of light. These red-, green-, and blue-sensitive cones are interconnected to _____ (47) cells in such a way as to produce opponent process effects. For example, long-wavelength light stimulates the _____ (48)-sensitive cones, which excites the _____ _____ (49) ganglion cells, whereas medium-wavelength light stimulates the green-sensitive cones, which _____ (50) the red-green ganglion cells. Short-wavelength light excites blue cones, which _____ (51) the yellow-blue ganglion cells, leading to a sensation of blue. Finally, red and green cones both stimulate the yellow-blue ganglion cells, leading to a sensation of yellow. Staring at a red stimulus eventually _____ (52) the red-green ganglion cells, resulting in inhibition and the experience of green. This explains the phenomenon of negative color _____ (53). Physical evidence for this theory was produced by studies involving shining different wavelengths of light onto the retinas of human eyes and measuring which wavelengths were absorbed. This finding shows that there are _____ (54) distinct color response curves; each receptor has a sensitivity peak but its response range significantly _____ (55) with that of its neighbors. The _____ (56) for red and green cone photopigments are probably the most recently evolved and may have diverged around the time in primate evolution when visual signals became important to differentiate _____ _____ (57) and to locate young, tender leaves. Color-opponent _____ (58) cells have been located in the retina and _____ _____ (59) nucleus of the thalamus in monkeys. This theory was considered successful because it was able to demonstrate that it was _____ (60) with the known facts, could _____ (61) those facts, and could _____ (62) new findings.

The study of color blindness, or color vision _____ (63), can also reveal information about how the visual system works. People who are completely color-blind with nonfunctional cones are limited to vision from rods, though thankfully this is a very rare condition. There are two more common types of color blindness. A person who is red-green color blind sees both colors but is unable to _____ (64) between them. People in the second color-blind group do not perceive the color _____ (65), so they see the world in variations of red and green. Many people who are partially color-blind are not even _____ (66) that they see the world differently from other people.

Short Answer and Essay Questions

Answer the following questions.

3. Summarize how Figure 10.7 demonstrates that our perception of color does not perfectly correspond to the wavelength of light we sense.

4. Illustrate how the opponent process theory explains the negative aftereffect.

5. Explain the three ways in which Hurvich and Jameson's combined theory has demonstrated that it is successful as a theory; include a specific example for each.

6. Demonstrate what we can conclude about the color receptors in a person who cannot distinguish between red and green but is especially sensitive to green light.

Form Vision

Summary and Guided Review

After studying this section in the text, fill in the blanks of the following summary.

The visual cortex contains a(n) _____ (67) map, which means that the spatial relationships among visual stimuli are conserved from retina to cortex. Form vision allows us to detect the boundaries of objects and is the first step in _____ (68) perception.

To perceive a form or object, we must first be able to detect its boundaries. The visual system is designed to respond to boundaries so that they stand out from the rest of the visual field. This fact is demonstrated by the _____ _____ (69) illusion, in which contrast between bands that differ in brightness appears greater at their edges. This illusion, and the visual system's ability to detect contrast in general, is explained by _____ _____ (70) of activity in ganglion cells. In mammals, the ganglion cells have concentric circular receptive fields. _____-_____ (71) cells respond by increasing the rate of firing when light stimulates the receptors in the central portion of the receptive field and _____ (72) their rate of firing when light stimulates the surrounding portion. Other ganglion cells have an off-center and an on-surround. Cells with opposed centers and surrounds are particularly responsive to the edges of objects because edges typically have a high _____ (73) in lighting.

Whereas cells in the lateral geniculate nucleus also have _____ (74) receptive fields, those in the cortex respond quite differently, as discovered by Nobel laureates _____ and _____ (75). They identified different types of cells in the cortex that respond to different aspects of these stimuli. _____ (76) cells in V1 cortex respond to a line or edge at a specific orientation in a specific location in the visual field. A simple cell receives input from several

_____ (77) cells with adjacent receptive fields arranged in a line.

_____ (78) V1 cortical cells receive input from several simple cells with adjacent and similarly oriented fields; these complex cells are responsive to lines in a particular orientation over a larger area of the retina; some complex cells can also detect _____ (79).

Hubel and Wiesel's theory accounts for the detection of edges, but it cannot account for other surface details by which we identify objects such as texture. Edges represent _____-_____ (80) changes in brightness, whereas subtle shading represents low-frequency changes; according to De Valois, complex cells are responsive to low-frequency as well as high-frequency changes. His _____ _____ (81) theory suggested that sensitivity to a range of edges and shading accounts for our ability to make out the varied details of a visual stimulus. In other words, visual cortical cells perform a(n) _____ (82) frequency analysis of luminosity variations in a scene, like auditory cortical cells perform on complex sounds.

Short Answer and Essay Questions

Answer the following questions.

7. Summarize the phenomenon of lateral inhibition and how it explains the Mach band illusion.

8. Demonstrate what will happen to an on-center, off-surround ganglion cell when light stimulates the entire receptive field, only the surround, and the center and only part of the surround.

9. Compare the receptive fields of simple and complex cells. Explain their differences in function and how this comes about.

The Perception of Objects, Color, and Movement

Summary and Guided Review

After studying this section in the text, fill in the blanks of the following summary.

The text takes the position that visual processing of objects, color, and movement is both modular and _____ (83), while acknowledging that the representation of some functions in multiple areas means that the modularity is tempered somewhat by the fact that any visual function is _____ (84) across a relatively wide area of the brain.

Beginning in the _____ (85), visual information processing is divided, to some extent, between two parallel systems. The _____ (86) system includes ganglion cells located in the fovea with small and color opponent receptive fields. These cells are sensitive to the fine _____ (87) of objects. By contrast, the _____ (88) system includes cells with large and _____ (89) opponent receptive fields. This system is involved in our perception of movement and contrast. Under poor lighting conditions, the _____ (90) system is most active, and we are particularly sensitive to movement in our _____ (91) visual field. At the same time, determining the color and details of objects, functions of the _____ (92) system, become difficult or impossible.

After the retina, both pathways continue to the _____
_____ (93) nucleus of the thalamus and then to the cortex. The first
cortical area for vision is the primary visual cortex, also known as _____ (94).
After passing through this area, the parvocellular system makes up the majority
of the _____ (95) stream of information that projects to the
_____ (96) lobes; along this route, color perception and object recognition
occur. The magnocellular system forms the majority of the _____ (97)
stream that projects to the _____ (98) lobes; along this route, spatial
information about visual stimuli is processed. Movement perception involves the areas
V5/MT and _____ (99); these are active even when viewing photos
implying action such as pictures taken during sporting events. Activity of cells in these areas
is _____ (100) during eye movements, so that stationary objects do not
appear to move. The dorsal and ventral streams converge on the _____
_____ (101) cortex, where the information is used, for example, in
planning actions. The ventral/dorsal distinction can be observed in the effects of brain damage
in the different pathways. People with damage to the _____ (102) stream
can identify objects but have trouble orienting and reaching toward them. People with damage
to the _____ (103) stream have trouble identifying objects, but they can
move toward and reach for them accurately.

Damage to one or more areas of the cortex involved in vision can lead to a specific
type of _____ (104), which is an impairment of some type of
visual perception. For example, people with object agnosia have difficulty recognizing
objects; object agnosia includes having difficulty recognizing the faces of familiar
people, called _____ (105), which can occasionally occur alone.
One brain region implicated in both forms of agnosia is the _____
_____ (106) cortex, which contains individual cells that respond to
specific types of objects, including geometric forms, animals, and faces. In addition, there is
evidence that the _____ _____ (107) area in the
inferior temporal cortex is especially important for recognition of faces; this area begins
helping in identification of familiar faces at about two years of age. However, evidence that
individuals with prosopagnosia respond to familiar faces _____ (108)
suggests that there are alternate pathways for recognition and identification in the brain.
An interesting example of this distinction is _____ (109), a condition in
which cortically blind individuals respond to objects they cannot see, including tracking object
movements and discriminating colors. A nearby area of the inferior temporal cortex is called
the _____ (110); it responds to written words as whole objects. Reduced
activity in this area occurs in dyslexia, but this does not mean it causes the reading disorder.

Another impairment is color agnosia, as characterized by the description of Jonathan
in the introduction to the chapter. Our experience of color depends in part on color
_____ (111), the perceptual process that allows us to identify the color
of an object despite changes in lighting conditions. This ability seems to depend on cells in
area _____ (112), whose activity Zeki concluded were "color coded."
Nonfunctioning cones are not the only cause for color blindness; _____
_____ (113) occurs when people have damage in the visual cortex
between V1 and the fusiform face area.

_____ (114) agnosia is the impaired ability to detect motion;
damage to the MST may produce an inability to detect _____ (115)
movement, which informs us about movement of objects toward or away from us.
Individuals with damage to the posterior parietal cortex often display characteristics of
_____ (116), such as failing to notice or attend to objects or parts of the

body opposite the side of damage. This is not due to a defect in visual processing, but involves a deficit in _____ (117).

How are we able to make sense of all of the visual information we take in? So far, there is no evidence that a single _____ (118) area exists for incorporating visual information into conscious experience. The most likely answer is that our awareness of visual stimuli is the result of _____ (119) processing throughout the brain. The _____ _____ (120) is the question of how the brain combines information from different areas and pathways into a single perceptual experience. One way to approach this problem is to study a condition called _____ (121), in which stimulation in one sense triggers an experience in another sense or a concept evokes an unrelated sensory experience (for example, emotions might have colors). People with this condition seem to "overbind" sensory information, due to either excess connectivity between the brain areas involved or reduced _____ (122) in otherwise typical pathways. This is yet another example of how anomalies in brain functioning can help us understand the normal function of the brain.

Short Answer and Essay Questions

Answer the following questions.

10. Identify the aspects of vision that the parvocellular and magnocellular systems are specialized for. Give an example of each.

11. Assess the support for modularity in vision, including specific agnosias and blindsight.

Post-test

Use these multiple-choice questions to check your understanding of the chapter.

1. Electromagnetic energy includes
   a. visible light rays.
   b. gamma rays.
   c. infrared rays.
   d. all of the above

2. The range of visible light for humans is
   a. 38–80 nm.
   b. 3,800–8,000 nm.
   c. 380–800 nm.
   d. 38,000–80,000 nm.

3. Light with a wavelength on the lower end of the spectrum (e.g., 450 nm) is normally perceived as
   a. blue.
   b. green.
   c. yellow.
   d. red.

4. The _____ is a flexible tissue that allows us to focus on objects at different distances.
   a. cornea
   b. lens

   c. pupil

   d. iris

5. The _____ is actually muscle tissue that responds to different levels of light.

   a. cornea

   b. lens

   c. pupil

   d. iris

6. The conversion of light energy into energy the brain can use begins in the

   a. receptors.

   b. bipolar cells.

   c. ganglion cells.

   d. amacrine cells.

7. Photoreceptors

   a. contain photopigments that increase in quantity when stimulated by light.

   b. connect directly with ganglion cells.

   c. are found at the back of the eye.

   d. all of the above

8. Which of the following statements is NOT true?

   a. Iodopsin is the cone photopigment.

   b. Rods function better in dim light.

   c. Cones are responsive to light but cannot distinguish between wavelengths of different colors.

   d. Rhodopsin is the rod photopigment.

9. All of the following types of cells are found in the retina EXCEPT _____ cells.

   a. bipolar

   b. horizontal

   c. amacrine

   d. complex

10. The ganglion cells with the smallest receptive fields receive input from

   a. rods in the periphery of the retina.

   b. rods 20 degrees from the fovea.

   c. cones in the fovea.

   d. cones outside the fovea.

11. When light reaches the photoreceptors

   a. they release more glutamate.

   b. sodium channels open.

   c. calcium channels open.

   d. none of the above

12. The blind spot contains

   a. rods only.

   b. cones only.

   c. both rods and cones.

   d. neither rods nor cones.

13. Visual information from the _____ side of each retina crosses to the other hemisphere at the _____.

   a. right; optic chiasm

   b. nasal; optic chiasm

    c. right; lateral geniculate nucleus

    d. nasal; lateral geniculate nucleus

14. An object's image falls on slightly different parts of the two retinas, depending on the distance of the object. This is called

    a. hierarchical processing.

    b. modularity.

    c. neural inhibition.

    d. retinal disparity.

15. Color televisions produce color in accordance with the principles of

    a. the opponent process theory of color vision.

    b. the trichromatic theory of color vision.

    c. the combined theory of color vision.

    d. none of the above

16. If you stare at a yellow image for a long time and then look at a piece of white paper, you will see the image in

    a. blue.

    b. green.

    c. red.

    d. yellow.

17. Which of the following is NOT true of Hering's original opponent process theory?

    a. It is consistent with principles of mixing light.

    b. It is consistent with the negative color aftereffect.

    c. It proposed four types of color receptors.

    d. It proposed four primary colors.

18. With respect to the cones, yellow light produces

    a. less response in the yellow/blue ganglion cell.

    b. more response in the yellow/blue ganglion cell.

    c. less response in the red/green ganglion cell.

    d. more response in the red/green ganglion cell.

19. With respect to the evolution and genetic basis of color vision

    a. genes for short-wavelength cones evolved relatively recently from a common precursor gene.

    b. red and green genes are adjacent to one another on the Y chromosome.

    c. the development of trichromacy and the use of vision to separate fruit from leaves occurred at the same time.

    d. all of the above

20. Which of the following statements regarding people who lack cones is NOT true?

    a. They have poor visual acuity.

    b. They can distinguish only very bright colors.

    c. They are very sensitive to light.

    d. They are more rare than people with red-green color blindness.

21. People with red-green color blindness

    a. are usually aware of their unusual condition.

    b. can see neither red nor green.

    c. may have red photopigment in their green cones.

    d. are less common than those with complete color blindness.

22. Which of the following is NOT a part of form vision?
    a. formation of tonotopic maps
    b. edge detection
    c. contrast enhancement
    d. detection of orientation

23. The Mach band illusion is a result of
    a. object recognition.
    b. lateral inhibition.
    c. retinal disparity.
    d. modular processing.

24. Light in the _____ of an off-center receptive field will result in _____.
    a. center; excitation
    b. surround; excitation
    c. surround; inhibition
    d. center and entire surround; inhibition

25. Which of the following types of cells have bar-shaped receptive fields?
    a. retinal ganglion cells
    b. lateral geniculate cells
    c. simple cells
    d. horizontal cells

26. Which of the following types of cells have the largest receptive field?
    a. retinal ganglion cells
    b. lateral geniculate cells
    c. simple cells
    d. complex cells

27. Movement is detected by
    a. simple cells.
    b. complex cells.
    c. lateral geniculate cells.
    d. ganglion cells.

28. Hubel and Wiesel's theory accounts for the ability to detect
    a. texture.
    b. edges.
    c. movement.
    d. b and c

29. According to spatial frequency theory,
    a. low-frequency contrast in objects is detected by different cells than high-frequency contrast.
    b. the visual system is capable of detecting only medium- to high-frequency contrast.
    c. the visual system is capable of detecting only low- to medium-frequency contrast.
    d. the brightness of an object is irrelevant.

30. The BEST description of visual processing is that it is
    a. modular.
    b. distributed.
    c. both modular and distributed.
    d. neither modular nor distributed.

31. Which of the following is a characteristic of cells in the parvocellular system?
    a. They have small receptive fields.
    b. They are brightness opponent.
    c. They are responsive to movement.
    d. Their input comes mainly from rods.

32. The magnocellular system dominates the _____ stream, which flows into the _____ lobes.
    a. ventral; temporal
    b. ventral; parietal
    c. dorsal; temporal
    d. dorsal; parietal

33. Magnocellular cells in area V1 are responsive to all of the following EXCEPT
    a. orientation.
    b. movement.
    c. retinal disparity.
    d. color.

34. Movement perception is a function of area
    a. V2.
    b. V4.
    c. V5.
    d. V8.

35. The ventral and dorsal streams converge on the _____ cortex.
    a. posterior parietal
    b. prefrontal
    c. anterior occipital
    d. inferior temporal

36. Object agnosia is often a result of damage to the _____ cortex.
    a. inferior temporal
    b. prefrontal
    c. posterior parietal
    d. posterior occipital

37. People with prosopagnosia
    a. fail to recognize familiar faces.
    b. fail to recognize familiar voices.
    c. fail to respond emotionally to familiar faces.
    d. all of the above

38. Specialized face-recognition cells have been located in the
    a. dorsal stream.
    b. fusiform face area.
    c. V1 area.
    d. parietal lobe.

39. The ability to perceive that an object is the same color despite different lighting conditions is known as
    a. visual constancy.
    b. color agnosia.
    c. retinal disparity.
    d. color constancy.

40. Zeki concluded that light wavelength is coded in _____, and color is coded in _____.
    a. V4; V1
    b. V4; V4
    c. V1; V1
    d. V1; V4

41. Someone with damage to the right posterior parietal cortex would probably exhibit
    a. right-side neglect.
    b. left-side neglect.
    c. movement agnosia.
    d. color agnosia.

42. Neglect probably occurs because of
    a. a lack of attention to the space on one side of the body.
    b. an inability to perceive objects on one side of the body.
    c. both a and b
    d. neither a nor b

43. Which of the following is NOT true about people with synesthesia?
    a. The condition may affect up to 5% of the population.
    b. V4 has been implicated.
    c. Synesthetes may "underbind" sensory information, due to decreased connectivity of brain areas.
    d. There are multiple types of synesthesia, resulting in different perceptual experiences.

44. According to the text, visual awareness is probably due to
    a. master visual cells in the superior temporal gyrus.
    b. master visual cells in the parietal cortex.
    c. many processes distributed across the brain.
    d. master cells in some part of the cortex that has not yet been identified.

Answers

Guided Review

1. electromagnetic
2. infrared
3. wavelength
4. 380–800
5. billionth
6. colors
7. cornea
8. lens
9. iris
10. pupil
11. retina
12. photoreceptors
13. rods or cones
14. cones or rods
15. rhodopsin
16. iodopsin
17. fovea
18. acuity
19. sensitivity
20. receptive
21. glutamate
22. calcium
23. amacrine
24. axons
25. blind spot
26. optic chiasm
27. temporal
28. lateral geniculate
29. left
30. right
31. retinal disparity
32. inhibition
33. hierarchical processing
34. modularity
35. wavelength
36. trichromatic
37. Helmholtz
38. blue
39. opponent process
40. photochemicals
41. gray
42. negative
43. red
44. additive
45. retina
46. cones
47. ganglion
48. red
49. red-green
50. inhibits
51. inhibits
52. fatigues
53. aftereffects
54. three
55. overlaps
56. Genes
57. ripe fruit or red fruit
58. ganglion
59. lateral geniculate
60. consistent
61. explain
62. predict
63. deficiency
64. distinguish or differentiate
65. blue
66. aware
67. retinotopic
68. object
69. Mach band
70. lateral inhibition
71. On-center
72. decreasing
73. contrast
74. circular

75. Hubel and Wiesel
76. Simple
77. ganglion
78. Complex
79. movement
80. high-frequency
81. spatial frequency
82. Fourier
83. hierarchical
84. distributed
85. retina
86. parvocellular
87. details
88. magnocellular
89. brightness
90. magnocellular
91. peripheral
92. parvocellular
93. lateral geniculate
94. V1
95. ventral
96. temporal
97. dorsal
98. parietal
99. MST (medial superior temporal area)
100. suppressed or inhibited
101. prefrontal
102. dorsal
103. ventral
104. agnosia
105. prosopagnosia
106. inferior temporal
107. fusiform face
108. emotionally
109. blindsight
110. VWFA (visual word form area)
111. constancy
112. V4
113. cerebral achromatopsia
114. Movement
115. radial
116. neglect
117. attention
118. master
119. distributed
120. binding problem
121. synesthesia
122. inhibition

Short Answer and Essay Questions

1. Ganglion cells receiving input from foveal cones have smaller receptive fields than those receiving input from rods. Some cones in the fovea have a one-to-one correspondence with ganglion cells (meaning that a ganglion cell receives input from a single cone). This arrangement allows us to make fine discriminations of the details of objects in our visual field. Ganglion cells receiving input from rods have large receptive fields, because they receive input from several rods. They are highly sensitive to light and movements but are not useful for distinguishing fine details.

2. Natural lenses change shape when focusing on near and far objects. A plastic replacement lens would no longer be able to change shape, so one consideration would be what focal length would need to be chosen—a lens that focuses on near objects (good for reading) or a lens that focuses on far objects (good for driving and other tasks). Another consideration would be that the person would likely need to wear glasses to compensate for the fixed focal length—either for seeing near, or for seeing far, depending on the lens.

3. In this figure, the circles reflect the same wavelengths of light, but the background color of each leads to the perception that the circles are different colors.

4. Opponent process theory states that there are only two color receptors: one for red and green, and one for blue and yellow. This theory attempts to explain color vision in terms of opposing processes. Hering believed that the photochemical in the red-green receptor is broken down by red light and regenerates in green light. A similar process would work in the blue-yellow receptor. If someone stares at a red stimulus for a minute and then looks at a white wall or sheet of paper, the person will see a green version of the original object. This happens because overstimulating the eye with one light (red) will make it more sensitive to its complement (green). This is consistent with opponent process theory, which states that two wavelengths affect the same receptor in opposed directions.

5. The combined theory is consistent with what was previously known about color, including the principles of light mixing as well as complementary colors. The theory also explains these facts, whereas the trichromatic theory could not explain complementary colors or negative color afterimages. Finally, the theory was used to predict the different cone types and the connections among the ganglion cells before there was physical evidence for them, and these predictions have been confirmed.

6. If someone cannot distinguish red from green, but is highly sensitive to green, then she or he probably has the photopigment for green in the red cones.

7. Lateral inhibition is the result of the way in which receptors and ganglion cells are interconnected. A receptor will have an excitatory effect on one ganglion cell while it inhibits activity in adjacent ganglion cells. This produces the Mach band illusion, which is the perception that at areas of contrast, dark edges are darker and light edges are lighter. This occurs because ganglion cells receiving stimulation from the edge of the dark region are receiving more inhibition (from the receptors stimulated by the light edge) than those farther from the border, and ganglion cells receiving stimulation from the light edge receive less inhibition (from the receptors stimulated by the dark edge) than those farther away.

8. In an on-center, off-surround cell, light falling on the entire receptive field will produce no change in the rate of firing, because the effects of light on the two areas cancel each other out. When the surround is illuminated, the cell will be inhibited, whereas when the center and a portion of the surround are illuminated, the net effect will be excitation.

9. A simple cell receives input from several ganglion cells with adjacent receptive fields oriented in a line. It detects an edge of light contrast that is aligned with its receptive field because the edge stimulates all (or almost all) of its ganglion cells. A complex cell receives input from several simple cells with receptive fields that have the same orientation and are adjacent to each other. Thus, as the edge moves across the receptive fields of these simple cells, the complex cell will continue responding, as long as the orientation doesn't change. This means that, compared to simple cells, complex cells have a larger receptive field; that is, they can detect edges over a wider area of the retina.

10. The parvocellular system is specialized for seeing in color and fine detail; reading and detecting ripe fruit are dependent on this system. The magnocellular system is specialized for perceiving movement and depth; detecting movement in the periphery of the visual field is dependent on this system.

11. The different agnosias (object, color, movement) exist because different parts of the brain are responsible for processing these aspects of visual stimuli. When a specific area is damaged, such as the inferior temporal cortex, the person may experience object agnosia and prosopagnosia but will not experience movement agnosia. Because these functions are handled

in relatively distinct areas of the brain, they are disrupted only by damage to specific areas. Blindsight is a phenomenon in which people with damage to the primary visual area perform as if they can see objects, even though they have no awareness of them. This may occur because some parts of the visual system handle unconscious processing of visual stimuli and they may be disconnected from parts of the visual system that perform conscious visual processing.

Post-test

1. d 2. c 3. a 4. b 5. d 6. a 7. c 8. c 9. d 10. c 11. d 12. d 13. b 14. d
15. b 16. a 17. c 18. a 19. c 20. b 21. c 22. a 23. b 24. b 25. c 26. d
27. b 28. d 29. a 30. c 31. a 32. d 33. d 34. c 35. b 36. a 37. a 38. b
39. d 40. d 41. b 42. a. 43. c 44. c

11 The Body Senses and Movement

Learning Objectives

After reading this chapter, you will be able to

1. Identify the receptors involved in each type of skin sensation

2. Describe the methods by which the brain gets information about the body and the environment

3. Illustrate how the cortical areas for sensation correspond to portions of the body

4. Assess the mechanisms by which pain is generated

5. Summarize the brain structures involved in the production of movement

6. Predict how movement is impaired in specific movement disorders

The Body Senses

Summary and Guided Review

After studying this section in the text, fill in the blanks of the following summary.

Unlike vision and _____ (1), which tell us about things and conditions external to ourselves, the body senses convey information about things we are directly in contact with as well as our own internal conditions. Because the body senses provide information about spatial position, posture, and balance, they are intimately tied in with _____ (2), behavior that allows us to interact with the environment.

We get information about the body from the _____ (3) system and from the vestibular system. _____ (4) refers to our sense of position and movement of our limbs and body. These messages originate in the muscles and joints. The commonly accepted skin senses include touch, _____ (5), cold, texture, and _____ (6) as a result of extreme or damaging sensation; as such, they provide information about both internal and external events. An additional sense might be _____ (7), because it appears to have its own receptors and pathways.

There are several types of encapsulated receptors, each of which is sensitive to different aspects of _____ (8). _____ (9) corpuscles and _____ (10) disks in the superficial layers of skin detect the texture and fine detail, as well as movement, of objects against the skin. In the deeper layers, _____ (11) corpuscles and _____ (12) endings detect stretching of the skin and contribute to our perception of the shape of grasped objects. Free nerve endings are sensitive to temperature and _____ (13). The free nerve ending receptors for temperature are members of the _____ (14) family of protein ion channels. Detection of pain also requires several receptors; these sources are characterized as thermal, _____ (15), and mechanical. Thermal and chemical pain receptors are also members of the TRP family; the best known is the _____ (16) heat pain receptor, which also responds to capsaicin found in chili peppers.

The _____ (17) sense, whose receptors are located above the auditory system, is involved in maintaining balance as well as providing information about head position and movement. The three _____ _____ (18), located near the cochlea, are oriented differently in space, providing sensitivity to acceleration in different planes. When we accelerate, this force displaces the gelatinous mass or _____ (19), which in turn changes the firing rate of _____ (20) cells. The utricle and _____ (21) contain a jellylike mass and hair cells (in horizontal and vertical patches, respectively); they monitor head position in relation to gravity. In general, proprioception and the vestibular sense provide coordinated information about the movement and _____ (22) of our bodies. The vestibular system sends projections to midbrain vestibular nuclei, the _____ (23), brain stem, and parieto-insular-vestibular cortex (PIV; the last of which makes us nauseated when we get dizzy).

Each spinal nerve receives sensory information from a different _____ (24) of the body; the areas served by these nerves overlap, so if a nerve is injured, the dermatome may retain some sensation. Body sensory information is carried by spinal and cranial nerves to the _____ (25) and then to the somatosensory cortex, mostly on the _____ (26) side of the brain. There are many similarities in the organization and function of the somatosensory systems and the other sensory systems. The somatosensory cortex contains a(n) _____ (27) map of the body, with adjacent body parts represented by adjacent parts of the cortex. The _____ (28) somatosensory cortex plays a role in processing sensory information from the body and sends information to the _____ (29) somatosensory cortex that integrates information from both sides of the body. The latter structure is particularly responsive to stimuli that have acquired meaning, and it sends information to the _____ (30), contributing to memory formation when somatosensation is involved. Another target area is the _____ _____ (31) cortex, where information from several sensory modalities is integrated, and output allowing for coordinated movements is sent to the _____ (32) areas of the brain.

A unified _____ (33) image is critical to our ability to function and even to our self-concept. Damage to the somatosensory system can produce conditions such as neglect or denial that a particular limb exists; individuals with _____ _____ _____ (34) disorder lack superior parietal activation when a paralyzed limb is touched and will sometimes ask that it be amputated. The entire body can be incorporated into an illusion called the _____-of-_____ (35) experience, during which the person sees his or her body from another location, or a ghostly shadow just behind the body. This can be caused by either traumatic injury or epilepsy affecting the junction between the temporal and parietal lobes.

Painful stimuli such as intense _____ (36) or temperature, damage to tissue, and exposure to various chemicals are detected by free nerve endings. Pain neurons and nonneural cells release a wide array of signaling molecules referred to as the _____ _____ (37); the signaling molecules include proteins, neurotransmitters, lipids, histamine, and _____ (38). The body's response to a painful stimulus includes swelling and redness, and _____ (39) excitability of the pain neurons so much that they respond even to light touch. This effect is adaptive because it encourages one to protect the injured area.

Pain information first travels to the spinal cord. The immediate sharp, stinging pain sensed following an injury is a result of information traveling via large, myelinated _____ (40) fibers, whereas the more delayed and persistent _____ (41) pain experienced is the result of activity in smaller and unmyelinated C fibers. In the spinal cord, pain neurons release glutamate and _____ (42), a neuropeptide that increases pain sensitivity.

Reduction of pain can be accomplished by using local _____ (43) that block _____ (44) channels in the pain neurons and reduce their ability to fire. General anesthetics may be injected or inhaled, rendering the person _____ (45). The most frequently used drugs for pain are aspirin, naproxen (Aleve), _____ (46), and acetaminophen (Tylenol). Anti-inflammatory drugs work by blocking the synthesis of _____ (47) that are released in response to injury. However, _____ (48) has a weak effect on the enzymes, so it produces little anti-inflammatory effects, compared to the others. More powerful drugs are often required for intense pain, such as _____ (49), the gold standard for pain reduction and extracted from poppy plants. Because this drug causes rapid tolerance and addiction, researchers are studying alternatives such as tanezumab, an antibody for _____ _____ (50) factor that has shown promise for treating arthritis and back pain. There also is promising success with _____ _____ (51); individuals treated with a gene that increased endorphin production saw an 80% reduction in cancer pain.

People sometimes feel little or no pain following traumatic injury. For instance _____ _____ (52) felt no pain despite having been mauled by a lion. This is because under some conditions, the body releases internal, or _____ (53), substances to deal with pain. These substances are called _____ (54) and act on _____ (55) receptors in many parts of the nervous system. Several kinds of stimulation trigger release of these substances, which include _____ (56) stress, acupuncture, and vaginal stimulation, which might play a role in reducing pain during _____ (57) or intercourse. Pain relief from a placebo may also involve endorphins, as revealed by _____ (58) blockage of opiate receptors.

According to Melzack and Wall's _____ _____ (59) theory, pressure signals cause the brain to send a(n) _____ (60) message down the spinal cord, where it closes a neural "gate" in the pain pathway. This is one of the pathways by which endorphins reduce pain. Pain causes the release of endorphins in the brain stem structure called the _____ _____ (61) or PAG; the endorphins inhibit the release of _____ (62) in the spinal cord and "close" the pain gate.

Fortunately, _____ _____ (63) to pain is a rare condition, because those who are afflicted unknowingly hurt themselves and often engage in risky and dangerous behavior. This condition may be genetic. A mutation in the *SCN9A* gene renders one type of _____ (64) channel nonfunctional, disabling pain neurons, whereas neurons that sense pain fail to develop due to a mutation in the _____ (65) gene. A mutation in the gene for nerve growth factor results in considerable loss of neural fibers.

Chronic pain is defined as pain that persists after _____ (66) has occurred or would be expected to have occurred. Chronic pain patients frequently show signs of being clinically _____ (67) prior to injury, which tends to cause them to exaggerate the intensity and extent of pain. There also may be maladaptive responses to stressful events triggered by strengthened connections between the _____ _____ (68) and the frontal cortex, which have been related to pain sensitivity in patients one year after injury. Many changes occur in the nervous system during chronic pain, such as increased sensitivity of pain pathways and an increase in the amount of the _____ (69) cortex devoted to the painful area. Although many cortical areas are activated in patients with chronic back pain, there is a loss of _____ (70); this aging-related decrease in brain matter is also seen in patients with fibromyalgia.

Sensations from _____ (71) limbs are real for amputees and, despite the fact that signals are no longer being sent to the brain from the amputated limb, about _____% (72) of amputees report feeling pain in the missing limb. Anesthetizing the problematic nerves relieves this pain in no more than half of patients. As described in the Application, more successful strategies have involved techniques that reduce _____ _____ (73), such as using a functional prosthesis or a(n) _____ (74) illusion to replace sensations from the missing limb.

Short Answer and Essay Questions

Answer the following questions.

1. Melanie is driving along the interstate at 55 miles per hour (mph). She crosses into a 70-mph zone and accelerates up to 70. She can feel the difference in speed as she accelerates, but once she reaches 70 and sets the cruise control, her only sensation of movement is from the passing landscape. Explain how activity in the vestibular system results in these sensations.

2. List the different forms of encapsulated nerve endings and the types of touch to which they are sensitive.

3. Describe four similarities that somatosensation shares with other senses such as vision.

4. Describe the pathway by which endorphins are thought to control pain.

5. Identify the probable anatomical basis of phantom pain.

Movement

Summary and Guided Review

After studying this section in the text, fill in the blanks of the following summary.

Movement involves striated, or _____ (75), muscles. The two other types of muscles are _____ (76) muscles found in the heart, and _____ (77) muscles found in the internal organs. Striated muscle cells are controlled by motor neurons at the _____ (78) junction (NMJ) via the neurotransmitter _____ (79). A single neuron may control a few or many muscle cells; the ratio of muscle fibers per neuron determines the _____ (80) of movement possible. Each muscle fiber is made up of _____ (81) filaments that slide along the _____ (82) filaments to shorten the fiber and contract the muscle. _____ (83) connect muscles to bone, and movement occurs when muscles contract, pulling against the bone. In the limbs, muscles are paired in a(n) _____ (84) way so that they produce opposing movements at a joint. Most muscle tension adjustments occur due to fast reflexes at the level of the _____ _____ (85).

An example of a spinal reflex occurs when the _____ (86) tendon is tapped; this stretches the quadriceps muscle, where stretch receptors called _____ _____ (87) send signals up the sensory nerve into the spinal cord. The sensory neurons form synapses with interneurons, then to _____ (88) neurons inside the spine, and a motor message is sent back to the quadriceps, causing it to _____ (89). This allows for quick, automatic postural adjustments and prevents muscle or tendon damage due to over-contraction or forces acting on the tendon. Muscle contractions are detected by _____ _____ (90) organs, which respond by inhibiting motor neurons and limiting the contraction so that damage from over-contraction does not occur. The spinal cord also contains _____ _____ _____ (91), which are networks that produce a rhythmic pattern of motor activity such as walking or swimming. These networks free up the brain for more important activities.

There are several cortical and subcortical brain areas involved in movement, organized in a hierarchical manner. The _____ _____ (92) integrates auditory and visual information about the world with information about the body in order to plan for movement. Studies of brain activity in monkeys during different stages of a delayed _____-to-_____ (93) task indicate that certain cells in the prefrontal cortex become active when a stimulus is presented and continue firing after its removal, helping plan for which choice the monkey needs to make. Other cells start firing before activity begins in the premotor areas; this indicates that the _____ (94) cortex selects the target of behavior and the appropriate motor response. Information then proceeds to secondary motor areas for conversion to motor commands.

The _____ (95) cortex programs an activity by combining information from the prefrontal cortex and the posterior parietal cortex. One interesting demonstration of the activity of these neurons is called the _____ _____ (96) illusion, where a rubber hand is stimulated at the same time as the person's hidden hand. Soon, the person reports a sense of ownership of the rubber hand itself, due to activity in this cortex. Sequences of movement such as eating or playing a musical instrument are coordinated by the _____ _____ (97) area; activity of different cells in this area produces different types of movements. The _____ _____ (98) cortex receives input from secondary motor areas and is responsible for organizing and executing _____ (99) movements. Cells in this area are relatively unspecialized; each cell may contribute to a range of related behaviors.

Two brain areas do not produce motor actions themselves, but instead modulate the activity of the motor systems they connect. The first, called the _____ _____ (100), includes the caudate nucleus, putamen, and globus pallidus, which fine-tune and smooth out movements. It is also involved in learning _____ (101) of movement. This area is also severely affected by _____ (102) disease, which can cause learning disabilities, postural changes, and involuntary movements as described in the introduction. The cerebellum receives input from the motor cortex regarding planned movements, and it integrates body posture and movement information from the _____ (103) system. As a result, this area is involved in several functions related to balance and the control of _____ (104) movements. It coordinates the different components of complex movements and provides corrections as movements are being executed. It is also involved in motor learning, in nonmotor learning, as well as in making time and speed estimates about visual and auditory objects.

There are several neurologically based movement disorders. Parkinson's disease affects 0.3% of the population in industrial nations and 1% of individuals over the age of 60. This disorder is caused by deterioration of the _____ _____ (105), the source of dopaminergic neurons projecting to the _____ (106) composed of part of the basal ganglia and the nucleus accumbens. Symptoms of Parkinson's disease include tremor, rigidity, and problems with balance, coordination, and the initiation of movement. Some of the genes involved in Parkinson's disease control the production of deviant proteins in neurons called _____ (107), which may contribute to cognitive deficits and depression. Brain injury and environmental _____ (108) found in industrial chemicals and pesticides may be involved in causing Parkinson's disease, and some people may inherit a reduced ability to metabolize these chemicals. The risk of Parkinson's disease is reduced by 50% in _____ (109) and by 80% in

_____ (110) drinkers. One theory is that the active chemicals in these, nicotine and _____ (111), reduces the effects and accumulation of toxins, resulting in increased dopamine and acetylcholine release. Treatment of Parkinson's disease has traditionally involved administration of the dopamine precursor _____ (112). The use of embryonic stem cells has not produced clinically significant improvement, although treatment using adult _____ (113) stem cells has shown more promise. Other alternatives to drug treatment include strategically placed _____ (114) in the basal ganglia, performed in individuals unable to take dopaminergic drugs, but this approach can lead to deficits such as weakness. There has been better success with _____ _____ (115) stimulation, which improves motor functioning and increases levodopa for up to 10 years, though cognitive deficits remain and some patients exhibit compulsive behaviors.

Huntington's disease occurs as a result of progressive cell loss in the cortex and _____ (116), producing movement impairments that become more pronounced with time, as well as psychological changes. The disease is eventually fatal from extensive cell death, presumably from a buildup of the protein _____ (117); the gene responsible for this protein has been located, and a person inheriting the dominant mutated form of the gene will eventually develop Huntington's disease. A number of drugs have been used to treat symptoms, but only one drug has received FDA approval. It works by reducing excess _____ (118) that causes the abnormal movements. Drugs that silence the mutated gene also have shown short-term promise in animal studies.

Several autoimmune diseases also involve the disruption of movement. _____ _____ (119) occurs as a result of a decrease in the number or sensitivity of acetylcholine receptors, and it is characterized by muscular weakness that, if untreated, may cause death. A study using a snake venom that binds to acetylcholine receptors revealed that people with the disease have significantly fewer of these receptors. Treatment normally involves inhibiting the enzyme _____ (120), or AChE, but a more permanent treatment involves removal of the _____ (121) gland, the body's major source of antibody-producing lymphocytes. _____ _____ (122) involves the loss of myelin in CNS cells, producing scarring and reducing or eliminating the functioning of affected neurons. Weakness, tremor, and impaired coordination result. Evidence suggests that myelin is destroyed by the _____ (123) system, perhaps as a result of exposure to a virus such as measles, mumps, or the Epstein-Barr virus. One drug treatment that has just been approved for multiple sclerosis blocks _____ (124) channels and improves motor performance, particularly walking. New stem cell treatments also show promise; injecting stem cells from a patient's _____ _____ (125) reduced brain inflammation and improved brain function.

Short Answer and Essay Questions

Answer the following questions.

6. Explain, in terms of precision of movement, the consequences of the fact that a single motor neuron projecting to the biceps muscle serves 100 muscle cells, whereas a single motor neuron projecting to the eye muscles serves only three cells.

7. Indicate how researchers know that the primary motor cortex, and not other motor areas, is responsible for the execution of movement.

8. Compare Parkinson's and Huntington's diseases in terms of what is known about the genetic basis of each. For which disease does the environment seem to play a more important role? Why?

Post-test

Use these multiple-choice questions to check your understanding of the chapter.

1. The receptors in the body that convey information about muscle tension and limb position are part of which sensory system?
   a. vestibular sense
   b. audition
   c. proprioception
   d. none of the above

2. Pacinian corpuscles are found _____ the surface of the skin and detect _____.
   a. near; touch and shape
   b. far from; touch and shape
   c. near; warmth and cold
   d. far from; warmth and cold

3. Which of the following areas of the body probably contains the FEWEST touch receptors?
   a. tongue
   b. upper arm
   c. thumb
   d. foot

4. Which of the following senses is NOT detected by free nerve endings?
   a. warmth
   b. cold
   c. touch
   d. pain

5. Information about touch from the right side of the body projects
   a. only to the left hemisphere.
   b. only to the right hemisphere.
   c. to the left and right hemispheres equally.
   d. mostly to the left hemisphere.

6. The primary somatosensory cortex is located in the
   a. anterior parietal lobe.
   b. posterior frontal lobe.
   c. central sulcus.
   d. superior temporal lobe.

7. Capsaicin
   a. acts on the TRPV1 receptor.
   b. is an ingredient of chili peppers.
   c. can alleviate joint pain.
   d. all of the above

8. In the vestibular system, hair cells are found in the
   a. utricle.
   b. saccule.
   c. semicircular canals.
   d. all of the above

9. As part of a classroom exercise, you spin around on an office chair for numerous rotations, and then stop. You feel like you are still spinning because you are still bending the hair cells inside your _____. You still know which way up is, because you didn't affect your _____.
   a. semicircular canals; cochlea
   b. cochlea; utricle and saccule
   c. semicircular canals; utricle and saccule
   d. utricle and saccule; semicircular canals

10. The vestibular system projects to the _____ cortex, which is responsible for the disgust and nausea you feel when you are dizzy.
    a. premotor
    b. parieto-insular-vestibular
    c. somatosensory
    d. posterior parietal

11. The body segment served by a specific spinal nerve is called a
    a. dermatome.
    b. spinal area.
    c. cupula.
    d. Ruffini area.

12. Which of the following is NOT a similarity between the visual cortex and somatosensory cortex?
    a. mapping of adjacent sensory input on adjacent cortical areas
    b. cells with excitatory centers and inhibitory surrounds
    c. found in the occipital lobe
    d. cells with sensitivity to orientation

13. The _____ receives input from both sides of the body through the left and right primary somatosensory cortices, and is particularly responsive to stimuli that have acquired _____.
    a. primary somatosensory cortex; pain
    b. secondary somatosensory cortex; meaning
    c. posterior parietal cortex; emotions
    d. amygdala; reinforcement

14. Patients suffering from one of the weirder disorders, called _____, are convinced that a particular limb doesn't belong to them and sometimes ask to have it amputated.
    a. out-of-body disorder
    b. mismatched limb disorder
    c. body integrity identity disorder
    d. somnolence disorder

15. A-delta fibers are _____ and are responsible for our experience of _____ pain.
    a. myelinated; sharp
    b. myelinated; dull

    c. unmyelinated; sharp

    d. unmyelinated; dull

16. Mice that lack receptors for substance P appear to experience

    a. no pain.

    b. only mild pain.

    c. only intense pain.

    d. moderate pain all of the time.

17. Which of the following pain medications acts by reducing inflammation in tissues?

    a. caffeine

    b. morphine

    c. acetaminophen

    d. ibuprofen

18. Endorphins are LEAST likely to be released in response to which of the following?

    a. physical stress

    b. vaginal stimulation

    c. placebo

    d. escapable shock

19. Pain causes the release of endorphins in the _____, which in turn causes inhibition of the release of substance P in the _____.

    a. PAG; spinal cord

    b. spinal cord; PAG

    c. PAG; amygdala

    d. spinal cord; cingulate cortex

20. Which of the following is NOT true about pain disorders?

    a. Most amputees do not experience phantom limb pain.

    b. Congenital pain insensitivity is a rare disorder, most likely genetic in origin.

    c. Chronic pain can cause loss of gray matter in the brain.

    d. Successful treatment of phantom limb pain reverses cortical reorganization.

21. Movements of the stomach and intestines are produced by

    a. smooth muscle.

    b. skeletal muscle.

    c. striated muscle.

    d. cardiac muscle.

22. Which of the following muscles probably has the MOST individual muscle cells controlled by a single motor neuron?

    a. triceps muscle

    b. eye muscle

    c. index finger muscle

    d. tongue muscle

23. Which of the following statements regarding antagonistic muscle pairs is FALSE?

    a. Each muscle has opposing effects on a limb.

    b. Both muscles may be contracted simultaneously.

    c. Maintaining the balance between opposed pairs of muscles requires conscious, voluntary activity.

    d. Coordination of antagonistic muscles is controlled by the spinal cord.

24. Muscle tension (extent of contraction) is detected by
    a. Golgi tendon organs.
    b. muscle spindles.
    c. Lewy bodies.
    d. a and b

25. Central pattern generators
    a. are found in lower animals but not in humans.
    b. are present in young infants, but they atrophy by adulthood.
    c. work even when the spinal cord is severed.
    d. none of the above

26. In producing movement, the last cortical area to be activated is the
    a. premotor area.
    b. association cortex.
    c. supplementary motor cortex.
    d. primary motor cortex.

27. The "memory" of a stimulus used in the delayed match-to-sample task seems to be held in the
    a. primary motor cortex.
    b. supplementary motor cortex.
    c. premotor cortex.
    d. prefrontal cortex.

28. Selection of arm movement needed for reaching a specific target seems to occur in the
    a. primary motor cortex.
    b. supplementary motor cortex.
    c. premotor cortex.
    d. prefrontal cortex.

29. Sequences of movements, such as those involved in typing on a computer keyboard, are coordinated by cells in the
    a. primary motor cortex.
    b. supplementary motor cortex.
    c. premotor cortex.
    d. prefrontal cortex.

30. The actual execution of a movement is triggered by activity in the
    a. primary motor cortex.
    b. supplementary motor cortex.
    c. premotor cortex.
    d. prefrontal cortex.

31. Which brain areas contribute to the smoothness of movement?
    a. cerebellum and premotor cortex
    b. supplementary motor cortex and basal ganglia
    c. prefrontal cortex and premotor cortex
    d. cerebellum and basal ganglia

32. The cerebellum is involved in
    a. the order and timing of complex movements.
    b. the learning of motor skills.

    c. judging the speed of objects.

    d. all of the above

33. Parkinson's disease results from a loss of _____ neurons originating in the _____.

    a. dopaminergic; striatum

    b. dopaminergic; substantia nigra

    c. cholinergic; striatum

    d. cholinergic; substantia nigra

34. Currently, which of the following treatments for Parkinson's disease has been shown to have the FEWEST side effects?

    a. brain stimulation

    b. brain lesions

    c. L-dopa

    d. fetal tissue transplant

35. Which of the following statements is (are) TRUE of Huntington's disease?

    a. It is a degenerative disease, becoming progressively worse over time.

    b. Cognitive and emotional deficits always occur.

    c. Researchers know which gene is involved and how it works.

    d. all of the above

36. People with myasthenia gravis have fewer or less sensitive _____ receptors.

    a. dopamine

    b. serotonin

    c. endorphin

    d. acetylcholine

37. Myasthenia gravis is MOST effectively treated by

    a. acetylcholinesterase inhibitors.

    b. thymectomy.

    c. fetal tissue transplant.

    d. brain stimulation.

38. Multiple sclerosis involves

    a. loss of myelin in the central nervous system.

    b. loss of myelin in the peripheral nervous system.

    c. loss of myelin in both the central and peripheral nervous systems.

    d. none of the above

Answers

Guided Review

1. hearing or audition
2. movement
3. somatosensory
4. Proprioception
5. warmth or heat
6. pain
7. itch or pruriception
8. touch
9. Meissner's
10. Merkel's
11. Pacinian
12. Ruffini
13. pain
14. TRP (transient receptor potential)
15. chemical
16. TRPV1
17. vestibular
18. semicircular canals
19. cupula
20. hair
21. saccule
22. position or orientation
23. cerebellum
24. dermatome
25. thalamus
26. opposite
27. somatotopic
28. primary
29. secondary
30. hippocampus
31. posterior parietal
32. frontal
33. body
34. body integrity identity
35. out-of-body
36. pressure
37. inflammatory soup
38. cytokines
39. enhances
40. A-delta
41. dull or aching
42. substance P
43. anesthetics
44. sodium
45. unconscious
46. ibuprofen
47. prostaglandins
48. acetaminophen
49. morphine
50. nerve growth
51. gene therapy
52. David Livingston
53. endogenous
54. endorphins
55. opiate
56. physical
57. (child)birth
58. naloxone
59. gate control
60. inhibitory
61. periaqueductal gray
62. substance P
63. congenital insensitivity or congenital analgesia
64. sodium
65. *PRDM12*
66. healing
67. depressed
68. nucleus accumbens
69. somatosensory
70. gray matter
71. missing or phantom
72. 75
73. cortical reorganization

74. mirror
75. skeletal
76. cardiac
77. smooth
78. neuromuscular
79. acetylcholine
80. precision
81. actin
82. myosin
83. Tendons
84. antagonistic
85. spinal cord
86. patellar
87. muscle spindles
88. motor
89. contract
90. Golgi tendon
91. central pattern generators (CPGs)
92. prefrontal cortex
93. match-to-sample
94. prefrontal
95. premotor
96. rubber hand
97. supplementary motor
98. primary motor
99. voluntary

100. basal ganglia
101. sequences
102. Parkinson's
103. vestibular
104. eye
105. substantia nigra
106. striatum
107. Lewy bodies
108. toxins
109. smokers
110. coffee
111. caffeine
112. L-dopa or levodopa
113. neural
114. lesions
115. deep brain
116. striatum
117. huntingtin
118. dopamine
119. Myasthenia gravis
120. acetylcholinesterase
121. thymus
122. Multiple sclerosis
123. immune
124. potassium
125. bone marrow

Short Answer and Essay Questions

1. When your body accelerates, the increase in speed displaces the gelatinous masses (cupulas) in the vestibular organs, causing the hair cells to bend and change the rate of firing in their neurons. Once you reach a stable speed, the cupulas return to normal, and the hair cells return to their normal rate of firing, so you do not notice movement.

2. Meissner's corpuscles and Merkel's disks are located near the surface of the skin, and they can detect texture, fine detail, and movement of objects across the skin. Pacinian corpuscles and Ruffini endings are located deeper, and because they detect stretching of the skin, they can detect the shape of objects that are grasped.

3. The visual and somatosensory areas are similar in the following ways: They contain a map of their respective receptive fields (the body and the retina, respectively); the receptive fields of some of the cells are arranged with an excitatory center and inhibitory surround; processing is hierarchical, with certain subareas of the somatosensory cortex passing information along to other areas (similar to the sequential processing seen in the visual system); and both systems contain cells that are feature detectors.

4. When pain messages are received in the periaqueductal gray, endorphins are released onto neurons that project down the spinal cord; there these neurons inhibit the neurons responsible for releasing substance P, reducing the flow of pain. This type of descending pathway was predicted by the gate control theory of pain.

5. When a limb is amputated or no longer sends sensory input to the brain because of a spinal cord injury, the area of the somatosensory cortex served by that limb may be "taken over" by neurons from adjacent body areas. Activation of these neurons produces a painful sensation that feels as if it is in the amputated limb, because the portion of the somatosensory cortex that previously served the missing limb has been activated.

6. When the ratio of motor neurons to muscle cells is low, as in the case of eye muscles, it allows for a great deal more precision of movement than when the ratio is high, as in the biceps muscle.

7. Activity in the prefrontal and premotor cortices occurs prior to the onset of movement, whereas activity in the primary motor cortex corresponds with movement. This suggests that although the prefrontal and premotor areas are involved in planning movements, the primary motor cortex executes the movement. Tasks such as the delayed match-to-sample task have helped characterize the planning functions of the prefrontal cortex.

8. Huntington's disease is due to a single gene; the individual will develop the disease if the gene has more than 37 repetitions of the bases cytosine, adenine, and guanine, with more repetitions correlated with earlier development. The genetic basis of Parkinson's is not well understood. It is familial (inherited) in only a minority of cases. In familial Parkinson's disease, several different genes appear to be involved. Implicated genes are involved in the death of dopamine neurons, production of Lewy bodies, and ability to metabolize toxins that may cause Parkinson's. In the latter cases, exposure to the toxins is probably necessary in order for the disease to develop, so both environment and genetics are important.

Post-test

1. c   2. b   3. b   4. c   5. d   6. a   7. d   8. d   9. c   10. b   11. a   12. c   13. b   14. c   15. a   16. b   17. d   18. d   19. a   20. a   21. a   22. a   23. c   24. a   25. c   26. d   27. d   28. c   29. b   30. a   31. d   32. d   33. b   34. a   35. d   36. d   37. b   38. a

12 Learning and Memory

Chapter Outline

Learning Objectives

After reading this chapter, you will be able to

1. Explain how the brain is involved in the different types of memory

2. Diagram the neural involvement in processing of information that is stored in memory

3. Describe the changes that occur in the brain as learning proceeds

4. Examine how memory changes during aging

5. Contrast the impacts of normal aging and disorders on memory

Learning as the Storage of Memories

Summary and Guided Review

After studying this section in the text, fill in the blanks of the following summary.

To be useful for future behavior, experiences or learning must somehow be stored within the nervous system; without _____ (1), we would be capable of only very simple forms of behavior. This point is demonstrated by the case of Henry Molaison (HM) described in the introduction to the chapter. HM underwent removal of much of his _____ (2) lobes to reduce his debilitating seizures, and afterward suffered from both anterograde and retrograde _____ (3). Consequently, he had great difficulty forming new memories as well as remembering past events (although he could recall some events that occurred before the age of 16). Because of the extent of damage to HM's brain, it is not known exactly which structures were responsible for his amnesia, although the _____ (4) and associated areas were certainly involved. Moderate anterograde amnesia and minimal retrograde amnesia occur following bilateral damage to the hippocampal area known as _____ (5). Damage to the entire hippocampus produces severe _____ (6) amnesia, and severe retrograde amnesia occurs if the larger hippocampal _____ (7) is damaged as well. HM's story is considered one of the most important cases in the study of learning and memory. Although he died in 2008 at the age of 82, he continues to make a contribution; researchers at the University of California at San Diego have_____ (8) his brain and are making a 3-D digital _____ (9) available online.

Until information stored in memory undergoes _____ (10), which is the process of forming a permanent physical representation, it is subject to disruption. New memories are disrupted easily, and even old memories may be lost following trauma. Evidence from studies on rats placed in a murky water maze suggests that this process in the hippocampus requires the neurotransmitter _____ (11). The process by which stored memories are accessed, or _____ (12), also appears to involve the hippocampus. In humans, this process has also been shown to involve the hippocampus using _____ (13) scans during long-term free recall of information. However, because very old memories are less affected by hippocampal damage, some other mechanism must be responsible for maintaining and retrieving them. The fact that learning and effortful attempts at retrieval also activate the _____ (14) area suggests that it might also serve these functions.

The neurotransmitter _____ (15) is needed for consolidation of long-term memories. Specifically, release of dopamine prompts protein synthesis that is part of the brain _____ (16) important to memory. Dopamine neurons detect _____ (17) in the environment, reflecting the importance of learning in responding to a dynamic world.

The hippocampus is not the actual storage site of memories. Researchers believe that _____-_____ (18) memory depends on the hippocampus but that long-term memory depends on an interaction between the hippocampus and the _____ (19). For example, when subjects recalled recent news events, fMRI activity was highest in the _____ (20), but when asked to recall events over the past 30 years, activity increased in several _____ (21) areas. Consolidated memories are stored in the areas of the cortex where specific types of information are processed; for example, memories for pictures are stored in the _____ (22) region, whereas verbal memories are stored in the left _____ (23) lobe. A "map" of a rat's environment is stored in the hippocampus, where specialized _____ (24) cells are located; in humans these cells are involved in not only spatial memory but also context.

The fact that HM displayed some forms of _____ (25) without being consciously aware of his newly acquired skills suggests that the brain forms at least two kinds of memory. _____ (26) memory refers to information about facts, people, and events that we can verbalize, whereas _____ (27) memory refers to memory for behaviors (including skills learning, emotional learning, and stimulus-response conditioning). Put simply, declarative memories involve the "what" in memory, whereas nondeclarative memories concern the _____ (28). Studies with rats demonstrate that different brain areas are involved in each form of memory; declarative or relational memory is disrupted by damage to the _____ (29), whereas nondeclarative memory is disrupted by damage to the _____ (30). In humans, this latter form of learning is disrupted in people with _____ (31) and Huntington's diseases. The _____ (32) is involved in nondeclarative emotional learning. A subject with bilateral damage to this area responded to a loud sound with a skin conductance response, but could not be conditioned to respond to a colored slide that was paired with the sound. Activity in this area may also strengthen _____ (33) learning about emotional events through its connections with the hippocampus.

Both new and old information are held temporarily in _____ (34) memory while being used; this is somewhat similar to a computer's RAM, although the capacity of working memory is very small and it fades quickly. The neurological basis of working memory can be studied using the delayed _____-to-_____ (35) task. Following presentation and removal of the stimulus, cells continue firing in the cortical area appropriate for that stimulus; but if this activity is disrupted, the animal still makes a correct choice, so these are not the location of working memory. Working memory apparently is located in the _____ (36) cortex; cells there continue firing during the delay, even in spite of a distracting stimulus, and they respond selectively to the stimulus and task conditions. The prefrontal cortex seems to be responsible for managing information in working memory by acting as a central _____ (37) rather than merely serving as a storage facility for memory.

Short Answer and Essay Questions

Answer the following questions.

1. Identify the brain areas involved in memory consolidation and retrieval.

2. Explain what Bechara and colleagues discovered about the different roles of the hippocampus and the amygdala in learning.

3. Describe the location of place cells and how their function relates to learning.

Brain Changes in Learning

Summary and Guided Review

After studying this section in the text, fill in the blanks of the following summary.

_____ (38) rule states that if a presynaptic neuron is active while a postsynaptic neuron is firing, the synapse will increase in strength. The synaptic changes are the result of LTP, which stands for _____-_____ _____ (39); they are similar to the neural plasticity exhibited by neurons early in development as synapses are being formed. LTP has been studied mostly in the _____ (40) but has also been found in the visual, auditory, and motor cortices. In the laboratory, LTP is usually induced by simultaneously stimulating presynaptic and postsynaptic neurons with an electrical current. This change may last briefly or for several months. In contrast, LTD, or _____-_____ _____ (41), weakens a synapse; it occurs when stimulation of presynaptic neurons is insufficient to activate postsynaptic neurons. LTD may be an important mechanism for modifying memories and _____ (42) old memories to free synapses for new information.

Presynaptic stimulation also influences the sensitivity of nearby synapses; if a weak synapse and a strong synapse on the same postsynaptic neuron are active simultaneously, the weak synapse will be _____ (43), or strengthened. This effect is called _____ (44) LTP. Researchers believe that this type of potentiation is the basis for _____ (45) conditioning. These three phenomena, LTP, LTD, and associative LTP, all illustrate the expression "cells that fire together _____ (46) together."

LTP induction involves a cascade of events at the synapse involving the neurotransmitter _____ (47), which has several different types of receptors. Initially glutamate activates _____ (48) receptors but not _____ (49) receptors, because the latter are blocked by _____ (50) ions. Partial depolarization of the membrane causes displacement of these ions, which then allows the _____ (51) receptors to be activated. This results in an influx of sodium and _____ (52) ions, which further depolarizes the neuron and activates the _____ (53) enzyme necessary for LTP. Mice that are _____ (54) for a mutant gene for this enzyme show no LTP. Mice that are heterozygous produce some enzyme, and show LTP, but it is not consolidated into _____-_____ (55) memory formation.

LTP induction is followed by changes in _____ (56) activation and silencing, and synthesis of _____ (57), resulting in changes at the synapse and growth of new connections. Within 45–60 minutes after LTP, structural changes occur at the synapse. These include increased numbers of synaptic _____ (58) on dendrites that make the synapse more sensitive. Other changes include transport of _____ (59) receptors from the dendrites into the spines. Furthermore, the birth of new neurons, or _____ (60), occurs in the hippocampus. Over the course of a lifetime these new cells may make up _____ %–_____% (61) of the total population of cells. These changes are long term, and they may explain why London cabbies who have memorized the layout of the city had a larger posterior part of their hippocampi, which is known to be involved in spatial _____ (62).

There is evidence that some transfer of information from the hippocampus to the cortex occurs during _____ (63). During this "offline" period, the replay of neural firing that occurred while learning a task provides the cortex the opportunity to undergo _____ (64) at the more leisurely pace that it requires. During sleep, more than 100 genes increase their activity and many have been implicated in _____ _____ (65), synaptic changes, and memory consolidation. Even a 90-minute daytime nap can trigger these changes.

Finally, it is important to understand that although memories may be long lasting, the brain has mechanisms for eliminating or changing information. _____ (66) is a process in which a learned association is slowly eliminated; the memory is actually still available but has been replaced by new learning, which involves the activation of NMDA receptors. The enzyme protein phosphatase 1 and the gene *Drac1(V12)* apparently mediate _____ (67). The gene's protein product _____ (68) causes memory to decay after learning. _____ (69), which normally occurs after a memory has been retrieved, is a very vulnerable period during which memories can be disrupted. Rats that were given a drug that interfered with _____ _____ (70) lost their learned fear responses to a tone that was originally paired with electric foot shock. Finally, retrieved memories may be _____ (71), for example, by being blended with other memories; Loftus and colleagues have shown that _____ (72) memories of experiences that did not occur may be implanted by suggestion. As stated in the In the News feature, stimulating the trigeminal nerve using a process called Targeted Neuroplasticity Training releases the neurotransmitter _____ (73), which enhances sensory functioning. This noninvasive treatment stimulates nerves through the skin and may eventually be marketed as wearable devices that improve your memory.

Short Answer and Essay Questions

Answer the following questions.

4. Contrast LTP and LTD in their impacts on synapses and learning.

5. Describe three different processes that show that memories are malleable or not "fixed in stone."

6. Winona witnessed a bank robbery by two men but was able to provide little more than general information in her description. Over the two years since the robbery and following repeated questioning, she has recalled several details. On the witness stand, the defense attorney questions the accuracy of these memories, but Winona insists her memories are vivid and accurate. Based on information in the text, what problems do you see with her testimony?

Learning Deficiencies and Disorders

Summary and Guided Review

After studying this section in the text, fill in the blanks of the following summary.

Until recently, it was believed that loss of memory and cognitive skills was a natural consequence of _____ (74); however, studies indicate that these losses are not inevitable (though it is unclear whether successful aging is due to choosing an active lifestyle or is an inherent characteristic of the individual). Another misconception is that when memory loss does occur, it results from neuron loss, particularly in the cortex and the _____ (75). What is more likely responsible for age-related declines in memory and cognition is that the hippocampus loses synapses and neuronal genes exhibit altered _____ (76) levels, both of which likely cause diminished LTP and learning. There have been 17 genes in the _____ _____ (77) that undergo changed levels of expression with aging; animal models with reduced expression of RbAp48 (a protein made by one of the genes) exhibited similar memory problems.

Environment appears important in protecting against the effects of aging. Age-related reductions in cortical thickness, neurogenesis, and dendritic branching have been minimized by providing _____ (78) environments to animals or by reducing calories or engaging in _____ _____ (79). Diets containing _____ (80) in fruits and vegetables have been associated with improved LTP in nonhuman animals and reduced cognitive decline in people. The _____ _____ (81) has found improvements in episodic memory through training elderly people in photography or quilting.

_____ (82) refers to the loss of memory and cognitive abilities. _____ (83) disease, in which the brain progressively deteriorates, is a form of dementia. In the early stages, _____ (84) memory is impaired, a symptom that becomes worse over time. Many behaviors become affected over the course of the disease, which eventually results in _____ (85).

The brains of people with Alzheimer's contain _____ _____ (86) (Aβ) plaques, which interfere with neuron functioning, and _____ (87) tangles; both are associated with cell death. Over time, deficits in brain tissue and functioning can be observed in most of the brain, especially the frontal lobes and the temporal lobes, where they effectively isolate the _____ (88). Over the past decade, scientists have realized they need to distinguish whether or not the amyloid is _____ (89); if it is, the concentration in the brain increases 70-fold and has been linked to memory failure, loss of synapses, and impaired LTP in the hippocampus.

Because plaques and tangles are also a characteristic of _____ (90) syndrome, Alzheimer's researchers looked for genes on chromosome 21, where they found the _____ (91) gene; mice engineered with a mutation of this gene that increases plaques also had deficits in LTP and learning. Of the four known genes for Alzheimer's disease, the E4 allele of the _____ (92) gene is associated with plaques and tangles. An additional 22 genes have been implicated in Alzheimer's, and although the particular identities of those loci are unknown, they are involved in inflammation, immune response, cell migration, and other _____ (93) functions.

Environmental factors can increase the likelihood of developing Alzheimer's disease: _____ (94) exposure, deficiencies in vitamin D, obesity, hypertension, _____ (95), and smoking all carry increased risks. Sports players and combat veterans with _____ _____ _____ (96) have shown Alzheimer's-like symptoms. Some new research has linked beta amyloid to past _____ (97) of *Chlamydophila pneumoniae* and spirochetes. Due to the aging population of the United States, the rate of Alzheimer's disease is predicted to _____ (98) in the coming years; thankfully, increasing education level in this country is reducing the percent likelihood per individual by 26%.

Five drugs are currently approved for treatment of Alzheimer's disease, although none of them provides a cure. Alzheimer's patients have a significant loss of neurons that release _____ (99), an important neurotransmitter for the hippocampal theta rhythm, impairing learning and memory. Three drugs that prevent the breakdown of acetylcholine are currently used to relieve cognitive and behavioral symptoms in mild cases of Alzheimer's. Moderate to severe cases may be treated with _____ (100), which reduces neurons' sensitivity to excessive glutamate, which overexcites and kills neurons. There are three current major fronts of developing treatments: removing amyloid, reducing inflammation, and preventing tangles. While the first two approaches have been unsuccessful, there is promise with the tangle-preventing drug _____ (101), which has reduced symptom progression by 90%. Scientists are also exploring treatments with gene therapy and _____ _____ (102). Clinical trials are examining the impacts of genes for _____ _____ _____ (103) such as BDNF. In mice, stimulating the brain with _____ (104) eliminated plaques.

Diagnosing Alzheimer's disease involves a battery of tests, but one of the most important steps is to rule out other forms of _____ (105) that may be more treatable. One strategy involves using PET scanning and tracers that specifically target _____ (106). This technique might help predict the disease and follow its course over time. Because PET scans diagnose only one-third of individuals with mild impairment, a more accurate approach is to test for _____ (107) for the disease found in blood and cerebrospinal fluid. A study of Catholic nuns found that the disease might start long before the diagnosis actually occurs and that individuals who did not develop Alzheimer's disease had higher _____ (108) density in autobiographical essays written decades before. This was despite similar number of *APOE4* alleles and healthy women showing signs of neurofibrillary tangles in autopsies following death. According to the _____ (109) hypothesis, lifelong learning (as evidenced in the healthy Roman Catholic sisters with high idea densities) increases a person's cognitive reserve, giving him or her increased resistance to the degenerative effects of dementia.

_____ _____ (110) is associated with thiamine deficiency, which is usually related to _____ (111) abuse. This degenerative disorder results in anterograde and retrograde amnesia due to damage to the _____ (112) bodies, medial thalamic area, and _____ (113) lobes. In the early stages, _____ (114) supplements can relieve the symptoms but cannot reverse the damage. Korsakoff patients often exhibit _____ (115), or the fabrication of stories, probably as an attempt to fill in information they can no longer recall. This characteristic seems to be related to damage to a specific area of the _____ (116) lobe, rendering patients unable to distinguish current reality and memories of prior events.

Short Answer and Essay Questions

Answer the following questions.

7. Contrast Alzheimer's disease and general age-related memory decline in terms of their neural correlates.

8. Evaluate the current treatments for Alzheimer's disease, including their effectiveness.

9. Describe the causes and characteristic effects of Korsakoff syndrome.

Post-test

Use these multiple-choice questions to check your understanding of the chapter.

1. Which of the following was NOT a result of HM's surgery?
   a. lowered IQ
   b. anterograde amnesia
   c. retrograde amnesia
   d. relief from seizures

2. Which of the following deficits is an example of anterograde amnesia?
   a. being unable to recall events occurring just prior to brain injury
   b. being unable to recall events occurring after brain injury
   c. being unable to recall events occurring many years prior to brain injury
   d. none of the above

3. Bilateral brain damage that is limited to hippocampal area CA1 results in
   a. moderate anterograde amnesia and profound retrograde amnesia.
   b. moderate anterograde amnesia and minimal retrograde amnesia.
   c. profound anterograde amnesia and profound retrograde amnesia.
   d. profound anterograde amnesia and minimal retrograde amnesia.

4. Consolidation is the process of
   a. accessing stored information.
   b. altering memories during retrieval.
   c. fabricating information missing from memory.
   d. making memories long lasting or permanent.

5. Which of the following is TRUE about the role of dopamine in learning?
   a. Dopamine is involved only in retrieval of memories.
   b. Dopamine disrupts consolidation in the hippocampus.
   c. Dopamine assists in consolidation of memories.
   d. Dopamine is important only for spatial learning.

6. Researchers found that, over 25 days of being tested for retention of a spatial discrimination task, mice showed
   a. increased activity in the hippocampus and increased activity in the cortex.
   b. increased activity in the hippocampus and decreased activity in the cortex.
   c. decreased activity in the hippocampus and increased activity in the cortex.
   d. decreased activity in the hippocampus and decreased activity in the cortex.

7. Effortful attempts at retrieval are associated with increased activity in
   a. the prefrontal area.
   b. the hippocampus.
   c. both the prefrontal area and the hippocampus.
   d. neither the prefrontal area nor the hippocampus.

8. Researchers believe that in most cases memories are stored
   a. in the hippocampus.
   b. in a single storage area of the cortex.
   c. evenly throughout the cortex.
   d. none of the above

9. Which of the following is NOT a type of declarative memory?
   a. memory for your 21st birthday
   b. memory of the fear you experienced at a haunted house
   c. memory of the facts from this textbook
   d. memory for the location of the dining hall on campus

10. People with damage to the striatum (as in Parkinson's and Huntington's diseases) have difficulty with
    a. procedural memory.
    b. declarative memory.
    c. relational memory.
    d. b and c

11. Incorporating emotional information into memory probably depends on the
    a. amygdala.
    b. cingulate gyrus.
    c. basal ganglia.
    d. cerebellum.

12. Which of the following statements regarding working memory is FALSE?
    a. It holds information temporarily.
    b. It has an unlimited capacity.
    c. It provides the basis for problem solving and decision making.
    d. It can hold new information as well as memories already stored.

13. The brain area that seems to be MOST important for working memory is the
    a. inferior temporal cortex.
    b. parietal cortex.
    c. prefrontal cortex.
    d. superior frontal cortex.

14. Following the simultaneous stimulation of presynaptic neurons and postsynaptic neurons, postsynaptic neurons will
    a. decrease their firing rate.
    b. produce larger EPSPs.
    c. produce smaller EPSPs.
    d. produce larger IPSPs.

15. LTP occurs
    a. only in the hippocampus.
    b. only in the visual cortex.

    c. only in the motor cortex.

    d. none of the above

16. Classical conditioning most likely involves

    a. LTP.

    b. associative LTP.

    c. LTD.

    d. associative LTD.

17. Low-frequency stimulation of presynaptic neurons, which results in no responses in postsynaptic neurons, results in

    a. LTP.

    b. LTD.

    c. more EPSPs.

    d. more postsynaptic action potentials.

18. Which of the following is TRUE about LTD?

    a. It allows unneeded memories to be removed.

    b. It is the same thing as LTP.

    c. It cannot occur in the hippocampus.

    d. It serves no purpose.

19. Which of these follows LTP induction?

    a. growth of new dendrites

    b. gene activation

    c. release of dopamine

    d. all of the above

20. In order for NMDA receptors to be activated, _____ must be dislodged.

    a. glutamate

    b. magnesium

    c. sodium

    d. nitric oxide

21. Which of the following occurs after LTP in the hippocampus?

    a. appearance of new AMPA receptors

    b. increased number of dendritic spines on postsynaptic neurons

    c. neurogenesis

    d. all of the above

22. Which of the following is TRUE about neurogenesis?

    a. It occurs only in the cortex.

    b. Over the life span, it produces less than 5% of neural cells.

    c. It is important to consolidation of memories in the cortex.

    d. It plays no role in learning.

23. A study of the brains of London taxicab drivers revealed that

    a. the entire hippocampus was larger than in other people.

    b. all of the spatial areas of the brain were larger than in other people.

    c. the posterior portion of the hippocampus was larger than in other people.

    d. none of the above

24. The presence of which of the following would MOST likely lead to reduced LTP?

    a. removal of magnesium block on the NMDA receptor

    b. X-radiation

c. α CaMKII

d. increased glutamate receptors

25. Which of the following statements regarding LTP is MOST likely true?
    a. It is only a laboratory (or experimental) phenomenon.
    b. Hippocampal LTP is permanent.
    c. Cortical LTP is responsible for long-term memory.
    d. Only humans exhibit LTP.

26. Mice heterozygous for a defective CaMKII gene
    a. are better learners than normal mice.
    b. are incapable of retaining information for more than a few hours.
    c. show no LTP.
    d. have more CaMKII than mice homozygous for the gene.

27. What is the MOST accurate statement about sleep and memory?
    a. During sleep, neurons in the hippocampus are silent.
    b. During sleep, more than 100 genes decrease their activity.
    c. "Offline" replay that occurs during sleep helps the cortex undergo LTP.
    d. Contrary to what researchers expected, sleep has no measurable effect on memory.

28. Memories seem to be vulnerable to change during
    a. reconsolidation.
    b. reconstruction.
    c. extinction.
    d. suppression.

29. Which of the following is FALSE about the process of forgetting?
    a. It has no apparent benefit; it would be better to remember everything, if possible.
    b. It involves the enzyme protein phosphatase 1.
    c. It is a different process from extinction.
    d. It may involve the protein Rac, which causes a memory to decay after learning.

30. Where is there significant brain cell loss in typical aging?
    a. basal forebrain
    b. hippocampus
    c. mammillary bodies
    d. medial thalamic area

31. Which of the following dietary changes can protect against age-related memory decline?
    a. calorie restriction
    b. sugar restriction
    c. vegetable consumption
    d. a and c

32. The MOST common cause of dementia is
    a. Alzheimer's disease.
    b. Korsakoff syndrome.
    c. nutritional deficiencies.
    d. Huntington's disease.

33. Which of the following is eventually disrupted in Alzheimer's disease?
    a. language
    b. spatial cognition

    c. reasoning

    d. all of the above

34. One of the most reliable ways to diagnose Alzheimer's disease (>90% accuracy) is to test the
    a. brain directly using a biopsy.
    b. cerebrospinal fluid for biomarkers.
    c. skin for degenerative peptides.
    d. level of amyloid using a PET scan.

35. In Alzheimer's patients, plaques and tangles found in the _____ lobes disrupt connections between the hippocampus and other structures.
    a. frontal
    b. parietal
    c. temporal
    d. occipital

36. Which of the following statements regarding Alzheimer's disease is FALSE?
    a. There are at least four different genes that cause it.
    b. People with Down syndrome will develop it if they live past 50.
    c. The amyloid precursor protein gene is found on chromosome 21.
    d. Symptoms of Alzheimer's disease do not appear before the age of 60.

37. Which of the following is the most common treatment for Alzheimer's disease?
    a. gene therapy
    b. cholinesterase inhibitors
    c. injection of amyloid to trigger an immune response
    d. memantine

38. One of the environmental triggers for Alzheimer's disease has been exposure to
    a. thiamine.
    b. smoking (nicotine).
    c. alcoholic beverages.
    d. animal dander (fur, skin).

39. Supporting the reserve hypothesis is the finding that
    a. memory failure is an inevitable, normal consequence of aging.
    b. engaging in mental but not physical activity reduces memory loss in older adults.
    c. there is no relationship between aging and memory loss.
    d. remaining mentally active is associated with better cognitive functioning.

40. Which of the following structures is NOT damaged in Korsakoff syndrome?
    a. hippocampus
    b. mammillary bodies
    c. medial thalamic area
    d. frontal lobes

41. Korsakoff patients are believed to engage in confabulation because
    a. their sense of right and wrong has deteriorated, and they do not care if they lie to others.
    b. they have difficulty distinguishing between current reality and their memories of the past.
    c. they are completely out of touch with reality.
    d. none of the above

Answers

Guided Review

1. memory
2. temporal
3. amnesia
4. hippocampus
5. CA1
6. anterograde
7. formation
8. dissected
9. reconstruction
10. consolidation
11. glutamate
12. retrieved
13. PET
14. prefrontal
15. dopamine
16. plasticity
17. novelty or change
18. short-term
19. cortex
20. hippocampus
21. cortical
22. occipital
23. frontal
24. place
25. learning
26. Declarative
27. nondeclarative
28. "how"
29. hippocampus
30. striatum
31. Parkinson's
32. amygdala
33. declarative
34. working
35. match-to-sample
36. prefrontal
37. executive

38. Hebb's
39. long-term potentiation (LTP)
40. hippocampus
41. Long-term depression (LTD)
42. clearing or forgetting
43. potentiated
44. associative
45. classical
46. wire
47. glutamate
48. AMPA
49. NMDA
50. magnesium
51. NMDA
52. calcium
53. CaMKII or αCaMKII
54. homozygous
55. long-term
56. gene
57. proteins
58. spines
59. AMPA
60. neurogenesis
61. 10–20
62. navigation
63. sleep
64. consolidation
65. protein synthesis
66. Extinction
67. forgetting
68. Rac
69. Reconsolidation
70. protein synthesis
71. reconstructed
72. false
73. norepinephrine
74. aging

75. hippocampus
76. expression
77. dentate gyrus
78. enriched
79. physical exercise
80. flavonoids
81. Synapse Project
82. Dementia
83. Alzheimer's
84. declarative
85. death
86. beta amyloid
87. neurofibrillary
88. hippocampus
89. soluble
90. Down
91. *APP*
92. *APOE*
93. cellular
94. Pesticide
95. diabetes

96. traumatic brain injury
97. infections
98. triple
99. acetylcholine
100. memantine or Namenda
101. LMTX
102. stem cells
103. nerve growth factors
104. ultrasound
105. dementia
106. plaques
107. biomarkers
108. idea
109. reserve
110. Korsakoff syndrome
111. alcohol
112. mammillary
113. frontal
114. thiamine
115. confabulation
116. frontal

Short Answer and Essay Questions

1. Consolidation of declarative or relational memory primarily involves the hippocampus, but other areas, such as the striatum and amygdala, are needed for nondeclarative memory consolidation. Retrieval of memories involves the hippocampus for a relatively short period of time following an event. The prefrontal cortex seems to direct retrieval and is important for working memory, whereas other cortical areas such as the temporal and parietal cortex are used for recalling older memories. Visual memories are stored in the occipital lobe, auditory memories in the temporal lobe, spatial memories in the parietal area and hippocampus, and verbal memories in the left frontal lobe.

2. A patient with bilateral hippocampal damage and one with bilateral amygdala damage underwent a conditioning procedure in which a loud sound was paired with a blue slide. Both patients showed a normal physiological response (SCR) to the sound. The hippocampal patient showed conditioning without being able to verbalize the association. (This patient showed a response to the blue slide but could not state which slide was paired with the sound.) The amygdala patient did know which slide was paired with the sound but did not show an increased SCR to that slide. What this suggests is that the hippocampus is necessary for declarative memory, whereas the amygdala is necessary for emotional learning, a form of nondeclarative learning.

3. Place cells increase their rate of firing when the individual is in a specific location in the environment. These cells are found in the hippocampus, whereas other memories are stored in different cortical areas. The primary role of place cells is to assist in memory for spatial locations.

4. Long-term potentiation is the strengthening of synapses through simultaneous activation of presynaptic and postsynaptic neurons. Following long-term potentiation, postsynaptic neurons show increased dendritic spines and AMPA receptors, which help support the strengthened connection between neurons. Long-term potentiation is important for long-term memory formation. Long-term depression is the weakening of a synapse as a result of a presynaptic neuron firing when the postsynaptic neuron is not depolarized. It is believed that this is an important mechanism in learning because it prevents LTP from becoming permanent and frees synapses for new associations. LTD may be particularly important for clearing the hippocampal area of old memories so that new memories can take their place.

5. Extinction, forgetting, and reconsolidation are three such processes. Extinction involves learning that a previous association no longer exists, so that an animal can respond differently to a changing world. Forgetting is the removal of learned information, which likely frees synapses to learn more relevant information. Reconsolidation is the process of storing memories after they have been retrieved, and memories are particularly vulnerable to change during this time, as shown in the studies by Loftus and her colleagues.

6. The jury should not consider her current statement to be accurate. Because she did not recall the details until after multiple chances for reconsolidation and reconstruction of the memory, it is likely that her memory for the event has been altered.

7. In general, aging results in the hippocampus losing synapses, which probably accounts for impaired LTP. There is decreased activity in the entorhinal cortex, which provides connections between the hippocampus and other brain areas. The basal forebrain region also undergoes neuron loss; this is an important area because its cells connect to the hippocampus, amygdala, and cortex. Finally, there are deficits in frontal lobe functioning, which suggests damage there. In contrast, Alzheimer's disease involves the accumulation of Aß plaques and neurofibrillary tangles that begins in limbic areas such as the hippocampus and progresses to the neocortex, eventually impacting most of the brain. Since Alzheimer's disease progressively involves large portions of the brain, the memory deficits become much more severe than seen with typical aging.

8. One current type of drug inhibits the breakdown of acetylcholine. Another reduces sensitivity to glutamate (which is overactive in affected neurons). Other potential treatments include anti-inflammatory drugs (unsuccessful), anti-amyloid injections (unsuccessful to date), tangle-preventing drugs (successful in phase 2 trials), injecting stem cells (some improvement), and gene therapies (promising).

9. Korsakoff syndrome is a disease caused by low thiamine (B1) vitamin, usually due to chronic alcoholism. Major symptoms include anterograde amnesia, some retrograde amnesia, and more impairment in declarative memory. Reductions of mammillary bodies, thalamus, and frontal lobes are seen in patients. Behavioral problems include confabulation (making up details to forgotten declarative memories), usually due to damage to a specific location in the frontal lobe.

Post-test

1. a   2. b   3. b   4. d   5. c   6. c   7. a   8. d   9. b   10. a   11. a   12. b   13. c   14. b   15. d   16. b   17. b   18. a   19. d   20. b   21. d   22. c   23. c   24. b   25. c   26. d   27. c   28. a   29. a   30. a   31. d   32. a   33. d   34. b   35. c   36. d   37. b   38. b   39. d   40. a   41. b

13 Intelligence and Cognitive Functioning

Chapter Outline

Learning Objectives

After reading this chapter, you will be able to

1. Describe how scientists have defined intelligence

2. Critique the scientific methods for measuring intelligence

3. Identify how the structure of the nervous system relates to intelligence

4. Appraise the relative contributions of heredity and environment to intelligence

5. Assess the impact of the typical aging process on cognitive functioning

6. Compare the impacts of intellectual disability, autism, and attention-deficit/hyperactivity disorder on intelligence

The Nature of Intelligence

Summary and Guided Review

After studying this section in the text, fill in the blanks of the following summary.

_____ (1), defined as the capacity for reasoning, understanding, and benefiting from experience, is challenging to measure. Originally, the intelligence quotient (or IQ) was determined as the ratio of a child's mental and _____ (2) age, multiplied by 100. Currently, a person's IQ represents personal performance compared with that of the general population; the average IQ score is arbitrarily set at _____ (3) for both children and adults, and most scores fall near this number. Only 2% of the population score above 130 or below 70. The first intelligence test, developed by Alfred _____ (4), was used to identify French children with special needs. IQ scores are positively correlated with school grades, level of education, job performance, and income level; and negatively correlated with juvenile _____ (5). Because of the correlation between IQ and both academic success and socioeconomic status, critics argue that IQ tests are designed to reflect these forms of success. Some observers believe the _____ _____ _____ (6) test, a culture-free test, provides a better measure of "pure" intelligence. Another criticism of IQ tests is that they do not measure cognitive skills that people use in their everyday lives, or _____ (7) intelligence ("street smarts").

There is also controversy over the structure of intelligence. _____ (8) are intelligence theorists who assume that there is a unitary capability underlying intelligence, often referred to as the _____ _____ (9), or "g." This argument is supported by the fact that different abilities such as math and verbal skills are correlated. On the other hand, _____ (10) argue that mental abilities are distinct from one another; this perspective is supported by the fact that brain damage often impairs one type of skill and not others.

Short Answer and Essay Questions

Answer the following question.

1. Describe two criticisms of intelligence tests.

The Biological Origins of Intelligence

Summary and Guided Review

After studying this section in the text, fill in the blanks of the following summary.

The search for a biological origin of intelligence led some researchers to ask whether more intelligent people have bigger brains. However, the brain of the genius _____ _____ (11) was rather small and did not differ from other brains in most respects. Exceptions were that his _____ (12) lobes, which are associated with mathematical skills and visual-spatial processing, were larger and that there were increased numbers of glial cells in that lobe. Scans of brain-damaged individuals support the idea that "g" requires a(n) _____ (13) system, spanning and connecting areas in several lobes of the brain.

If we compare across species, brain size alone is not a good predictor of intelligence. Among humans, there is some evidence for a relationship between IQ and brain size, although it is small (6%). There is a gender difference in the ratio, with males' brains being somewhat _____ (14) than females' brains, although men and women do not differ in intelligence. One possible reason for the gender difference is that women's brains, which have more densely packed neurons and relatively more _____ _____ (15), are more efficient. How the brain is organized appears to be more important than how big it is.

The speed at which people process information may be an indication of general intelligence; in fact, IQ and _____ _____ (16) are correlated. An even stronger correlation exists between IQ scores and _____ _____ (17) velocity, which may lead to more efficient processing. _____ (18), which speeds neural impulses and prevents inappropriate communication between adjacent neurons, is also believed to be related to intelligence. People who are higher in IQ use less brain _____ (19); people with higher IQs show less _____ _____ (20) while playing Tetris, whereas people with mild _____ _____ (21) exhibit more brain activity than above-average individuals while performing a mental task. These results suggest that IQ is related to the _____ (22) of neural processing. One current theory, called the _____-_____ _____ (23) Theory (P-FIT), suggests that information processing takes place in four stages. First, sensory information is processed in secondary areas, then passed to parietal areas for abstraction and integration, then to the frontal lobes for problem solving and evaluation. In the final step, the _____ _____ (24) cortex selects the response and inhibits alternative responses. More intelligent individuals have been shown to have more numerous interconnections and shorter paths between steps.

Individual components of intelligence may be identified by _____ _____ (25), which involves giving people a variety of tests and then looking for correlations among clusters of related abilities. Although performance on all mental tests tends to be correlated, _____ (26), logical-mathematical, and spatial components have emerged as major components of intelligence. One brain-based explanation for these different components is that they evolved separately and consist of different _____ (27) or complex networks to support a particular function. For example, performing calculations from memory depends on activity in the left _____ (28) cortex, while estimating values involves both _____ (29) areas. Research involving human infants and nonhuman _____ (30) suggests that the brain is "wired" for numbers.

There are also many examples of complex behaviors in the animal world that most people assume are unique to humans, including their ability to make and use _____ (31). Ingenuity and "planfulness" have also been observed in chimps and in some birds, such as _____ (32). In spite of these examples, humans' brains seem to be unique in possessing specialized structures for tool use, or the ability to develop them through _____ (33).

Because intelligence is complex, identifying its genetic and environmental components has proven to be extremely difficult. Most studies have examined the correlation between brain structure characteristics determined by genetics and intelligence. One twin study found a heritability of _____% (34) for brain volume, 82% for gray matter, and 88% for white matter. Another study demonstrated a higher heritability for _____ (35) intelligence than for more specific abilities like verbal and spatial abilities. These arguments support a strong _____ (36) basis for g. Locating specific genes involved in intelligence has been frustrating due to the failure to _____ (37) promising findings. Possibilities include the _____ (38) gene, which is related to brain size, and the *PACAP* precursor gene, which is involved in _____ (39) and neural signaling. Researchers are now combining genetic data with brain morphological measurements to try to identify genes and alleles correlated with brain pathways, cortical thickness, and IQ results.

The fact that intelligence is highly heritable does not mean that it cannot be influenced by the _____ (40); rather, genes set a range of potential intelligence levels, and the environment determines where in that range intelligence will fall. Furthermore, it has been necessary to adjust IQ test norms to maintain the average at 100 as people's performance on intelligence tests has steadily _____ (41). Some observers argue that twin studies are not a fair assessment of the heritability of IQ, because parents and others may treat identical twins as being more similar based on appearance, and hence provide similar learning experiences that could result in more highly correlated IQs (higher concordance rates). However, studies show that parents' belief as to whether their twins are fraternal or identical has no influence on the twins' intellectual similarity, whereas the twins' true _____ (42) relationship does.

The reasons behind racial differences in IQ scores are hotly debated. Some researchers such as Arthur Jensen argue that IQ differences between ethnic groups are largely _____ (43), while others contend that this is not the case. For example, Scarr and colleagues failed to show any cognitive test difference among African Americans with different degrees of African _____ (44), and the American Psychological Association has concluded that there is little evidence for a genetic explanation of the racial differences.

Environmental contributions to intelligence are also difficult to identify, in part because environmental and genetic factors are _____ (45); because children share both genes and environment with their parents, it is difficult to separate their influences. Also, environmental factors are numerous and individually _____ (46). Some forms of environmental intervention have been successful in improving achievement in at-risk children. Although there are long-term educational and career benefits among children participating in the _____ _____ (47) program, the IQ gains disappear over time. The _____ (48) project seems to produce longer-lasting IQ improvement, possibly because this program starts intervention at the time of _____ (49). Children who are _____ (50) show stronger IQ correlations with their biological parents than with their adopted parents, but African American children from impoverished backgrounds adopted into middle-class homes showed IQ score increases from 90 to about _____ (51) points.

Environmental factors can increase, intelligence, but they can reduce them as well. For instance, children who had prenatal exposure to organophosphate _____ (52) had significantly lower IQs than did children without that exposure. In addition, there is a strong correlation between intelligence and _____ _____ (53); improved access to health care might explain the IQ increases seen in the _____ (54) effect.

Short Answer and Essay Questions

Answer the following questions.

2. Identify several features of brain structure and neural processing that are related to intelligence.

3. Explain why it is incorrect to assume that because intelligence is highly heritable, it is influenced very little by the environment.

4. Describe what adoption studies have revealed about the genetic and environmental contributions to intelligence.

Deficiencies and Disorders of Intelligence

Summary and Guided Review

After studying this section in the text, fill in the blanks of the following summary.

As we age, activity decreases in genes that are involved in _____- _____ _____ (55) and memory storage. Particularly affected are genes responsible for _____ (56) and GABA receptors. However, the degree of loss of cognitive functioning has been _____ (57). When older adults are given tests on material relevant to their lives, they show much less deterioration than on meaningless tasks such as memorizing lists of words. Also _____ (58) studies of the same people as they age reveal less decline than cross-sectional studies of people of differing ages. The loss also depends on the type of intelligence measured: Skills and overlearned knowledge, called _____ (59) intelligence, remain stable throughout life, but problem solving and learning new information (fluid intelligence) starts declining beyond the third decade. In normal aging there is a loss of coordination in the _____ _____ (60) network (portions of the frontal, parietal, and temporal lobes active when the brain is at rest or focused internally). This loss appears to be related to a decline in _____ _____ (61) connections between these areas in the brain. Elderly adults may compensate for less efficient processing by using additional brain areas to complete tasks, or by increasing _____ (62). Elderly individuals can regain lost skills through practice and enhancement of _____-_____ (63). Cognitive decline can be lessened by changing dietary habits, for example, by increasing _____ (64) intake. Vitamin supplements also might help performance; individuals with mild cognitive impairment slowed declines in brain atrophy and cognition by increasing their vitamin _____ (65) intake. Sex hormones may also play a role. Older women who take estrogen are at lower risk for _____ (66) disease. Many neurons contain _____ (67) receptors, and therefore this hormone may play a role in several cognitive tasks. Men receiving testosterone therapy show improvement in _____ (68) memory; additional skills are improved by dihydrotestosterone, which is converted into estrogen through the process of _____ (69).

Retardation is a term that has strong negative connotations, causing practitioners and authorities to use the term _____ _____ (70). ID covers limitations in reasoning, learning, problem solving, and adaptive behavior that is _____ (71) in origin. The *DSM*-5 considers a person to have an intellectual disability if the person's IQ is below _____ (72), he or she has impaired social participation and communication, and the impairments occurred during development. Intellectual disability can be caused by infections, birth complications, severe malnutrition, and maternal _____ (73) abuse during pregnancy. So far, more than _____ (74) genes have been convincingly linked to ID, but each one seems to have minimal effects by itself.

_____ (75) syndrome, which usually results from an extra 21st chromosome, is the most common genetic cause of intellectual disability. Individuals with this condition typically have IQs in the _____ to _____ (76) range, although some are less impaired than most. In some cases of Down syndrome, only some of the body's cells possess the extra chromosome; this condition is called _____ _____ _____ (77). The Ts65Dn mouse strain is a model for Down syndrome; these animals are similar to humans with the disorder in that their _____ (78) cells secrete less proteins that support cell survival. Another frequent genetic cause of intellectual disability is _____ _____ syndrome (79), due to a mutation of the X chromosome *FMR1* gene. This gene may be important in the pruning or elimination of excess _____ (80). A genetic disorder that interferes with myelination, _____ (81), may not lead to intellectual impairment if the affected individual avoids foods with phenylalanine, as well as the artificial sweetener (found in blue packets) _____ (82). The buildup of cerebrospinal fluid in _____ (83) may also lead to impairment, but it can be treated if caught early. However, many affected individuals have surprisingly normal IQs. One newsworthy environmental cause for ID may be carried by mosquitoes; insects carrying the _____ (84) virus can slow brain development and reduce head size (microcephaly) in children from infected mothers.

Autism spectrum disorder (ASD) is a set of neurodevelopmental disorders characterized by social deficits, communication difficulties, and _____ (85) behaviors. ASD includes the previous diagnostic criteria for autism, Asperger syndrome, pervasive developmental disorder, and childhood disintegrative disorder. There is some debate over whether the incidence of autism has actually _____ (86) over time; although the prevalence of ASD increased from 2000 to 2010, it could be due to improved detection and broader diagnostic criteria. In addition, _____% (87) of children with ASD had intellectual disabilities, and 31% had average or above average intelligence. Children with ASD usually prefer to be alone, and when interacting with other people tend to treat them as _____ (88). ASD children perform more poorly on _____ of _____ (89) tasks, compared to younger typical children and even to children with Down syndrome. Researchers have suggested that autistic individuals' difficulty empathizing and learning language through imitation involves impairments with _____ (90) neurons. There is some evidence that people with autism and Asperger syndrome have insufficient activity in the

_____ (91) stream connections that provide input to brain areas associated with imitation (inferior frontal cortex and motor cortex).

Although originally thought to be purely psychological in origin, autism is now considered a disorder of the _____ (92). However, because not all autistic individuals show the same pattern of abnormalities, there are probably several ways in which the disorder can develop. Although the brain of an autistic individual is normal or slightly reduced in size at birth, it undergoes dramatic _____ (93) during the first year, particularly in the _____ (94) and _____ (95) areas. One of the differences in the autistic brain is an alteration in brain _____ (96), with some studies highlighting reduced connections in the _____ _____ (97) and prefrontal cortex whereas other studies have shown hyperconnectivity in _____ (98) areas. These conflicting findings may occur due to differences in the times of _____ (99) of the brain regions that have been studied.

Several neurotransmitters have been implicated in autism, particularly _____ (100), because of its contribution to neural development. Children with ASD have reduced synthesis of the neurotransmitter, and treatment with reuptake inhibitors such as _____ (101) decreases repetitive and obsessive behaviors in some individuals. Additionally, high levels of _____ (102) (decreased by the antipsychotic risperidone) and glutamate have been found in autistic children. But symptoms are not just the result of too much neurotransmitter. _____ (103), known as the "sociability molecule," is found in reduced levels in many autistic children. In addition, decreases in repetitive behavior and fear were seen following treatment.

Many environmental factors have been associated with autism, including _____ (104) due to agriculture and automobile traffic. Other influences originate in the mother herself; mothers who got sick during the second trimester of pregnancy had _____ (105) the chance of bearing a child with ASD. The current obesity epidemic is also linked to autism. Mothers of children with ASD were _____% (106) more likely to be obese than mothers of intellectually average children, though mothers who supplemented their diets with _____ _____ (107) during pregnancy reduced the risk to the child by 50%. One factor that has been definitively ruled out as a cause of autism is the normal procedure of giving children _____ (108) against common childhood diseases: The original study showing a link was retracted due to unethical behavior by the authors. Despite the lack of any credible link between vaccinations and subsequent diagnosis of autism spectrum disorder, immunization rates continue to _____ (109) in several countries.

Autism has a(n) _____ (110) component, as autistic children have a much higher chance of having an autistic sibling than normal children, and the concordance rate for identical twins is 60%. When analyses consider additional abnormal symptoms found in _____ (111), the concordance rate for identical twins increases to _____% (112). The genes implicated in ASD tend to be involved in neuronal development, neurotransmitters, and migration. Genes for the receptors of the neurotransmitters _____ (113), glutamate, and oxytocin have all been linked to autism. Many of the affected genes interfere with the development of _____ (114) between cortical layers. One gene in particular, the _____ (115) gene, targets more than 2,500 other genes (some involved in neural development) and is sensitive to sex-specific hormones, which may explain some of the gender differences in ASD incidence.

Some individuals with ASD, referred to as autistic _____ (116), are extremely talented in one area, such as music, drawing, painting, computation, or memorizing, but have overall functioning that is below normal. The most likely explanation for these skills is that the individual with ASD lacks _____ (117) or integrative functions within the brain, and this gives the savant access to speedy lower levels of processing. The best-known savant was Kim Peek, who was the basis for the character in the movie *Rain Man*. There are also _____-_____ (118) individuals with ASD, such as Temple Grandin, who have normal or above normal intelligence but who still show autistic characteristics such as poorly developed theory of mind.

_____ (119) is characterized by impulsive and hyperactive behavior as well as problems with attention and learning. Three subtypes are currently recognized; combined inattention and hyperactivity-impulsivity, inattention alone, or hyperactivity-impulsivity alone. The sex ratio for this disorder is also skewed: _____ (120) are more than twice as likely to be diagnosed with attention-deficit/hyperactivity disorder. Those diagnosed with ADHD as children often continue to have problems as adults, including increased rates of criminal behavior, drug abuse, and _____ _____ (121) disorder. The link between ADHD and later drug use led to concerns that treating ADHD in children with _____ (122) drugs such as methylphenidate (Ritalin) and amphetamine was encouraging subsequent addiction to drugs like cocaine. However, there is no evidence that these drugs increase the risk of addiction; if anything, they have a(n) _____ (123) effect.

Regarding brain abnormalities in ADHD, one of the most consistent findings is that there is reduced brain volume overall and in structures involved in emotion, motivation, and reward processing such as the hippocampus, caudate nucleus, putamen, and, most important, the nucleus _____ (124). As is true of ASD, there are _____ (125) reductions in ADHD and obsessive-compulsive disorder, both between brain hemispheres and from the front to the back of the brain. Scientists think these impairments in brain connections around the amygdala are responsible for _____ (126) behavior in people with ADHD.

There is strong evidence for a genetic basis to ADHD; the concordance rate for ADHD among identical twins is much higher than among fraternal twins. Heritability averages _____% (127) across studies. One interesting finding is that a number of copy number variations (CNVs) found in ADHD are also found in individuals with _____ (128) and autism, implying that gene changes affect common brain processes and are not disease specific. Several genes have been identified as being involved in ADHD and are found in the dopamine, serotonin, and _____ (129) transmission systems.

Given that stimulant drugs used to treat ADHD also increase _____ (130) activity, it is not surprising that researchers have found _____ (131) activity in pathways for this neurotransmitter, particularly in the _____ (132) cortex and striatum. These areas are involved in impulse inhibition, movement, and reward, which could account for many ADHD symptoms. For example, people with ADHD have difficulty foregoing _____ (133) rewards for better, but delayed, rewards. Stimulant drugs are the drugs most commonly used to treat ADHD, but they do not work for everyone. Two other drugs that are used, modafinil and atomoxetine, block the _____ (134) of norepinephrine.

Environmental factors that play a role in ADHD are often parental in nature, such as maternal _____ (135) and stress during pregnancy, parental abuse of drugs, and parental mood and _____ (136) disorders. Other environmental influences include stroke, pregnancy complications, and exposure to toxins such as _____ (137), air pollution, and organophosphate pesticides.

Environmental factors may alter risk for ADHD by changing _____ (138) functioning. For example, maternal diets high in fat and sugar were associated with increased _____ (139) of the *IGF2* gene and increased ADHD symptoms in children.

Short Answer and Essay Questions

Answer the following questions.

5. Identify common causes of intellectual impairment that occur early in life (other than autism and ADHD). Describe one of them in detail in terms of what is known about cause(s), symptoms, and treatment.

6. Describe the brain anomalies (structural, developmental, and functional) associated with autism.

7. Explain why researchers believe there is a strong genetic component to autism.

8. Describe the controversy about whether there is a link between childhood vaccinations and autism.

9. Describe the evidence that points to dopamine as an important factor in ADHD. Address the issue of the role of dopamine in treatment.

10. Evaluate the contributions of both genetics and environment in the risk for ADHD.

Post-test

Use these multiple-choice questions to check your understanding of the chapter.

1. The intelligence quotient was originally based on
   a. the ratio of intellectual capacity to the population average.
   b. the ratio of mental age to chronological age.
   c. the ratio of chronological age to mental age.
   d. none of the above

2. IQ scores are correlated with which of the following?
   a. grades earned in school
   b. income
   c. job performance
   d. all of the above

3. The Raven Progressive Matrices test is designed to
   a. be culture free.
   b. measure nonverbal abilities.
   c. measure practical intelligence.
   d. a and b

4. Robert Sternberg argues that
   a. intelligence tests measure a general, underlying factor of cognitive ability that contributes to specific mental skills.
   b. intelligence tests are completely useless.
   c. intelligence is how a culture defines people's ability to succeed.
   d. tests that measure practical intelligence are better than traditional intelligence tests.

5. An intelligence theorist who proposes that there are seven different components of intelligence would BEST be described as a
   a. lumper.
   b. splitter.
   c. general factor theorist.
   d. reaction time theorist.

6. Which of the following is TRUE regarding Albert Einstein's brain?
   a. It had fewer glial cells.
   b. It was larger (heavier) than the average person's brain.
   c. It contained more neurons than the average brain.
   d. Its parietal lobes were larger than those of the average brain.

7. Studies of people with brain damage have shown that general intelligence or "g" requires
   a. a distributed network.
   b. a system involving the frontal, parietal, and temporal lobes.
   c. the ability to integrate different types of processing from several areas of the brain.
   d. all of the above

8. Which of the following statements regarding brain size is FALSE?
   a. Species with the largest brains are the most intelligent.
   b. Brain size alone accounts for only a small amount of the variability in intelligence.
   c. Men's brains are proportionately larger than women's brains.
   d. Elephants' brains are larger than humans' brains.

9. Which of the following is probably the BEST predictor of IQ score?
   a. brain size
   b. reaction time
   c. nerve conduction velocity
   d. frontal area activity

10. Which of the following statements about myelination is TRUE?
    a. People with more gray matter and less white matter tend to have higher IQs.
    b. Myelination increases from childhood to maturity.
    c. Myelination increases cross-talk between neurons.
    d. Myelination is at its peak in the elderly.

11. People with higher IQs tend to
    a. have faster nerve conduction velocity.
    b. use less energy when processing information.
    c. have a high white matter/gray matter ratio.
    d. all of the above

12. Which of the following is NOT one of the components of intelligence frequently identified by factor analysis?
    a. practical intelligence
    b. linguistic intelligence
    c. logical-mathematical intelligence
    d. spatial intelligence

13. Which of the following MOST specifically engages the parietal lobes?
    a. language functions
    b. tool use

    c. spatial ability

    d. rote arithmetic tasks, such as using times tables

14. What area(s) of the brain is (are) involved in mathematical abilities such as calculation and estimation?

    a. frontal lobe only

    b. parietal lobe only

    c. both the frontal and parietal lobes

    d. none of the above

15. Which of the following is NOT true with respect to intelligence in animals?

    a. Nonhuman primates are able to demonstrate language skills but not mathematical abilities.

    b. Chimps show evidence of intelligence by using tools to acquire food.

    c. Crows and owls show planfulness in their methods for obtaining or "luring" food.

    d. Mirror neurons are activated in monkeys when they watch someone retrieve an object with a hand or a tool.

16. The proportion of variability in intelligence due to heredity is HIGHEST in

    a. infancy.

    b. childhood.

    c. adolescence.

    d. adulthood.

17. Which of the following is TRUE with respect to the genetic basis of intelligence?

    a. The heritability of intelligence is about 70%.

    b. The *PACAP* precursor gene is a major determinant of brain size.

    c. In a twin study, estimated heritability was highest for brain volume as a structural contributor to intelligence.

    d. There are probably 50 candidate genes that have been linked to some aspect of cognitive ability.

18. IQ scoring standards have been adjusted in the past 50 years to reflect the fact that

    a. people are scoring more poorly on the tests than they have in the past.

    b. the average performance on IQ tests has risen.

    c. fewer people are intellectually impaired now.

    d. our genes are making us more intelligent.

19. Studies of identical and fraternal twins reveal that the STRONGEST correlation for IQ scores is between

    a. identical twins, but only if correctly identified by their parents as identical.

    b. fraternal twins, but only if correctly identified by their parents as fraternal.

    c. identical twins, regardless of whether their parents identified them as identical or fraternal.

    d. identical twins incorrectly identified by their parents as fraternal.

20. Scarr's study of IQ scores among African Americans revealed that

    a. there was no relationship between degree of African ancestry and IQ.

    b. those with more African ancestors had lower IQs than those with fewer African ancestors.

    c. there were no differences between African Americans and Whites.

    d. none of the above

21. Which of the following statements regarding environmental contributions to intelligence is FALSE?
    a. Environmental factors may be confounded with genetic factors.
    b. The results from the Abecedarian project suggest that the environment is not as important as genes when it comes to intelligence.
    c. Many environmental factors may contribute weakly to intelligence.
    d. Illness is an important factor in explaining worldwide differences in IQ.

22. Which of the following statements regarding Head Start is FALSE?
    a. There are long-term benefits in IQ scores.
    b. There are long-term benefits in career accomplishments.
    c. There are long-term benefits in mathematics.
    d. There are long-term benefits in educational attainment.

23. Adoption studies reveal that adopted children's IQ scores are
    a. relatively unaffected by the adoptive home.
    b. most strongly correlated with their biological parents' scores in childhood and adulthood.
    c. most strongly correlated with their adopted parents' scores in childhood and adulthood.
    d. initially more similar to their biological parents' scores but become more similar to their adopted parents' scores in adulthood.

24. Which of the following has been identified as a possible way to enhance cognitive functioning?
    a. electrical stimulation of the scalp over the prefrontal cortex
    b. using working memory by playing video games
    c. consuming flavanols
    d. all of the above

25. With respect to aging and intelligence,
    a. the declines are significant and irreversible.
    b. loss occurs, but it has been overestimated.
    c. much of the decline has been attributed to loss of glutamate.
    d. performance speed is not affected as much as verbal memory.

26. Which of the following is FALSE about the default mode network?
    a. It is involved in a person's preparedness for action.
    b. The elderly show loss of coordination in this network.
    c. The network primarily involves gray matter.
    d. It involves activity and communication between the frontal, temporal, and parietal lobes.

27. The elderly could compensate for loss of cognitive function by
    a. eating more fish.
    b. practicing skills.
    c. taking drugs that increase GABA.
    d. all of the above

28. Which of the following is TRUE concerning hormones and cognitive function in the elderly?
    a. Testosterone works better than dihydrotestosterone at improving cognitive abilities.
    b. Estrogen plays a role in increasing cognitive function in females but not males.

    c. Estrogen most likely exerts the majority of its beneficial effects in the parietal lobes of the brain.

    d. Estrogen lowers the risk of Alzheimer's disease in menopausal women.

29. What percentage of the population falls in the IQ range for intellectual impairment?
    a. 0.02%
    b. 0.2%
    c. 2%
    d. 5%

30. The leading genetic cause of intellectual impairment is
    a. prenatal exposure to cigarette smoke.
    b. prenatal exposure to alcohol.
    c. Down syndrome.
    d. hydrocephalus.

31. Down syndrome
    a. is caused by the *FMR1* gene, according to new studies.
    b. can be studied in a mouse model that has been engineered to produce more norepinephrine.
    c. may be caused by more than just the genes on the 21st chromosome.
    d. cannot be identified until the baby is born.

32. Phenylketonuria
    a. is typically diagnosed by amniocentesis.
    b. can be controlled by diet.
    c. is caused by a lack of phenylalanine.
    d. if untreated, can lead to mild mental impairment.

33. Which of the following statements regarding hydrocephalus is (are) TRUE?
    a. It is treatable.
    b. If untreated, it usually causes intellectual disability, but not in all cases.
    c. It results from a buildup of cerebrospinal fluid.
    d. all of the above

34. Autism
    a. is caused by poor parenting.
    b. has become more prevalent, increasing from 1% of the population in the 1960s and 1970s to 5% currently.
    c. is one disorder in the autism spectrum that includes Asperger syndrome.
    d. involves the least intellectual impairment in the spectrum.

35. Which of the following is NOT a common characteristic of autism?
    a. locked in a world of fantasy
    b. delayed language development
    c. repetitive behaviors
    d. limited interactions with others

36. Theory of mind
    a. is lacking in autistic individuals.
    b. may involve activity in mirror neurons.
    c. has been explained by both the "theory theory" and "simulation theory."
    d. all of the above

37. Which of the following statements regarding savants is TRUE?
    a. Their skills usually result from a great deal of concentrated practice.
    b. Their skills typically generalize to other related tasks.
    c. Their skills may involve speedy access to lower levels of cognitive processing.
    d. All savants are autistic.

38. Which of the following is NOT true of Temple Grandin, the high-functioning autistic described in the textbook?
    a. She has a PhD in animal science.
    b. She gives lectures about her condition.
    c. She had normal language development as a child, which explains her high-functioning adult state.
    d. She exhibits a poorly developed theory of mind.

39. Which of the following brain areas was NOT listed in the textbook as being implicated in autism?
    a. occipital lobe
    b. temporal lobe
    c. brain stem
    d. cerebellum

40. What characterizes early brain development in autism?
    a. an initial stage of degeneration, followed by some recovery
    b. a rapid growth in size during the first year
    c. overgrowth in parietal and occipital areas
    d. very small brains that develop to adult size by adolescence

41. Although research has been inconsistent, which of the following has/have been studied as playing a role in autism?
    a. cells in the medial occipital lobe
    b. mirror neurons
    c. functional connectivity between the caudate and basal ganglia
    d. all of the above

42. With respect to the genetic basis of autism,
    a. the fraternal twin concordance rate for autistic individuals is 92%.
    b. the identical twin concordance rate for autistic individuals is at least 60%.
    c. relatives of autistic individuals have a concordance rate of 10%.
    d. the heritability rate is probably overestimated because parents stop having children.

43. The impairment of sociability in autistic individuals has been linked to
    a. oxytocin.
    b. vasopressin.
    c. GABA.
    d. a and b

44. What is the MOST accurate statement about vaccines and autism?
    a. There is strong evidence that childhood vaccinations cause autism.
    b. There is a causal link between autism and the mercury preservative in autism, but not to the vaccines.
    c. The initial study supporting the link between the MMR vaccine and autism has been retracted due to being methodologically flawed.
    d. Because most parents of autistic individuals agree that there is no link between immunizations and autism, there has been a worldwide increase in childhood vaccinations.

45. Which of the following is NOT a symptom of ADHD?
    a. attentional problems
    b. impulsiveness
    c. lack of theory of mind
    d. hyperactivity

46. When children with ADHD grow up,
    a. they are usually normal.
    b. they are normal only if they were medicated as children.
    c. they are more likely to exhibit personality disorders.
    d. they are unlikely to have children who are subsequently diagnosed with ADHD.

47. Children who take stimulant drugs to treat ADHD
    a. are more likely to become addicted to drugs like amphetamine or cocaine.
    b. may be protected from drug abuse.
    c. are more likely to smoke marijuana, because stimulant drugs act as gateway drugs.
    d. are more likely to become addicted to alcohol but not to other drugs.

48. In people with ADHD, dopamine activity is typically
    a. low.
    b. higher than normal.
    c. normal.
    d. lower than normal when the person takes Ritalin.

49. Which of the following show(s) that the prefrontal lobes play a key role in ADHD?
    a. People with ADHD tend to be impulsive.
    b. People with ADHD prefer immediate rewards over delayed rewards.
    c. There is reduced dopamine activity in the area in people with ADHD.
    d. all of the above

50. Studies of people with ADHD have shown reduced brain volume in all of the following areas EXCEPT for the
    a. thalamus.
    b. prefrontal areas.
    c. caudate nucleus.
    d. cerebellum.

51. Which of the following drugs has NOT been used to treat ADHD?
    a. methylphenidate
    b. modafinil
    c. atomoxetine
    d. risperidone

52. Which of the following genes has been implicated in ADHD?
    a. a serotonin receptor gene
    b. a gene for the serotonin transporter
    c. a gene for the nicotinic acetylcholine receptor
    d. all of the above

53. Which of the following has NOT been considered an environmental contributor to ADHD?
    a. thimerosal
    b. lead
    c. parental drug abuse
    d. pesticides

Answers

Guided Review

1. Intelligence	38. *ASPM*
2. chronological	39. neurogenesis
3. 100	40. environment
4. Binet	41. increased
5. delinquency	42. genetic
6. Raven Progressive Matrices	43. inherited (genetic)
7. practical	44. ancestry
8. Lumpers	45. confounded
9. general factor	46. weak
10. Splitters	47. Head Start
11. Albert Einstein	48. Abecedarian
12. parietal	49. birth
13. distributed	50. adopted
14. larger	51. 106
15. gray matter	52. pesticides
16. reaction time	53. infectious disease
17. nerve conduction	54. Flynn
18. Myelin	55. long-term potentiation
19. energy	56. glutamate
20. glucose metabolism	57. overestimated
21. intellectual disabilities	58. longitudinal
22. efficiency	59. crystallized
23. Parieto-Frontal Integration	60. default mode
24. anterior cingulate	61. white matter
25. factor analysis	62. metabolism
26. linguistic	63. self-esteem
27. modules	64. fish
28. prefrontal	65. B
29. parietal	66. Alzheimer's
30. primates	67. estrogen
31. tools	68. spatial
32. crows	69. aromatization
33. experience	70. intellectual disability
34. 90	71. developmental
35. general	72. 70
36. biological	73. alcohol
37. replicate	74. 700

75. Down
76. 40 to 55
77. mosaic trisomy 21
78. glial
79. Fragile X
80. synapses
81. phenylketonuria or PKU
82. aspartame (NutraSweet or Equal)
83. hydrocephalus
84. Zika
85. repetitive
86. increased
87. 55
88. objects
89. theory of mind
90. mirror
91. dorsal
92. brain
93. growth
94. frontal/temporal
95. temporal/frontal
96. connectivity
97. corpus callosum
98. sensory
99. maturation
100. serotonin
101. Prozac
102. dopamine
103. Oxytocin
104. pollution
105. triple
106. 40
107. folic acid
108. vaccinations
109. decline
110. genetic
111. relatives
112. 92
113. GABA
114. connections
115. *RORA*
116. savants
117. executive
118. high-functioning
119. ADHD
120. Boys or Males
121. antisocial personality
122. stimulant
123. protective
124. accumbens
125. connectivity
126. impulsive
127. 76
128. schizophrenia
129. norepinephrine
130. dopamine
131. reduced
132. prefrontal
133. immediate
134. reuptake
135. smoking
136. anxiety
137. lead
138. gene
139. methylation

Short Answer and Essay Questions

1. One criticism of intelligence tests is that they are designed to measure academic and socioeconomic success and thus do not measure important things like practical intelligence. Another criticism is that people who are highly successful sometimes score in the mediocre range on these tests, suggesting that the content of the tests is too narrow. Another is that performance on most intelligence tests is too dependent on familiarity with the culture and language for which the test was designed.

2.   People with higher intelligence typically have a larger brain and a thicker cortex, and they may have more columns; functionally, they have better short-term memory, shorter reaction times, and higher nerve conduction velocity (possibly related to greater myelination). As a result, people with greater intelligence might be better at transferring short-term memory to long-term memory, and use less energy to do so. In other words, their brains are more efficient at accomplishing cognitive tasks.

3.   If a particular trait is highly heritable, the environment can still have profound influence over it. For example, people's IQ scores have been increasing steadily over the past few generations, most likely as a result of improved environment. In addition, studies have found large IQ increases following adoption into a richer environment. A better way of thinking about how genes influence intelligence is that they provide a range of possibilities, and whatever environment a person is exposed to will then determine where within that range his or her intelligence will fall.

4.   Adoption studies have shown that children's IQs are more strongly correlated with their biological parents' IQs than with their adoptive parents' IQs. However, they have also shown that disadvantaged children's IQs can be dramatically improved in an adoptive home.

5.   Conditions that cause intellectual impairment early in life are Down syndrome, phenylketonuria (PKU), hydrocephalus, and fragile X syndrome. Down syndrome is caused by an additional 21st chromosome. Individuals typically have IQs in the range of 40–55. There is currently no treatment, although research with animal models is being conducted, and some individuals with Down syndrome can function quite well with support. PKU involves an inability to metabolize the amino acid phenylalanine, which accumulates and destroys myelin, leading to profound intellectual disability. These serious effects can be prevented by limiting the amount of phenylalanine in the diet. Hydrocephalus is a condition in which cerebrospinal fluid builds up in the ventricles of the brain and compresses brain tissue against the skull, producing brain damage that leads to intellectual impairment. This condition can be treated by using a shunt to drain the fluid out of the ventricles. Fragile X syndrome is due to a mutation in the *FMR1* gene, resulting in IQs below 75. This gene may play a role in synaptic pruning during development. Males are more likely than females to have this condition.

6.   Brain changes in autism include a rapid period of growth in the first year of life, particularly in the frontal and temporal lobes, followed by some degeneration. Activity deficiencies have been reported in the mirror neuron system, but this may be due to deficits in synchronization in the default mode network. This lack of functional connectivity is correlated with deficits in social, communication, and task performance in autistic individuals. Connectivity appears reduced in the corpus callosum and prefrontal cortex and increased in sensory areas, possibly explaining why so many people with autism also have synesthesia.

7.   A genetic basis is confirmed for autism: Identical twin concordance rates are about 60%, and when the comparison groups include nonautistic relatives who show symptoms, concordance is 92% for identical twins and 10% for fraternal pairs. Genes that have been implicated in autism are involved in neurotransmitter activity, neuron development and migration, and synapse formation.

8.   A 1998 study by Wakefield and colleagues suggested that autism was linked to MMR vaccinations or mercury-based preservative. This study was later discredited as being methodologically flawed and was retracted by the journal that published it. Two reviews of all the available literature have found no credible association. However, many parents remain convinced that the link is "real" and causal, and some are refusing to immunize their children against these serious childhood diseases, despite the lack of any supporting evidence.

9. Dopamine activity is lower in people with ADHD, particularly in the striatum and pre-frontal cortex; deficits in these areas may contribute to the associated impulsive behavior and learning difficulties. The mechanism may be excess transporters, which remove dopamine from the synapse before it has time to work. Stimulant drugs used to treat ADHD, such as methylphe-nidate (Ritalin) and amphetamine, increase dopamine levels; drugs that affect norepinephrine (such as atomoxetine) are more effective for some individuals.

10. ADHD clearly "runs in families," with a heritability of 75% across studies. Several of the genes that have been implicated in ADHD are involved with dopamine receptors and transporters. Genes that affect serotonin receptors and the serotonin transporter have also been identified as playing a role in the disorder. Parental factors correlated with ADHD that may be environmental or genetic include maternal smoking and stress, parental abuse of alcohol and other drugs, and parental mood and anxiety disorders. Definite environmental contributors include brain injury, stroke, birth/pregnancy complications, and neurotoxins such as lead and pesticides.

Post-test

1. b 2. d 3. d 4. c 5. b 6. d 7. d 8. a 9. c 10. b 11. d 12. a 13. c 14. c 15. a 16. d 17. c 18. b 19. c 20. a 21. b 22. a 23. b 24. d 25. b 26. c 27. d 28. d 29. c 30. c 31. c 32. b 33. d 34. c 35. a 36. d 37. c 38. c 39. a 40. b 41. b 42. b 43. a 44. c 45. c 46. c 47. b 48. a 49. d 50. a 51. d 52. d 53. a

14 Psychological Disorders

CONCEPT CHECK

Personality Disorders

    Obsessive-Compulsive Disorder

    OCD-Related Disorders

APPLICATION | Of Hermits and Hoarders

    Borderline Personality Disorder

CONCEPT CHECK

In Perspective

Chapter Summary

Study Resources

Learning Objectives

After reading this chapter, you will be able to

1. Name and describe the various categories of psychological disorders

2. Understand the characteristics and neurological causes of schizophrenia

3. Describe how heredity and environment interact to produce psychological disorders

4. Understand the symptoms and causes of the affective disorders

5. Understand and describe the symptoms and physiological causes of the anxiety disorders

6. Explain the causes and features of the various personality disorders

Schizophrenia

Summary and Guided Review

After studying this section in the text, fill in the blanks of the following summary.

    According to recent estimates, one out of every _____ (1) people in the United States currently suffers from a diagnosable mental disorder, and 46% will suffer from at least one. Schizophrenia is a mental disorder marked by a number of perceptual, emotional, and _____ (2) deficits along with a loss of contact with reality and an inability to function in life. Schizophrenia is a(n) _____ (3), meaning that there are severe disturbances in reality, orientation, and thinking. It affects about _____% (4) of the population, regardless of gender or socioeconomic status, but the costs associated with this disorder have reached $156 billion annually in the United States.

    Schizophrenia literally means "split mind" and reflects a distortion of _____ (5) and emotion, which are not based in reality. Symptoms include hallucinations, false and unfounded beliefs called _____ (6), and paranoia. The use of diagnostic categories based on predominant symptoms, such as paranoia, is now discouraged in favor of neural or genetic mechanisms as patients often have _____ (7) symptoms and multiple diagnoses. People exhibiting sudden _____ (8) symptoms generally respond to treatment better than those who suffer from gradually developing chronic symptoms. Although in the early 20th century, schizophrenia was believed to have a(n) _____ (9) basis, the technology for determining this did not become available until the 1960s; in the meantime, social explanations held sway for decades.

Twin and adoption studies suggest a strong genetic component to schizophrenia; heritability has been estimated at _____%–_____% (10). Furthermore, being _____ (11) out of a family with a history of schizophrenia provides little or no protection from the disorder's development. Despite _____ (12) among identical twins for schizophrenia, research has demonstrated that children of "normal" twins are as likely to exhibit schizophrenia as children of the twin with schizophrenia.

Researchers have identified at least _____ (13) genes suspected of a role in producing schizophrenia, most of which are related to neurodevelopment and plasticity, immune response, neurotransmission, and hormonal activity. Although linked genes have minor individual effects, the _____-in-_____ (14) (*DISC1*) gene impacts mood and memory by altering neuron development. _____ _____ (15), such as deletions or rearrangements of the information on chromosomes, have larger effects and are largely inherited. The genetic changes associated with schizophrenia go back millennia, as psychotic-like symptoms have been documented in individuals as far as _____ (16) years ago. Such a maladaptive behavior may have persisted because of its association with an ability to cope with rapid cultural evolution and because the disorder fosters creative thinking (exhibited by many Nobel laureates such as Albert Einstein).

It is more accurate to think of genes as conferring risk for schizophrenia rather than as the single cause. According to the _____ (17) model, a person will become schizophrenic if the combined genetic and environmental causal factors reach or exceed a threshold. Environmental factors might be _____ (18), such as job difficulties or divorce, or _____ (19), such as poor nutrition, infection, or exposure to toxic substances. There is evidence that environmental influences work in part by _____ (20) means through altering gene expression.

The symptoms of schizophrenia may be classified as either _____ (21) (including hallucinations and delusions) or _____ (22) (including lack of emotion or motivation). While positive symptoms tend to have a(n) _____ (23) onset and respond well to drug treatments, negative symptoms tend to be _____ (24) and are associated with brain deficits.

Until the mid-1950s, little could be done to help individuals with schizophrenia. The first effective _____ (25) drugs were introduced at that time, although researchers did not know why these drugs worked. Later, it was discovered that _____ (26) overdoses produce psychotic behavior via increased dopamine activity, suggesting that excess dopaminergic activity was involved. This was supported by the fact that drugs that _____ (27) D_2 dopamine receptors are effective in reducing the positive symptoms of schizophrenia. Together, these observations support the _____ _____ (28) of schizophrenia. Some researchers have suggested that the extra dopamine in schizophrenia heightens attention so that internal thoughts and everyday events become highly important and hard to distinguish from each other; this idea is called the _____ _____ (29) hypothesis.

However, 30%–40% of patients with schizophrenia fail to respond to dopamine-blocking antipsychotics; some individuals, especially those with chronic symptoms, appear to have a dopamine _____ (30). A significant problem with prolonged use of dopamine blockers is that they often lead to _____ _____ (31), producing involuntary tremors and movement because of dopamine receptor death in the basal ganglia. Newer antipsychotic drugs, referred to as _____ (32) drugs, target D$_2$ receptors to a lesser degree and produce fewer _____ (33) disturbances. _____ (34) has also been implicated in schizophrenia; hallucinogenic drugs such as psilocybin and LSD trigger schizophrenic-like responses. However, PCP induces strong negative symptoms, and since the drug strongly inhibits the _____ (35) receptor, which has led to the _____ (36) theory of schizophrenia. _____ (37), which activates the NMDA receptor, alleviates both positive and negative symptoms where this neurotransmitter is implicated. The fact that three major neurotransmitters have been implicated in schizophrenia suggests that focusing on a single one might not be wise. Plus, there are additional structural and functional _____ (38) in the brain that can also cause schizophrenia symptoms.

A signature characteristic of the schizophrenic brain is a _____ (39) in both white and gray matter volume. Enlarged _____ (40), indicating loss of brain tissue, are often associated with schizophrenia and other neurological conditions. Although tissue loss has been found in at least 50 areas, deficits in the _____ (41) and temporal lobes are particularly important. Although activity is decreased in the dorsolateral prefrontal cortex, it is increased in the orbitofrontal cortex, as well as a subregion of the _____ (42). The symptoms of schizophrenia have been associated with _____ (43), a condition in which working memory and other functions of the prefrontal cortex are impaired. This may be due to a deficiency of _____ (44) in the prefrontal cortex; administering amphetamine increases blood flow into that area, improving performance on the _____ (45) Card Sorting Test. The behavioral results of hypofrontality in schizophrenics include flat affect, social withdrawal, impaired attention, and difficulty with problem solving.

Schizophrenia may also involve lack of coordination in activity between the _____ (46) and the _____ (47) cortex and across the brain in general. Since brain functioning depends on linking activity within and across cortical and subcortical areas, it requires _____ (48) firing of neurons, and it is no surprise that patients with schizophrenia have disruptions in this process. In patients with positive symptoms, these oscillations are enhanced in some areas and reduced in others. For instance, _____ (49) areas are active during auditory hallucinations, and visual areas during visual hallucinations. These areas are activated during "inner speech" in people without schizophrenia, but in those with the disorder this activation might result in misperceiving self-generated thoughts. Another effect associated with altered synchrony is the schizophrenic's inability to suppress _____ (50) sounds; this is an impairment of sensory _____ (51). Antipsychotic drugs may improve gating, but _____ (52) normalizes it; although the _____ (53) rate has declined by more than half, to 15%, in the United States in the past 50 years, it remains at 80% among people with schizophrenia, likely as a form of self-medication.

Many environmental factors, such as maternal stress and birth complications, have been associated with schizophrenia. The _____ (54) effect refers to the fact that more people who eventually develop schizophrenia are born in

January to May. The factor implicated is not the temperature but that mothers are at greater risk for prenatal exposure to infectious disease in the second trimester of pregnancy. In these cases, the culprit is probably not the disease itself but the _____ (55) reaction that is triggered. An original study of mothers in the Netherlands during World War II had some limitations, but recent evidence from a study in China confirmed that prenatal _____ (56) may also play a role. A nonmaternal factor that may contribute to schizophrenia is the father's _____ (57) at the time of conception. These factors suggest epigenetic changes are occurring.

Some brain deficits, such as failed _____ (58) of neurons in the frontal and temporal lobes, occur during pregnancy. Evidence comes from studies of children, who later exhibited schizophrenia, demonstrating deficits in physical coordination and positive affect compared to their siblings. By the time a person is diagnosed with schizophrenia, physical changes in the brain have already occurred, probably during _____ (59) and young adulthood. However, some studies of schizophrenic adolescents have found progressive loss of _____ (60) matter following diagnosis.

Short Answer and Essay Questions

Answer the following questions.

1. Evaluate the genetic and environmental factors that contribute to the development of schizophrenia. Be sure to address both twin studies of schizophrenia heritability and the vulnerability model of schizophrenia.

2. Indicate how dopamine, glutamate, and serotonin are thought to be involved in schizophrenia. Consider how antipsychotic medications affect these neurotransmitters.

3. Describe the anatomical and functional brain deficits that occur in schizophrenia. Why do some researchers believe that schizophrenia is a disorder of synchrony? When do these deficits develop?

Affective Disorders

Summary and Guided Review

After studying this section in the text, fill in the blanks of the following summary.

Major depression, which is more severe than normal _____ (61) depression, is characterized by hopelessness, loss of ability to enjoy life, slowed thought, and sleep disturbances. _____ (62) disorder involves cycling between depression and mania or agitation, which is characterized by periods of excess energy and confidence and development of grandiose schemes. Unipolar depression (major depressive disorder, or MDD) is more common in _____ (63), but bipolar disorder is equally common in men and women. Recent data indicate that _____ (64) out of 10 individuals will suffer a mood disorder in their lifetime (most likely depression).

Although there is an environmental contribution to affective disorders, concordance rates are 69% for _____ (65) twins and 13% for fraternal twins, and adoption has little effect on these rates. There is a sex difference in heritability (29% for men, 42% for women), as well as the genes implicated in depressive symptoms (seven exclusive to men, nine to women, and only three in both). As in schizophrenia, the genes implicated are many and of small effect individually, which has forced researchers to perform large-scale meta-analyses to identify candidate genes. For instance, individuals with the *5-HTTLPR* portion of the *SLC6A4* _____ _____ (66) gene have an increased vulnerability to depression, along with reduced gray matter in the _____ (67) and part of the cingulate cortex. These changes may also increase susceptibility to chronic _____ (68), which can lead to depression. The effect of this variation may be suppressed by another gene, a process called genetic _____ (69); the protective gene in this case is an allele of the gene for _____ (70), a protein that encourages neuron growth and survival. A common characteristic of depression is disruption of the _____ (71) (day-night) rhythm, and at least 11 genes involved in this rhythm have also been associated with depression. Bipolar disorder is also _____ (72), even more so than depression, with heritability estimates of at least 85%. Few genes have been confirmed, though large-scale studies have found common genes across bipolar disorder, major depressive disorder, autism spectrum disorders, and attention-deficit/hyperactivity disorder. One notable difference is that three _____ (73) found in circadian rhythm genes are not found in those other disorders.

Early drugs for depression were discovered accidentally. For instance, iproniazid was a drug developed to treat _____ (74), but it also elevated mood and had a strong antidepressive effect. This drug's ability to raise the levels of the neurotransmitters norepinephrine and _____ (75) led to the _____ (76) hypothesis of depression. Some antidepressant drugs, such as the tricyclic and atypical antidepressants, act by blocking _____ (77) at the synapse, while others (such as monoamine oxidase inhibitors, or MAOIs) block the enzymatic inactivation of many neurotransmitters in the terminals. Atypical antidepressants are more targeted in their actions; Prozac increases _____ (78) levels, improving mood, activity level, daily rhythms, eating, sex drive, and cognition, whereas Cymbalta increases both serotonin and _____ (79) levels. A non-nicotine component of tobacco smoke serves as an MAOI, which may explain why so many depressed people smoke and have difficulty quitting. The drug _____ (80), which blocks NMDA glutamate receptors, shows some promise as a temporary treatment for depressive symptoms that fail to be alleviated with standard drug treatments. A nondrug treatment that is as effective as drug therapy is _____-_____ (81) therapy (CBT); in patients receiving CBT, there was an almost twofold improvement in depression scores.

Electroconvulsive therapy (ECT) is sometimes used to treat depression in extreme cases of nonresponsiveness to traditional therapy or in those who exhibit _____ (82) behaviors. This requires applying an electrical current to the brain to produce a brief _____ (83) and is performed under anesthesia and muscle relaxers. It is safer and more effective than many drug treatments, its effects are experienced more quickly, and _____ (84) improvements can even exceed pre-depression levels. The one disadvantage of ECT is that it often conveys short-term benefits, so its use is often combined with drug treatment over the longer term. ECT is effective with depression, mania, and schizophrenia, suggesting that ECT has complex effects in the brain. Two known effects are increasing the _____ (85) of postsynaptic serotonin receptors, while decreasing it on autoreceptors of norepinephrine and dopamine neurons. ECT also seems to _____ (86) neural firing throughout the brain.

ECT and antidepressant drugs may also relieve depression by enhancing _____ (87) in the hippocampus. These new neurons then migrate to their new locations and show more _____ (88) than the existing one, but ECT may increase plasticity independently of neurogenesis. The time required for the new neurons to migrate and assume functions coincides with the delay in symptom improvement that occurs with most antidepressant drugs.

People with depression often suffer from _____ (89) rhythm disturbances, including feeling sleepy early in the evening, waking early in the morning, or spending more time in _____ (90) sleep. Readjusting one's circadian rhythm by altering sleep habits may bring relief, as may reducing REM sleep. In many depressed individuals, sleep _____ (91) can temporarily alleviate symptoms, and most antidepressant drugs also reduce the amount of REM sleep. People with _____ _____ _____ (92), or SAD, experience depression either in the summer or winter and improve or experience hypomania in the other season. This disorder accounts for 10% of all affective disorders and is much more common in _____ (93). Depression in SAD is usually characterized by excess sleepiness, increased appetite and _____ (94) intake, and weight gain. Winter depression is associated with a reduced amount of natural _____ (95); moving to or visiting a more tropical region (even for a few days) often brings some relief. Heat is associated with _____ (96) depression; finding ways to stay cool seems to relieve this form of depression. Winter depression is often treated with _____ (97), which involves exposure to high-intensity light for a few hours each day. The light exposure must mimic bright sunlight, and it seems to work by _____ (98) the circadian rhythm. In addition, people suffering from winter depression may self-medicate by eating more carbohydrates, which increases brain _____ (99) levels.

People with _____ (100) disorder exhibit a great deal of variability in their moods. Stress often triggers the transition from depressive to _____ (101) phases, although over time the switch tends to occur more spontaneously. Bipolar disorder is most often treated with _____ (102), which stabilizes both manic and depressive episodes; it is believed that this is accomplished through normalization of several neurotransmitter and receptor systems. However, one specific effect of lithium, and an alternative drug valproate, is the inhibition of _____ (103), a family of intracellular messengers that regulate neural excitability.

Structural abnormalities in affective disorders include larger _____ (104), which is indicative of decreased tissue volume. Frontal areas show decreases in size, as does the hippocampus, but the _____ (105) is actually larger. Gray matter is reduced in the cingulate cortex, the prefrontal cortex, the basal forebrain, and the _____ (106) cortex, an area associated with emotional regulation. Depression is associated with an overall reduction in brain activity, but increased activity is seen in the _____ _____ (107) cortex, which may indicate the state of depression. Mania is also characterized by increased brain activity; the _____ (108) prefrontal cortex may control cycling and could be referred to as a "bipolar switch" that cannot be turned off during emotionally neutral activities. There is also evidence that both depressed and bipolar patients have anomalies in functional brain _____ (109), which return to more normal levels as an individual's symptoms improve.

People with affective disorders, particularly those with bipolar disorder, are at greater risk for suicide than others in the population. According to the _____-_____ (110) model, the individual has a genetic predisposition for suicide, and the stress of a psychiatric disorder may be the environmental "trigger" for suicide. Suicide, even among nondepressed individuals, is associated with low levels of the _____ (111) metabolite 5-HIAA. Low levels of 5-HIAA are linked to suicidal behavior, particularly in _____ (112) suicide attempters. Recently, prescriptions for _____ (113) have decreased among teens over concerns about the drugs' link to suicide; this drop in the prescription rate was followed by an increase in suicide rate among depressed teens in the United States and the Netherlands.

Short Answer and Essay Questions

Answer the following questions.

4. Contrast the mechanisms of monoamine oxidase inhibitors, tricyclic antidepressants, and atypical (second-generation) antidepressants.

5. Describe the role of serotonin in major depressive disorder (MDD) and identify how this relates to the attempts of people with MDD to self-medicate.

6. Describe the similarities and differences between unipolar depression (MDD) and bipolar disorder in terms of symptoms, genetic basis, and treatment.

7. Identify the ways that brain stimulation can be used to treat depression. How might these treatments exert their therapeutic effects on the brain?

Anxiety, Trauma, and Stress-Related Disorders

Summary and Guided Review

After studying this section in the text, fill in the blanks of the following summary.

Anxiety disorders include generalized anxiety disorder, panic disorder, and _____ (114). Whereas _____ (115) is an adaptive response to real objects or events in the environment, anxiety involves the anticipation of stressful events and inappropriate reactions to objects and events. Anxiety disorders may be treated with benzodiazepines, which increase sensitivity to _____ (116), though they have a high addiction potential. Reduced _____ (117) activity is also implicated in anxiety disorders, and as a result _____ (118) such as selective serotonin reuptake inhibitors (SSRIs) are now the treatment of choice for anxiety disorders.

Posttraumatic stress disorder, or PTSD, is characterized by recurrent thoughts or images of a traumatic event, called _____ (119). Individuals also demonstrate lack of concentration, and overreactivity to environmental stimuli. PTSD is observed in individuals exposed to combat and other traumatic experiences, and it is four times more likely to occur in _____ (120) when they are exposed to trauma. PTSD is not easy to treat with traditional approaches; one alternative is _____ (121) therapy, which allows confrontation of the anxiety-provoking stimuli under safe conditions. Another therapeutic technique that capitalizes on reconsolidation is called _____ _____ (122). Psychotherapy used in combination with _____ (123) drugs has also demonstrated reduced PTSD symptoms in 66% of patients in one study.

Anxiety and related disorders share a common set of brain anomalies: The _____ (124) and the anterior cingulate are hyperactive in general anxiety, phobia, and panic disorders, whereas the _____ (125) cortex is overly responsive in phobias and PTSD. In addition, the _____ (126) decreases its activity in PTSD patients, which could explain memory problems associated with the disorder. The key to whether a traumatic event will be followed by PTSD does not appear to be related to the severity of the event or the emotional state of the individual. Rather, it seems to be the person's _____ (127) to PTSD, due to decreases in _____ (128) matter in the orbitofrontal cortex, hippocampus, and anterior cingulate cortex.

Researchers are now identifying four faulty networks that contribute to anxiety disorders. Together, the _____ _____ (129) network and the salience network prompt people with anxiety disorders to attend too greatly to stimuli and respond more than is needed while the _____ (130) network and the _____ _____ (131) network show reduced activity that results in diminished emotional regulation and executive control.

Many people with anxiety disorders have other psychiatric problems, especially _____ (132) disorders. The genetic bases for anxiety disorders include mechanisms that influence the activity of the neurotransmitter _____ (133), but other substances such as adenosine and cholecystokinin are also involved.

Short Answer and Essay Questions

Answer the following question.

8. Explain why some people who are exposed to traumatic events develop PTSD while others do not.

Personality Disorders

Summary and Guided Review

After studying this section in the text, fill in the blanks of the following summary.

_____-_____ (134) disorder is marked by recurring thoughts (obsessions) and resulting compulsive actions over which the person claims to have no control. These behaviors are often repetitive and _____ (135), such as checking locks or appliances multiple times, or engaging in unnecessary routines. OCD runs in families: About a fourth of OCD patients have a family member with the same condition.

OCD is associated with increased activity in the _____ (136) cortex and the caudate nuclei, which decreases following both successful drug and behavior therapy. OCD occurs with a number of diseases that damage the _____ _____ (137), which is involved in impulse control. Millionaire Howard Hughes displayed OCD later in his life, after a series of airplane and automobile _____ (138), and included a crippling obsession with avoiding germs. Serotonin activity is _____ (139) in OCD, and SSRI drugs reduce symptoms in some individuals, apparently through compensatory decreases in sensitivity of receptors. Other effective drug treatments include antipsychotics and antiglutamate drugs. One controversial psychosurgical procedure is to remove the _____ _____ (140) cortex, though deep brain stimulation to the same area has had equal efficacy.

OCD is related to _____ _____ _____ (141), a disorder in which animals overgroom themselves; this can result in loss of fur, hair, and feathers, and can increase the risk of skin infections. The human version of this condition involves nail biting and obsessive _____

_____ (142), or trichotillomania. A compulsive collecting behavior found among many people with OCD (but that can occur on its own) is _____ (143); this disorder can result in injury, unsanitary living conditions, and even death to individuals trapped in and by their own belongings. Apparently this disorder is characterized by high activity levels in areas of the brain that evaluate behavior and a sense of _____ (144); throwing out anything, even garbage, would seem like throwing out parts of the individual. OCD is also related to _____ _____ (145), which is characterized by recurring _____ (146), which are sudden, rapid, nonrhythmic facial expressions, body movements, and noises. Other symptoms include mirroring facial expressions and gestures, though the popularly reported tendency to blurt out profanity and insults is relatively rare. The disorder, which affects approximately 0.3% of the U.S. population, typically emerges in _____ (147) and becomes more pronounced over time; _____ (148) are three times more likely to have this disorder than the other sex. The heritability for Tourette syndrome is high, with a concordance rate of 53% for identical twins, suggesting a strong _____ (149) basis. Tourette syndrome involves increased activity in the _____ _____ (150), and although the _____ (151) blocker haloperidol is the treatment of choice, newer drugs with fewer side effects are increasingly being used. One report suggests the naturally high levels of neurotransmitter overstimulate the _____ _____ (152) portion of the basal ganglia in Tourette patients.

A poor self-image, impulsivity, and erratic interpersonal relationships are seen in individuals with _____ _____ (153) disorder. Although only 0.5%–5.9% of the population has this disorder, the risk is partially genetic with a heritability of approximately _____% (154). Some of the genes linked to this disorder impact functioning of the neurotransmitters serotonin and _____ (155). The "warrior gene" _____ (156) is also associated with risk for borderline personality disorder, but environmental exposures determine which genetically predisposed individuals develop this disorder.

Short Answer and Essay Questions

Answer the following questions.

9. Describe the symptoms and brain changes that occur in OCD. Indicate how the brain changes are addressed in typical OCD treatment.

10. Describe the other disorders that are related to OCD, including why these disorders are believed to be related.

11. Describe the symptoms and neurological causes of borderline personality disorder. What could be a potentially effective treatment?

Post-test

Use these multiple-choice questions to check your understanding of the chapter.

1. How many people in the United States are estimated to be suffering from a diagnosable mental illness?
   a. 1 out of every 3 people
   b. 1 out of every 4 people

   c. 1 out of every 5 people

   d. 1 out of every 10 people

2. Which of the following is TRUE about the 5th edition of the *Diagnostic and Statistical Manual of Mental Disorders?*

   a. Bipolar disorder is no longer characterized as a mood disorder.

   b. Bipolar disorder is now considered a form of depression.

   c. Obsessive-compulsive disorder is now considered a form of depression.

   d. Schizophrenia is no longer considered to have a biological basis.

3. Schizophrenia is typically characterized by all of the following EXCEPT

   a. loss of contact with reality.

   b. perceptual, emotional, and intellectual deficits.

   c. periods of intense excitement.

   d. an inability to function in life.

4. If an individual has severe disturbances of reality, orientation, and thinking, he or she is suffering from a(n)

   a. psychosis.

   b. tic.

   c. OCD.

   d. affective disorder.

5. Schizophrenics with _____ symptoms are MORE likely to recover.

   a. chronic

   b. negative

   c. violent

   d. acute

6. In the 1940s, emphasis shifted from biological to _____ causes of schizophrenia.

   a. genetic

   b. emotional

   c. hormonal

   d. social

7. When spectrum disorders are NOT considered, the concordance rate for schizophrenia among identical twins is

   a. 48%.

   b. 17%.

   c. 89%.

   d. 28%.

8. Jerry and Jason are identical twins. Jerry has schizophrenia, but Jason does not. Which of the following statements is correct?

   a. Jerry's children are more likely to develop schizophrenia than Jason's children.

   b. Jason's children are more likely to develop schizophrenia than Jerry's children.

   c. Jerry and Jason's children are equally likely to develop schizophrenia.

   d. Jerry and Jason's children are no more likely to develop schizophrenia than other members of the population.

9. Schizophrenia is a very old disorder, with symptoms having been documented 4,000 years ago and some genes developing over 100,000 years ago. What is one hypothesis for why the genes have persisted despite their negative effects?

   a. They are found alongside highly beneficial genes and therefore are hitchhiking on them.

   b. They are the result of rapid mutation, so that when one is eliminated through evolution, another one appears to take its place.

    c. They may help individuals cope with a rapidly developing social culture.

    d. They encode vital proteins and become damaging only when mutated.

10. Which of the following genes have been implicated in schizophrenia, according to a large database analysis?

    a. genes involved in hormonal activity

    b. genes that affect the immune response

    c. genes that play a role in neural development and plasticity

    d. all of the above

11. Schizophrenia research indicates that

    a. genes are more important than the environment.

    b. the environment is more important than genes.

    c. most of the implicated genes protect the individual from environmental causes of schizophrenia.

    d. environmental factors work in part by epigenetic means.

12. A person with genes linked to schizophrenia might be normal until an environmental challenge occurs (such as a death, loss of a job, or infection), pushing the person over a threshold that triggers schizophrenic symptoms. This idea is called the

    a. epistasis model.

    b. traumatic model.

    c. depressive model.

    d. vulnerability model.

13. Which of the following symptoms is MOST likely to respond to treatment with antipsychotic medication?

    a. hallucinations

    b. impaired attention

    c. poverty of speech

    d. lack of affect

14. The first effective antipsychotic drugs were

    a. dopamine antagonists.

    b. dopamine agonists.

    c. serotonin antagonists.

    d. serotonin agonists.

15. Which of the following statements does NOT support the dopamine hypothesis of schizophrenia?

    a. Amphetamines can produce a psychosis that resembles schizophrenia.

    b. Schizophrenia can be treated by drugs that block NMDA receptors.

    c. Effective drugs block the D_2 type of receptors.

    d. Schizophrenics have higher dopamine activity in the striatum.

16. Tardive dyskinesia results from

    a. the blocking of serotonin receptors in the prefrontal cortex.

    b. enhancing dopamine release throughout the brain.

    c. compensatory sensitivity of dopamine receptors in the basal ganglia.

    d. activating NMDA glutamate receptors.

17. Enlarged ventricles are associated with

    a. schizophrenia.

    b. Alzheimer's disease.

    c. Huntington's chorea.

    d. all of the above

18. Hypofrontality is a decrease in dorsolateral prefrontal activity caused by _____ deficiency, which impairs performance in the _____ task.

    a. dopamine; Wisconsin Card Sorting

    b. serotonin; delayed match-to-sample

    c. norepinephrine; knee reflex

    d. glutamate; anger avoidance

19. One of the key functions disrupted in schizophrenia is

    a. synchrony between the prefrontal lobes and the hippocampus.

    b. coordination of activity between auditory and visual areas.

    c. oscillation synchrony at low frequencies.

    d. none of the above

20. Auditory gating, the filtering out of environmental noise, is normalized in schizophrenics by which activity?

    a. drinking

    b. smoking

    c. breathing the gas from whipped cream containers

    d. laughing loudly

21. All of the following are linked to brain and transmitter anomalies associated with schizophrenia EXCEPT

    a. prenatal exposure to influenza (flu).

    b. maternal stress during pregnancy.

    c. prenatal starvation of the mother.

    d. prenatal exposure to alcohol.

22. Which of the following statements regarding the development of schizophrenia is TRUE?

    a. Gray matter deficits are a result of lack of pruning, caused by glutamate excess.

    b. Cortical neurons fail to migrate to the appropriate locations in the second trimester of pregnancy.

    c. Ventricle enlargement is evident at birth.

    d. Brain damage associated with schizophrenia does not begin until after 40.

23. Edna had to put her cat Fluffy down due to kidney failure, and as a result she felt very sad and depressed. Although her depression felt severe, after a few days she remembered happier times with Fluffy, and the dark cloud eventually went away. What form of depression did she suffer from during that low time?

    a. major depression

    b. bipolar disorder

    c. monoamine disorder

    d. none of the above

24. Women are MORE likely than men to suffer from

    a. unipolar depression.

    b. bipolar disorder.

    c. both unipolar depression and bipolar disorder.

    d. bipolar depression and schizophrenia.

25. The concordance rate for depression among identical twins raised apart
    a. is much lower than for those raised together.
    b. is about the same as for fraternal twins raised together.
    c. is about the same as for those raised together.
    d. none of the above

26. If you have tested positive for the *5-HTTLPR* portion of the *SLC6A4* serotonin transporter gene, what substance created by the *VAL66MET* allele can protect you against its negative effects?
    a. glutamate
    b. L-dopamine (L-dopa)
    c. Prozac
    d. brain-derived neurotrophic factor

27. Which antidepressants appear to support the monoamine hypothesis for depression in their impacts on depressive symptoms?
    a. MAOIs
    b. tricyclics
    c. NDRIs
    d. all of the above

28. Prozac (fluoxetine), because of its effects on a single neurotransmitter, is a
    a. monoamine oxidase inhibitor.
    b. tricyclic antidepressant.
    c. first-generation antidepressant.
    d. selective serotonin reuptake inhibitor.

29. Reduced norepinephrine is associated with
    a. sleep.
    b. lack of motivation.
    c. body temperature dysregulation.
    d. sexual activity.

30. A treatment that produces improvement in treatment-resistant depression in less than two hours of administration is
    a. glycine.
    b. nicotine.
    c. phototherapy.
    d. ketamine.

31. Which of the following is NOT true of ECT?
    a. It typically involves profound memory loss.
    b. It must result in a brain seizure in order to be effective.
    c. It must be repeated multiple times.
    d. Its therapeutic effects are equal or better than those of antidepressant drugs.

32. Which of the following brain change(s) is(are) associated with ECT?
    a. increased sensitivity to serotonin
    b. decreased sensitivity in norepinephrine autoreceptors
    c. widespread synchrony of neural firing
    d. all of the above

33. All of the following are existing or potential treatments for unipolar depression EXCEPT
    a. cognitive-behavioral therapy.
    b. lithium.
    c. smoking cigarettes.
    d. SNRIs.

34. What mechanism(s) may be responsible for the effectiveness of antidepressant treatments?
    a. neurogenesis
    b. migration of new cells in the hippocampus
    c. greater plasticity in new cells
    d. all of the above

35. Unipolar depression is associated with
    a. early-onset REM sleep.
    b. REM sleep deficit.
    c. a heightened sense of arousal in the evenings.
    d. late REM onset.

36. Which of the following statements regarding SAD is TRUE?
    a. It is more likely to improve if a person moves away from the equator.
    b. It affects people only in the winter.
    c. It is more common in men.
    d. It can be associated with hypomanic periods during the "good" season.

37. Regarding the role of light in SAD,
    a. the length of exposure to light is more important than the amount or intensity of light.
    b. the amount of light is more important than the length of exposure to light.
    c. phototherapy works only if it is used early in the morning.
    d. phototherapy is more effective than drug therapy because it lowers serotonin levels.

38. People with SAD sometimes self-medicate by
    a. eating a lot of carbohydrates.
    b. smoking.
    c. limiting their intake of junk food.
    d. all of the above

39. All of the following are true about bipolar disorder EXCEPT
    a. lithium is the medication of choice.
    b. the manic phase usually lasts longer than the depressive phase.
    c. stress is a common trigger for cycling between depression and mania.
    d. effective drug treatments share the effect of inhibiting the PKC family of enzymes.

40. Which of the following brain areas shows heightened activity during depressive episodes?
    a. caudate nucleus and inferotemporal cortex
    b. dorsolateral prefrontal cortex and anterior cingulate cortex
    c. subgenual prefrontal cortex and hippocampus
    d. ventral prefrontal cortex and amygdala

41. Which of the following brain areas has been referred to as the bipolar "switch"?
    a. hippocampus
    b. subgenual prefrontal cortex
    c. amygdala
    d. ventral prefrontal cortex

42. Which of the following groups is MOST at risk for suicide?
    a. people with unipolar depression
    b. people with bipolar disorder
    c. people with substance abuse
    d. people with schizophrenia

43. Trevor becomes anxious whenever he is near water, so he avoids going to lakes, rivers, and other large bodies of water. What type of anxiety disorder does he MOST likely have?
    a. generalized anxiety disorder
    b. phobia
    c. panic disorder
    d. OCD

44. Which of the following relieve(s) anxiety by enhancing GABA activity?
    a. atypical antidepressants
    b. neuroleptic drugs
    c. lithium
    d. benzodiazepines

45. Which of the following is NOT true about PTSD?
    a. It is characterized by flashbacks and nightmares.
    b. Men are more vulnerable than women.
    c. It involves the *VAL66MET* allele.
    d. It has been linked to changes in the hippocampus that might be caused by childhood abuse.

46. Which of the following treatments is NOT particularly effective with PTSD?
    a. SSRIs
    b. exposure therapy
    c. therapy involving psychedelics
    d. fear erasure

47. Howard Hughes suffered from
    a. generalized anxiety disorder.
    b. phobia.
    c. panic disorder.
    d. OCD.

48. Ryan was diagnosed with OCD when he was 21. He feels like every surface is contaminated, so when he touches something, he must immediately wash his hands with hot water and soap from a fresh pack to get the "germs" off. In this example, handwashing is the
    a. obsession.
    b. compulsion.
    c. disorder.
    d. MacGuffin.

49. Which of the following brain changes is (are) associated with OCD?
    a. increased activity in the orbitofrontal cortex
    b. a decrease in white matter in the circuit connecting the cingulate gyrus with other brain areas
    c. increased activity in the caudate nucleus
    d. all of the above

50. Which drug is MOST likely to be used in treating OCD and related disorders such as hair pulling and nail biting?
    a. serotonin reuptake inhibitors
    b. benzodiazepines
    c. haloperidol
    d. monoamine oxidase inhibitors

51. Tourette syndrome probably results from increased _____ activity in the _____.
    a. dopamine; prefrontal cortex
    b. serotonin; prefrontal cortex
    c. serotonin; basal ganglia
    d. dopamine; basal ganglia

52. Which of the following neurotransmitter systems appears to be dysfunctional in borderline personality disorder?
    a. glutamate
    b. GABA
    c. dopamine
    d. acetylcholine

53. Which of the following statements MOST accurately reflects the risk factors for developing borderline personality disorder?
    a. Anyone with the *MAOA* gene will develop borderline personality disorder.
    b. Epigenetic factors determine which predisposed people develop borderline personality disorder.
    c. Borderline personality disorder risk is determined mostly by childhood diet.
    d. Borderline personality disorder heritability is 90%.

Answers

Guided Review

1. four
2. intellectual
3. psychosis
4. 1
5. thought
6. delusions
7. overlapping
8. acute
9. physical/biological
10. 60–90
11. adopted
12. discordance
13. 108
14. disrupted-in-schizophrenia 1
15. Copy number variations (CNVs)
16. 4,000
17. vulnerability
18. external
19. internal
20. epigenetic
21. positive
22. negative
23. acute
24. chronic
25. antipsychotic
26. amphetamine
27. block
28. dopamine hypothesis
29. aberrant salience
30. deficiency
31. tardive dyskinesia
32. atypical/second-generation
33. motor/movement
34. Serotonin
35. NMDA
36. glutamate
37. Glycine
38. anomalies
39. decrease
40. ventricles
41. frontal
42. hippocampus
43. hypofrontality
44. dopamine
45. Wisconsin
46. hippocampus
47. prefrontal
48. synchronized
49. language
50. environmental
51. gating
52. nicotine
53. smoking
54. winter birth
55. immune
56. starvation
57. age
58. migration
59. adolescence
60. gray
61. reactive
62. Bipolar
63. women
64. 3
65. identical
66. serotonin transporter
67. amygdala
68. stress
69. epistasis
70. BDNF (brain-derived neurotrophic factor)
71. circadian
72. heritable
73. mutations
74. tuberculosis

75. serotonin
76. monoamine
77. reuptake
78. serotonin
79. norepinephrine
80. ketamine
81. cognitive-behavioral
82. suicidal
83. seizure
84. cognitive
85. sensitivity
86. synchronize
87. neurogenesis
88. plasticity
89. circadian/biological
90. REM (rapid eye movement)
91. deprivation
92. seasonal affective disorder
93. women
94. carbohydrate
95. light
96. summer
97. phototherapy
98. resetting
99. serotonin
100. bipolar
101. manic
102. lithium
103. PKC (protein kinase C)
104. ventricles
105. amygdala
106. orbitofrontal
107. ventral prefrontal
108. subgenual
109. connectivity
110. stress-diathesis
111. serotonin
112. impulsive
113. SSRIs
114. phobias
115. fear

116. GABA
117. serotonin
118. antidepressants
119. flashbacks
120. women
121. exposure
122. fear erasure
123. psychedelic
124. amygdala
125. insular
126. hippocampus
127. vulnerability
128. gray
129. ventral attention
130. frontoparietal
131. default mode
132. mood
133. serotonin
134. Obsessive-compulsive
135. ritualistic
136. orbitofrontal
137. basal ganglia
138. accidents/crashes
139. high
140. anterior cingulate
141. acral lick syndrome
142. hair pulling
143. hoarding
144. self
145. Tourette syndrome
146. tics
147. childhood
148. men
149. genetic or heritable
150. basal ganglia
151. dopamine
152. caudate nuclei
153. borderline personality
154. 40
155. dopamine
156. *MAOA*

Short Answer and Essay Questions

1. Because the children of identical twins with schizophrenia were equally likely to develop the disorder as the children of identical twins whose siblings had schizophrenia, genes are clearly involved in the disorder. It is not something one gets exclusively from the environment; otherwise, the children of the "normal" twin would have a much lower rate of schizophrenia than the offspring of the affected twin. At the same time, because the normal twin possesses the same genes as the schizophrenic twin, the differences in environmental factors between the twins must account for the fact that one of them is more affected than the other. The vulnerability model suggests that schizophrenia develops as a result of the combined influence of genetic and environmental factors that reach or exceed some threshold. According to this model, someone with a low genetic predisposition may become schizophrenic if environmental factors, such as stressors, are strong enough to trigger the disorder. It also explains that someone with a high degree of genetic predisposition may not develop the disorder if he or she is exposed to low levels of environmental challenges.

2. Drugs that block D_2 receptors are effective in treating some cases of schizophrenia. However, atypical antipsychotics, which increase glutamate levels but block D_2 receptors less, are more effective (that is, they work in more cases). Glycine, which increases glutamate release, also produces better results when paired with conventional antipsychotics than these drugs alone. Glutamate increases have been linked to an improvement in negative symptoms. Some atypical antipsychotics also block serotonin receptors. It is likely that these three neurotransmitter systems interact to produce schizophrenia.

3. Anatomical deficits include reductions in brain tissue, particularly in frontal and temporal areas, which may lead to enlarged ventricles. In addition, neurons in the frontal and temporal lobes (including the hippocampus) are disordered and mislocated, indicating errors in migration. Functional deficits include increased dopamine and serotonin activity and decreased glutamate activity; hypofrontality (which apparently contributes to negative symptoms); and disordered connections between prefrontal areas and the hippocampus and between frontal and sensory areas. Some researchers believe schizophrenia is a disorder of synchrony in part because the disordered connections result in lack of synchrony among areas, which is associated with gating problems; in addition, excessive synchrony in sensory areas is associated with hallucinations.

4. Monoamine oxidase inhibitors work by preventing the breakdown of monoamines in the synapse. Tricyclics prevent reuptake of the monoamines. Second-generation antidepressants affect one specific neurotransmitter, rather than all of the monoamines; for example, fluoxetine (Prozac) prevents the reuptake of serotonin.

5. The serotonin transporter gene *SLC6A4* has been correlated with both depression and gray matter reductions in the amygdala, which some scientists think reflects a heightened susceptibility to stress. Drugs that increase serotonin can be effective in treating depression and serotonin is known to play a role in the behaviors linked with depression (sexual behavior, sleep, etc.). Many depressed people smoke, and an ingredient in tobacco smoke acts as a MAOI.

6. Unipolar depression and bipolar disorder share the symptom of severe depression, but in bipolar disorder the depression alternates with mania. Depression is more common in women than men, whereas there is no sex difference for bipolar disorder. Both disorders have a genetic basis, but the heritability for bipolar disorder is about 85%, compared to 37% for unipolar depression. Although it is well accepted that unipolar depression involves some imbalance in the monoamine transmitter, the biological basis of bipolar disorder is less clear. Unipolar depression is typically treated with drugs that increase serotonin and/or norepinephrine. Bipolar disorder has traditionally been treated with lithium, but newer drugs exist (valproate) or are being tested

for effectiveness (PKC inhibitors). Tissue loss is characteristic of depression (with the exception of the amygdala, which is larger), along with reduced brain activity; activity is also decreased during bipolar depression but increases during mania. Activity in the ventral prefrontal area comes and goes with depression, and the area may be a "depression switch"; the subgenual prefrontal cortex is active during mania and appears to be a "bipolar switch."

7. ECT causes seizure activity in the brain, which appears to facilitate synchronous firing throughout the brain that may help with depression. ECT and drugs used to treat affective disorders may exert their effects on correcting imbalances in transmitters, such as increasing sensitivity to serotonin. They may also affect neurogenesis in the hippocampus and plasticity in the brain.

8. PTSD is characterized by flashbacks, nightmares, lack of concentration, and overreactivity to environmental stimuli. The reason some people develop PTSD while others do not has to do with vulnerability, which seems to be linked to reduced hippocampal volume, genetic factors, and childhood abuse.

9. The symptoms of OCD are primarily obsessions (recurring thoughts) and compulsions (repetitive and ritualistic acts). Brain changes in OCD occur in a circuit involving the cingulate gyrus's connections to the basal ganglia, thalamus, and cortex. OCD also involves excess serotonin. Treatments include SSRIs, antipsychotics, glutamate blockers, surgical disconnection of the orbitofrontal cortex from the anterior cingulate cortex, and deep brain stimulation.

10. OCD-like behaviors include acral lick syndrome in animals, hair-pulling or trichotillomania in humans, hoarding, and Tourette syndrome. These conditions are similar in that the behaviors exhibited are so compulsive. In Tourette syndrome, a person can control the behavior, but only for a while. Tourette syndrome, OCD, and trichotillomania co-occur in families, and OCD and Tourette syndrome both involve increased activity in the basal ganglia. Serotonin reuptake inhibitors are used to treat OCD and trichotillomania, but not Tourette syndrome. Hoarding can be seen in patients with OCD but is considered a separate disorder that involves the anterior cingulate cortex.

11. Borderline personality disorder (BPD) is characterized by unstable relationships with others, a poor self-image, and impulsive behaviors. An individual will have strong feelings of attachments and love that alternate with a fear of abandonment and distrust. Evidence of impulsivity can be seen in compulsive gambling and other risky behaviors like reckless driving and daredevil acts. There also is increased risk of suicidality and drug overdose. Neurological causes include problems in serotonin transporters (5HHTLPR), dopamine transporters (DAT1), neurotransmitter-creating enzymes (tyrosine hydroxylase), and neuronal survival chemicals (brain-derived neurotrophic factor). In addition, genes linked to aggression (like *MAOA*) are also linked to BPD. Treatment options could include one or more of the following: SSRIs, dopamine agonists, depressants, and potentially antipsychotics. Behavioral therapy is likely more useful (such as cognitive-behavioral therapy, as discussed in the section on schizophrenia), given that individuals with BPD have a higher likelihood to overdose on drugs.

Post-test

1. b   2. a   3. c   4. a   5. d   6. d   7. a   8. c   9. c   10. d   11. d   12. d   13. a   14. a
15. b   16. c   17. d   18. a   19. a   20. b   21. d   22. b   23. d   24. a   25. c   26. d
27. d   28. d   29. b   30. d   31. a   32. d   33. b   34. d   35. a   36. d   37. b   38. a
39. b   40. d   41. b   42. b   43. b   44. d   45. b   46. a   47. d   48. b   49. d   50. a
51. d   52. c   53. b

15 Sleep and Consciousness

Chapter Outline

Learning Objectives

After reading this chapter, you will be able to

1. Summarize the characteristics of the rhythms that occur during sleep and waking

2. Describe the neural controls of sleep and waking rhythms

3. Examine the functions of sleep and shorter rhythms

4. Assess the causes of sleep disorders

5. Explain how researchers are approaching the issue of consciousness

6. Indicate the neural processes that contribute to consciousness

Sleep and Dreaming

Summary and Guided Review

After studying this section in the text, fill in the blanks of the following summary.

The study of consciousness within psychology has been controversial. The use of _____ (1) to study consciousness, popular at the end of the 19th century, fell out of favor when the _____ (2) attempted to rid psychology of subjective methods during the first half of the 20th century. When _____ (3) psychology emerged in the mid-20th century, mental experiences were once again acceptable to study if they could be examined objectively. However, because of lack of technology as well as lack of consensus concerning the meaning of consciousness, this topic has remained controversial. Psychologists who do study it often work with researchers from other disciplines, including _____ (4), philosophy, and computer science; of the conscious states, _____ (5) is most commonly studied, because it can be objectively observed and measured.

Although sleep is one of our most basic needs, researchers who study it have been unable to fully explain its functions. One explanation is that sleep is _____ (6); it allows us to conserve energy and repair our bodies. Because amount of sleep is correlated with a species' body size, food availability, metabolic rate, and vulnerability, the _____ (7) hypothesis suggests the amount of sleep is a function of needs for energy conservation and safety. In a study of 39 species, the factors of body size and danger accounted for _____% (8) of the variability in sleep time. One interesting finding is that when you sleep, that is when the brain increases CSF flow to cleanse itself of _____ (9). There is also considerable evidence that getting adequate sleep at the right time is important. People who are _____ (10) workers experience difficulty getting enough sleep during the day. In addition, rates of vehicle and work-related accidents are higher in the early morning hours than at other times. Finally, _____ _____ (11) baseball teams playing games in East Coast cities seem to be at a disadvantage if they are not given adequate time to adjust to the time shift. This difficulty in adjustment while traveling across time zones is often referred to as _____ _____ (12).

Our sleep-wake cycle is an example of a(n) _____ (13) rhythm, and the sleep period corresponds with decreases in several physiological measures

such as urine production and body temperature. These cycles are controlled by the
_____ _____ (14); rats with lesions in this region
no longer exhibit regular daily cycles of sleep. When daylight cues are unavailable, people's
circadian rhythms tend to increase to _____ (15)-hour cycles. This
suggests that natural light is the critical _____ (16) for entraining the
SCN to a 24-hour cycle. Furthermore, being exposed to _____ (17)
light during wakefulness and darkness during sleep are important for coordinating the
different biological rhythms associated with sleep. The fact that we tend toward a 25-
hour cycle may explain why it is easier to adjust to _____ (18) times
for falling asleep and waking up. Shift workers whose shifts rotate according to phase
_____ (19) are able to adjust more easily than those who must
accommodate phase advance changes. Light controls the sleep cycle through its influence on
the pineal gland's secretion of _____ (20); in totally blind individuals,
a failure to produce this substance in response to changing levels of light is associated with
_____ (21). Blind individuals with normal melatonin cycling probably rely
on signals from the _____ (22) pathway to the SCN. This pathway may
be mediated not by rods and cones but by retinal ganglion cells containing the photopigment
_____ (23), which is sensitive to the overall level of light. The internal
clock itself consists of two major groups of _____ (24) and their
_____ (25) products. The groups alternate in activity as a group's proteins
turn those genes off and turn the other group of genes on. Every day the feedback loop that
comprises the circadian clock must be reset by _____ (26). Other clocks
in the body are entrained to the day-night cycle by the _____ (27), which
does not always operate properly, as discussed in patients with depression.

Several bodily rhythms in humans follow shorter, _____
(28) cycles. Some examples are hormone production, urinary output, and alertness.
The basic rest and activity cycle is a rhythm that is about _____-
_____ (29) minutes long. When the person is awake, the EEG is a
mixture of _____ (30) waves, associated with arousal and alertness,
and _____ (31) waves, characteristic of relaxed wakefulness.
_____ (32) waves occur during Stage 1, or light sleep. During Stage 2,
we exhibit _____ _____ (33) and K-complexes.
Slow-wave sleep (SWS) in Stages 3 and 4 is associated with _____ (34)
waves; movement, including sleepwalking, often occurs during this time. The EEG activity
then indicates a reverse progression through the sleep stages until _____
_____ _____ (35) sleep is achieved. This type of sleep
is sometimes called _____ (36) sleep, because it is characterized by eye
movements, physiological arousal, dreaming, and brain waves that are similar to a waking
state. One unusual characteristic of REM sleep is that in spite of these signs of arousal, the
body is in a state of paralysis or _____ (37). The length of REM sleep
periods increases over the night as the amount of slow-wave sleep decreases.

Scientists are still debating the functions of the different stages of sleep. Because the
amount of SWS is associated with _____ (38) in the brain prior to sleep,
it has been suggested that SWS is more important for brain than body restoration. It may
be involved in cerebral recovery, particularly in the _____ (39) cortex.
Individuals given _____ (40) prior to a nap experienced less SWS during
the nap and had poorer cognitive performance following the nap than those given a placebo,
though they reported feeling vigorous and no sleepier than the control group. People deprived
of REM sleep will enter it more quickly on subsequent nights and spend more time in this
stage of sleep, which implies that there is a biological need for REM sleep. Researchers do

not agree on the function(s) of REM sleep. One suggestion is that because REM sleep is more common in infants and children than in adults, it promotes neural _____ (41).

Sleep serves another function by supporting _____ (42). One way the brain consolidates memory during REM sleep is through the theta rhythm in the _____ (43). Once that occurs, the replay shifts to the troughs of the theta rhythm, resulting in memory deletion. Therefore, REM sleep provides the mechanism by which memories are reconsolidated, made more efficient, or _____ (44). But it's not just REM; _____ (45) is likely a multistep process requiring both slow-wave and REM sleep. Based on recent research, evidence suggests that memories are _____ (46) during non-REM sleep and stored during REM sleep. Applying slow-oscillating potentials to the frontal and temporal lobes improved word association recall, presumably by increasing neuroplasticity. Even taking a brief _____ (47) that includes both types of sleep improves visual discrimination performance. Tononi and Cirelli postulate that sleep is also an opportunity to eliminate inaccurate connections through synaptic _____ (48); ripples, generated by the hippocampus and activating the default mode network, strengthen synapses that were used during _____ (49) learning.

Wakefulness is produced through two primary pathways: the _____ _____ _____ (50) and the forebrain arousal centers. The brainstem pathway has two branches and is _____ (51), meaning that signals originate in the brainstem and terminate in higher brain areas. The first branch consists of the PPT/LDT branch that fires most rapidly during REM sleep and _____ (52) and most slowly during _____ (53) sleep. The second branch originates in the locus coeruleus, raphé nuclei, parabrachial nucleus, and _____ _____ (54) nucleus. Forebrain arousal centers include the _____ _____ (55), which desynchronizes EEG and sends signals to the prefrontal cortex. Activity in the _____ _____ (56) nucleus inhibits arousal in several brain areas in the brain stem and the lateral hypothalamus, helping animals switch between wakefulness and sleep. One other area important to non-REM sleep is the _____ _____ (57) in the medulla.

Prior to REM sleep, _____ (58) waves travel from the pons to the lateral geniculate nucleus of the thalamus and then to the occipital lobe; these waves may account for the visual aspects of dreaming. These waves also synchronize with firing of PPT/LDT cells, suggesting coordination in control of sleep cycles. Within the pons, the _____ (59) nucleus (SDL) controls cycling in and out of REM sleep, including signals that result in sleep paralysis (atonia).

_____ (60) is the inability to sleep or to obtain quality sleep. People who get either too little or too much sleep typically have a shorter life span. Body mass index is higher in people who get too _____ (61) sleep, apparently because several eating-related hormones shift out of balance. Insomniacs apparently suffer from hyperarousal during sleep; their non-REM sleep contains excess _____-_____ (62) EEG, and secretion of excess _____ (63) and adrenocorticotropic hormone indicates disturbance of the hypothalamic-pituitary-adrenal axis. Many factors contribute to insomnia, but the disorder is often found in people with _____ (64) disorders. Insomnia has been associated with reductions in right hemisphere _____ _____ (65) and diminished gray matter in the parietal cortex and _____ (66) cortex. Many _____ (67) medications, while helpful, can cause rebound insomnia when people decrease the nightly dosage. Another reason for insomnia may be that a person's body temperature cycle is out of sync with the sleep cycle; going to sleep when the body temperature is high results in _____-_____ (68) insomnia, whereas a phase advance in body temperature results in early waking. The ideal time to go to sleep is when the body temperature is low. Whether your _____ (69) is synchronized to the 24-hour day depends on both genes and the environment. A mutation in the _____ (70) circadian clock gene is associated with advanced sleep phase disorder whereas the _____ (71) clock gene is linked to delayed sleep phase disorder. A counterintuitive treatment for _____ _____ (72) syndrome involves delaying each sleep cycle by three hours over several consecutive days.

Sleepwalking occurs during _____-_____ (73) sleep, as do bedwetting and night terrors. There have been cases in which sleepwalkers committed violent acts, including murder. This condition appears to have a genetic basis; the involvement of one particular gene suggests that in some cases cells important in sleep regulation have been attacked by the _____ (74) system. A sleep disorder that usually results in weight gain as well as daytime fatigue is _____-_____ _____ (75) disorder. One final non-REM disorder is _____ (76), in which 4% of women and 11% of men seeking treatment for a sleep disorder reported engaging in sexual behavior while asleep.

Disorders of REM sleep include _____ (77), in which a person enters REM sleep suddenly and directly from full consciousness. One symptom of this disorder is _____ (78), in which a person becomes suddenly paralyzed but remains conscious. Both of these conditions may stem from an abnormal form of a gene for the _____ (79) receptor. Extreme physical activity during REM sleep, such as leaping out of bed, is a symptom of REM sleep _____ _____ (80). This condition is often associated with a neurological condition, such as _____ (81) disease.

Francis Crick suggested that we are in a state of diminished consciousness during REM sleep and unconscious during non-REM sleep. However, the distinction between consciousness and unconsciousness during sleep is hardly clear. _____ (82) dreamers report awareness of their dreams as they happen and also seem to be able to control the content of their dreams. Sleepwalkers and those with REM sleep behavior disorder carry out complex behaviors while asleep (such as driving a car). Perhaps consciousness exists on a(n) _____ (83), and different states such as wakefulness, sleep, and dreaming reflect different levels of awareness.

Short Answer and Essay Questions

Answer the following questions.

1. Contrast the adaptive explanation and the synaptic homeostasis hypothesis for sleep functions and provide supporting evidence for each view.

2. Indicate the difference between circadian and ultradian rhythms.

3. Describe how blind individuals are able to synchronize their circadian cycle if the zeitgeber is light.

4. Describe the roles of the basal forebrain area, hypothalamus, and pons in sleep and arousal.

5. Identify possible causes and biological explanations for the sleep disorders insomnia and narcolepsy.

The Neural Bases of Consciousness

Summary and Guided Review

After studying this section in the text, fill in the blanks of the following summary.

Although experts disagree as to a specific definition of consciousness, most would probably concur that being conscious includes attention, _____ (84), and a sense of self. There is probably no single brain area responsible for consciousness, but rather it arises from the interaction of several different brain areas.

Investigations of people who had lost consciousness indicated that damage to the _____ _____ (85) of the thalamus and the rostral dorsolateral _____ _____ (86) would produce unconsciousness. Consciousness arises not from these structures alone, but from connections between these structures and higher brain areas such as the anterior cingulate cortex and the anterior _____ (87) cortex, which are part of the _____ _____ (88) detecting stimuli that require attention. Thus, consciousness structures determine when the default mode or _____ _____ (89) networks are active, based on environmental needs.

Most researchers believe consciousness requires a widely distributed neuronal network. For example, stimuli outside awareness activate only the sensory area, but when the stimulus enters consciousness, activation is more widespread. When the frontal and parietal cortices decrease activity, such as during deep sleep, general anesthesia, coma, and near-death experiences, coordinated activity disappears. Many theorists believe network activity is coordinated by gamma oscillations generated by a feedback loop between the _____ (90) and cortex. Some scientists believe that while there is no brain structure that houses consciousness, there must be something that acts as a(n) _____ (91), directing activity in other structures. Candidates for this role have included the thalamus, the _____ _____ (92) cortex, and the _____ (93). The latter structure, in particular, may _____ (94) information from various brain areas or even detect neural _____ (95) between areas, given that this structure is so highly connected with sensory, motor, and emotion brain regions.

Awareness and consciousness seem to depend on a group of brain areas called the _____-_____ (96) network, including the lateral prefrontal cortex, posterior parietal cortex, and the thalamus. How the brain integrates or binds information from different areas into a unitary whole most likely involves the _____ (97) of neural activity. This type of activity occurs mostly in the _____ (98) frequency range, between 30 and 90 Hz. For example, when researchers presented a light that had been paired with a shock, activity became synchronized between the _____ (99) cortex and the finger area of the somatosensory cortex. In one study, electrodes were implanted in the brains of people who were being evaluated for surgery to treat seizures. When words were presented, initial localized gamma activity was recorded from the _____ (100) area, but if the words were recognized there was synchronized activity in occipital, parietal, and temporal areas. However, awareness is not required for all of our behavior. For example, people with _____ (101) can locate objects that they claim not to see, and considerable learning occurs without conscious awareness.

_____ (102) is the brain's means of allocating its limited resources. Much of the stimuli around us go unnoticed, although highly relevant stimuli such as one's name may be attended to. _____ _____ (103), which occurs when the brain is presented with two different visual stimuli in the same location, results in attention being alternately focused on each object, as demonstrated in the _____ _____ (104) effect. PET scans revealed that when participants were instructed to attend to an object's color, _____ (105) became more active; when told to attend to the object's shape, the _____ _____ (106) cortex became more active; and when attention was directed toward the object's movement, the activity switched to _____ (107). The shifts were clearly due to _____ (108), because the particular area was active whether the object possessed the feature or not (colored vs. not colored, for example). The gateway for sensory information to the cortex is the _____ (109); the cortex can selectively inhibit input from this area to determine which information will reach it. Imaging suggests there are two networks involved in attention. The _____ (110) network operates under goal-directed control, whereas the ventral network responds to _____ _____ (111). In addition, the _____ _____ (112) cortex may play an executive role. This area is active during complex tasks, like the _____ (113) test, in which subjects are asked to identify the color of a word that spells out a conflicting color name (for example, saying "red" when the word _green_ is presented in a red color).

Our sense of self includes identity and the sense of _____ (114), in which we perceive ourselves as the source of actions or effects. Children over _____ (115) months of age appear to recognize themselves in mirrors, indicating that they have a sense of self. This is true of only a few other animal species. For example, among the primates, chimpanzees and orangutans pass the mirror test, but _____ (116) fail it. Damage to specific brain areas can result in impairment in self-awareness, including failure to recognize one's own reflection. The sense that we are causing an action or event may be due to activity in the _____ _____ (117) and the inferior parietal area. However, the sense of self is not represented in a single brain area, but probably results from several distributed functions.

The sense of loss in individuals who have undergone limb amputation, and people with body sensory disorders, suggests that an intact body image is a part of our sense of self. The majority of amputees experience some manifestation of the _____ _____ (118) phenomenon, such as the sense that the missing limb is stuck in a particular position or that one still has control over it. Even individuals born with missing limbs can experience this phenomenon; therefore, body image does not have to be _____ (119).

_____-_____ (120) memory is also a source of our sense of identity. People with severe retrograde _____ (121), such as that resulting from Alzheimer's disease or Korsakoff syndrome, may engage in _____ (122); this is hypothesized to result from a failure to suppress irrelevant information due to damage to the _____ (123) lobe. Sacks suggests that confabulators are constantly creating both a past and a present, interspersed with fragments of actual experiences.

The ability to empathize with others and understand others' intentions may lie in _____ (124) neurons; it has even been suggested that malfunction in this system is responsible for some of the symptoms of autism, such as the inability to develop a(n) _____ of _____ (125).

Studies of split-brain patients can tell us something about consciousness and the self. Although most of the time people whose hemispheres have been disconnected perform normally, occasionally they act as if they have two selves. In laboratory studies, when information is presented only to the nonverbal _____ (126) hemisphere, the person is unable to identify it verbally; and the left hand (controlled by the right hemisphere) must sometimes be restrained to prevent it from helping the right hand perform a(n) _____ (127) task. While some researchers speculate that each hemisphere is capable of a separate consciousness, Gazzaniga argues that the left hemisphere is the brain _____ (128), which integrates cognitive functions occurring throughout the brain. An alternative perspective is that because the right hemisphere lacks _____ (129) ability, it is simply unable to report on its own contents and therefore appears to be less conscious or aware than the left hemisphere.

Individuals with multiple personality, or _____ _____ (130) disorder, show shifts in consciousness and behavior that appear to be distinct personalities or selves. Diagnosis of this disorder is controversial, and some experts believe that patients who display it are conforming to their therapists' expectations. However, a few studies have found different physiological profiles (heart rate, immune functioning, EEG activity) when different "personalities" were present, which suggests that there may be a(n) _____ (131) basis for the disorder. For example, some studies indicate that this disorder may represent a case of state-dependent learning. There are several indications of possible involvement of the brain structures of learning, including hippocampal changes during personality switches and frequent backgrounds of childhood abuse (associated with hippocampal damage), and temporal lobe differences between personalities.

Short Answer and Essay Questions

Answer the following questions.

6. Describe a research study that indicates we can learn without being aware of what we have learned.

7. Explain why Gazzaniga argues that the left hemisphere is more highly conscious than the right hemisphere, including the significance of the brain interpreter in his argument.

8. Most researchers believe that consciousness is distributed across much of the brain. Describe their thinking about networks in relation to consciousness.

9. Evaluate the importance of understanding the nature of consciousness for patients with severe brain damage.

Post-test

Use these multiple-choice questions to check your understanding of the chapter.

1. In the late 19th century, consciousness was studied primarily
   a. by using introspection.
   b. with the EEG.

   c. by examining sleep and dreaming.

   d. by observing others' behavior.

2. Currently, brain researchers
   a. are interested only in studying sleep as a form of consciousness.
   b. agree on a definition of consciousness.
   c. integrate philosophical, biological, and computer science perspectives to study consciousness.
   d. agree that consciousness cannot be studied objectively.

3. Which of the following statements regarding shift work is TRUE?
   a. Night-shift workers perform their jobs as well as day-shift workers.
   b. Shift workers sleep less than day workers.
   c. Night-shift workers generally sleep through the day on their weekends or days off.
   d. Job-related accidents are most likely to occur between 10:00 p.m. and midnight.

4. Which of the following baseball teams is LEAST likely to win a game?
   a. the Boston Red Sox playing at the Houston Astros
   b. the Houston Astros playing at the Boston Red Sox
   c. the San Francisco Giants playing at the Atlanta Braves
   d. the Atlanta Braves playing at the San Francisco Giants

5. Circadian rhythms for sleep and waking arise in the
   a. suprachiasmatic nucleus.
   b. hypothalamus.
   c. pineal gland.
   d. medulla.

6. The MOST significant zeitgeber for the sleep-wake cycles appears to be
   a. moonlight.
   b. sunlight.
   c. clocks.
   d. social contact.

7. Research suggests that in order to increase worker productivity, night-shift workers should
   a. sleep in complete darkness.
   b. work in bright light.
   c. take naps every two hours while working.
   d. a and b

8. Assuming that the day shift is from 8:00 a.m. to 4:00 p.m., the swing shift is from 4:00 p.m. to midnight, and the night shift is from midnight to 8:00 a.m., which of the following shift-rotation schedules would be MOST beneficial to workers?
   a. day shift to swing shift to night shift
   b. day shift to night shift to swing shift
   c. swing shift to day shift to night shift
   d. night shift to swing shift to day shift

9. How have researchers explained evidence that the internal clock operates on a 25-hour cycle?
   a. The effect is related to the 30-day lunar cycle.
   b. It is just an artifact of allowing people to use alarm clocks to start their day.

    c. Body temperature moves the cycle from 24 to 25 hours.

    d. none of the above

10. _____ is a hormone released by the pineal gland that induces sleepiness.

    a. Melanopsin

    b. Adenosine

    c. Melatonin

    d. Hypocretin

11. Which of the following statements is NOT true?

    a. Mice lacking rods and cones are unable to show normal entrainment and cycling.

    b. Light is able to activate the SCN by way of the retinohypothalamic pathway.

    c. The small percentage of ganglion cells that respond to light directly contain melanopsin.

    d. Melanopsin has been found in the cells of humans.

12. The circadian clock for sleep and waking

    a. is found in the brain, but it may control clocks in other organs.

    b. involves a feedback loop of two groups of genes and their protein products.

    c. must be reset each day by light.

    d. all of the above

13. Which of the following cycle lengths would be considered an ultradian rhythm?

    a. 24-hour

    b. 3-hour

    c. 48-hour

    d. 36-hour

14. The basic rest and activity cycle

    a. is a circadian rhythm.

    b. is a 60-minute cycle that occurs throughout the day.

    c. shows up in a 90-minute daydreaming cycle.

    d. is controlled by temperature.

15. Which of the following statements is NOT true about sleep?

    a. It is an active process.

    b. It is the cessation of activity due to fatigue.

    c. It involves turning some brain structures on and other structures off.

    d. It includes both active and inactive periods of brain activity.

16. An EEG pattern showing low-amplitude, high-frequency (13–30 Hz) waves characterizes

    a. alertness.

    b. relaxation.

    c. light sleep.

    d. slow-wave sleep.

17. Sleep spindles and K-complexes are MOST likely to be observed in

    a. REM sleep.

    b. Stage 4 sleep.

    c. Stage 2 sleep.

    d. Stage 1 sleep.

18. What type of EEG characterizes Stages 3 and 4 of slow-wave sleep?
    a. alpha activity
    b. beta activity
    c. delta activity
    d. theta activity

19. Which of the following is NOT a typical characteristic of REM sleep?
    a. low-amplitude, moderate-frequency EEG
    b. eye movements
    c. arm and leg movements
    d. genital erection

20. Dreams
    a. occur only during REM sleep.
    b. are more vivid in slow-wave sleep.
    c. have no personal meaning.
    d. probably occur in all people.

21. Someone who is deprived of REM sleep will
    a. spend more time in REM and slow-wave sleep when allowed to sleep without interruptions.
    b. develop temporary narcolepsy or cataplexy.
    c. come to understand the symbolic contents of her dreams.
    d. spend more time in REM sleep when allowed to sleep without interruptions.

22. Which of the following does NOT occur during slow-wave sleep in children?
    a. bedwetting
    b. sleepwalking
    c. atonia
    d. night terrors

23. Infants spend about _____% of their total sleep time in REM sleep.
    a. 10
    b. 50
    c. 20
    d. 75

24. The developmental hypothesis of REM sleep
    a. states that REM sleep promotes neural development during childhood, especially during infancy.
    b. argues that REM sleep encourages maturation and myelination of higher brain structures.
    c. is supported by the finding that genes involved in neural plasticity are upregulated during REM sleep.
    d. all of the above

25. Slow-wave sleep
    a. promotes cerebral recovery, especially in the prefrontal cortex.
    b. occurs in response to low body temperature.
    c. occurs in response to low brain temperature.
    d. is not affected by caffeine, although REM sleep is.

26. Learning and memory
    a. decrease REM sleep in the night following the task.
    b. involve both REM and non-REM sleep.
    c. are related to the circadian cycle of sleep, but not the type of sleep.
    d. are linked to REM sleep in animals but not humans.

27. Which of the following structures is most important in neuronal replay that occurs during sleep?
    a. the visual cortex
    b. the hippocampus
    c. the pons
    d. the basal forebrain region

28. Which of the following hypotheses suggests that inappropriate neural connections are discarded during sleep?
    a. neural development
    b. synaptic homeostasis
    c. dual mode
    d. activation synthesis

29. Slow-wave sleep is LEAST likely to increase if a person
    a. swims 25 laps in a chilly pool.
    b. runs 10 miles on a hot day.
    c. has a fever.
    d. works in an overheated office.

30. Sleep involves all of the following structures EXCEPT
    a. the medulla.
    b. the basal forebrain region.
    c. the pons.
    d. the ventrolateral thalamus.

31. Muscular paralysis accompanying REM sleep is moderated by the
    a. magnocellular nucleus of the medulla.
    b. lateral geniculate nucleus of the thalamus.
    c. occipital cortex.
    d. basal forebrain area.

32. Which of the following statements about the arousal systems of the brain is NOT true?
    a. One arousal pathway includes the PPT/LDT.
    b. One arousal pathway projects to the thalamus.
    c. Melatonin is required for arousal.
    d. There are two arousal pathways.

33. PGO waves
    a. travel from the pons to the thalamus and on to the cortex.
    b. begin about 80 seconds before the start of a REM period.
    c. initiate the desynchrony of REM sleep.
    d. all of the above

34. Which of the following statements is NOT true about insomnia?
    a. It is associated with disorders such as obesity.
    b. It is usually diagnosed in a sleep laboratory.
    c. It may involve cortisol release during the night.
    d. It is common in people with depression.

35. The best treatment for delayed sleep syndrome is to
    a. take benzodiazepine sleep medications.
    b. stay up later on consecutive days.
    c. increase your body temperature at bedtime.
    d. go to bed three hours earlier for a few days.

36. Sleepwalking
    a. occurs during slow-wave sleep.
    b. may have a genetic basis.
    c. is most common during childhood.
    d. all of the above

37. Narcolepsy is a condition in which a person
    a. suddenly goes from being awake directly into slow-wave sleep.
    b. falls directly into REM sleep from wakefulness.
    c. has too much orexin.
    d. sleeps much more than people without narcolepsy.

38. Someone who literally acts outs dreams is probably experiencing
    a. lucid dreaming.
    b. cataplexy.
    c. REM sleep behavior disorder.
    d. insomnia.

39. All of the following are components that most researchers agree are part of consciousness EXCEPT
    a. attention.
    b. personality.
    c. sense of self.
    d. awareness.

40. A single center of consciousness may not exist, but the _____ has been proposed
to be an "executive" area that coordinates all of the areas involved in consciousness.
    a. thalamus
    b. anterior cingulate cortex
    c. claustrum
    d. all of the above

41. In which of the following conditions is default mode network activity MOST likely to
be normal?
    a. coma
    b. locked-in syndrome
    c. minimally conscious state
    d. vegetative state

42. Which of the following is evidence of learning without awareness?
    a. recognizing that our unconscious mind is capable of motivating our behavior
    b. following a coach's instructions for hitting a ball with a bat
    c. using proprioceptive information to sit erect and walk
    d. reading instructions for assembling a computer prior to putting it together

43. The Cheshire cat effect is an example of
    a. binocular rivalry.
    b. lucid dreaming.
    c. binocular disparity.
    d. unconscious learning.

44. Attention
    a. is the same as awareness.
    b. is a concept rather than a physiological process.
    c. is a reflection of changes in brain activity.
    d. all of the above

45. Which of the following is LEAST likely to recognize herself in a mirror?
    a. a 16-month-old human
    b. an adult rhesus monkey
    c. an adult chimpanzee
    d. a 24-month-old human

46. All of the following contribute to the sense of self EXCEPT
    a. arousal.
    b. body image.
    c. memory.
    d. mirror neurons.

47. Phantom limb sensations may be experienced
    a. by amputees.
    b. by people born with missing limbs.
    c. even before an individual has developed a learned body image.
    d. all of the above

48. Which of the following statements regarding confabulation is FALSE?
    a. It often includes elements of real memories.
    b. It is often consistent and meaningful.
    c. It is usually intentional.
    d. It is associated with long-term memory loss.

49. Split-brain patients
    a. are unable to perform behaviors requiring coordination from both sides of the body.
    b. are able to give verbal descriptions of objects in both visual fields.
    c. clearly demonstrate that the left hemisphere is more highly conscious than the right.
    d. usually perform spatial tasks better with the left hand than the right.

50. Which of the following statements regarding dissociative identity disorder is FALSE?
    a. It is not included in the *Diagnostic and Statistical Manual of Mental Disorders*.
    b. It was formerly called multiple personality disorder.
    c. It is believed to result from childhood abuse or trauma.
    d. Individuals exhibit different physiological patterns when manifesting different identities.

Answers

Guided Review

1. introspection
2. behaviorists
3. cognitive
4. biology
5. sleep
6. restorative
7. adaptive
8. 80
9. toxins
10. shift
11. West Coast
12. jet lag
13. circadian
14. suprachiasmatic nucleus (SCN)
15. 25
16. zeitgeber (or "time-giver")
17. bright
18. later
19. delays
20. melatonin
21. insomnia
22. retinohypothalamic
23. melanopsin
24. genes
25. protein
26. light
27. SCN
28. ultradian
29. 90–100
30. beta
31. alpha
32. Theta
33. sleep spindles
34. delta
35. rapid eye movement (REM)
36. paradoxical
37. atonia
38. temperature
39. prefrontal
40. caffeine
41. development
42. learning
43. hippocampus
44. deleted/forgotten
45. consolidation
46. recalled
47. nap
48. pruning
49. intensive
50. brainstem arousal centers
51. ascending
52. wakefulness
53. non-REM
54. tuberomammillary
55. basal forebrain
56. ventrolateral preoptic (VLPO)
57. parafacial zone
58. PGO
59. sublaterodorsal
60. Insomnia
61. little
62. high-frequency
63. cortisol
64. psychological/affective
65. white matter
66. orbitofrontal
67. sleep
68. sleep-onset
69. chronotype
70. *CKI*
71. *PER3*
72. delayed sleep
73. slow-wave
74. immune

75. sleep-related eating
76. sexsomnia
77. narcolepsy
78. cataplexy
79. orexin
80. behavior disorder
81. Parkinson's
82. Lucid
83. continuum
84. awareness
85. intralaminar nuclei
86. pontine tegmentum
87. insular
88. salience network
89. central executive
90. thalamus
91. executive
92. anterior cingulate
93. claustrum
94. bind
95. synchrony
96. prefrontal-parietal
97. synchronization
98. gamma
99. visual
100. occipital
101. blindsight
102. Attention
103. Binocular rivalry

104. Cheshire cat
105. V4
106. inferior temporal
107. V5
108. attention
109. thalamus
110. dorsal
111. stimulus demands
112. anterior cingulate
113. Stroop
114. agency
115. 15
116. monkeys
117. anterior insula
118. phantom limb
119. learned
120. Long-term
121. amnesia
122. confabulation
123. frontal
124. mirror
125. theory of mind
126. right
127. spatial
128. interpreter
129. verbal
130. dissociative identity
131. biological

Short Answer and Essay Questions

1. The adaptive explanation for sleep states that the amount of sleep is determined by safety considerations and access to food. Evidence for this hypothesis comes from studying sleep in different animals. For example, vulnerable animals like horses and cattle sleep very little, and those with low vulnerability, like lions, sleep much of the time. Bats and burrowing animals also sleep a lot because they can find safety by hiding. According to the synaptic homeostasis hypothesis, sleep is a time when unneeded or incorrect connections between neurons can be pruned. The ripples, slow waves, and sleep spindles of sleep are believed to identify rarely used synapses and weaken them. Evidence for this hypothesis comes from a study of mice; three-dimensional electron microscopy showed that during sleep, dendritic spine density was reduced only in synapses that had not been used regularly.

2. The circadian rhythm has the length of a day, whereas ultradian rhythms are shorter than a day. An example of an ultradian rhythm is the basic rest and activity cycle that has a rhythm of about 90–100 minutes. The circadian clock is located in the SCN (suprachiasmatic nucleus). Evidence for this is that when the SCN is lesioned in animals, they do not stop sleeping but they sleep in naps throughout the 24-hour day. The circadian cycle is entrained by cues in the environment such as light; when not synchronized to these zeitgebers, the cycle drifts. The SCN controls the pineal gland's secretion of melatonin, a sleep-inducing hormone that has been used to treat jet lag and insomnia in shift workers.

3. Apparently some blind individuals are able to entrain to the light-dark cycle because light stimulates the photopigment melanopsin in a small percentage of retinal ganglion cells, which signal the SCN via the retinohypothalamic pathway.

4. Areas involved in sleep include the basal forebrain and the ventrolateral preoptic area of the hypothalamus. Both regions inhibit arousal-producing neurons in the pons. There are two main arousal systems. One arises from specific nuclei in the pons that shifts the synchronous EEG to a desynchronized pattern, which is observed during both waking and REM sleep. The second pathway activates the cortex; both of these systems originate in the brain stem. Furthermore, neurons in the lateral hypothalamus send axons to the basal forebrain region and several brain stem areas. These cells release orexin, which seems to stabilize the sleep and waking system.

5. Insomnia is a disorder related to many factors, including stress, psychological disorders such as depression, disruption of the circadian and temperature cycles, and even sleep medications. There is no single biological cause of insomnia, but excess high-frequency activity in slow-wave sleep, increased release of cortisol, and genes involved in circadian rhythms have been studied. Narcolepsy is a disorder that occurs when the "stabilization switch" fails and the person falls asleep during the daytime and experiences REM sleep at inappropriate times. Low levels of orexin are found in people and animals with narcolepsy. Genetic factors affecting the immune system may play a role in the disorder, based on the study of canine narcolepsy.

6. The book describes two studies. In one, participants learned to predict where a target would appear on a screen, although they were unable to verbalize how they were predicting its location. In another study, people formed associations between facial features and personality characteristics but were unaware they had done so.

7. Gazzaniga argues that because the left hemisphere has language and inferential capabilities the right lacks, the right hemisphere's consciousness is more "primitive." In addition, he explains the tendency of the left hemisphere to confabulate reasons for behaviors generated by the right hemisphere (based on stimuli presented to it and not shared with the left) as evidence of a "brain interpreter."

8. According to Tononi, consciousness depends on the brain's ability to integrate information, and some of the results of studies of networks support this idea. For example, when a stimulus enters consciousness, activity spreads beyond the sensory area to other brain areas. Some theorists think awareness requires coordination in networks by gamma-frequency activity, which is generated in a thalamus-cortex loop; damage to the thalamocortical system produces unconsciousness. Recent attention has turned to the default mode network; coordination in this network decreases as a result of several conditions of altered consciousness, including sleep, sleep deprivation, anesthesia, unconsciousness, and brain damage that affects level of consciousness. The anterior cingulate cortex and anterior insular cortex are two cortical areas that are

part of the salience network, which shifts activity between the default mode network and central executive network to best respond to environmental needs.

9. People with brain damage may be in a coma, minimally conscious, in a persistent vegetative state, or in a locked-in state. They are often unable to communicate with caregivers and family due to the nature of the damage. Hence, it is difficult to make informed decisions about appropriate care, prognosis, and whether therapeutic intervention is possible. A rare but informative example is the case of locked-in syndrome, in which a person is fully conscious but with little or no ability to communicate. The ability to assess the individual's level of consciousness is necessary for deciding treatment strategies and goals.

Post-test

1. a   2. c   3. b   4. c   5. a   6. b   7. d   8. a   9. d   10. c   11. a   12. d   13. b   14. c
15. a   16. c   17. c   18. c   19. c   20. d   21. d   22. c   23. b   24. d   25. a   26. b
27. b   28. b   29. a   30. d   31. a   32. c   33. d   34. b   35. b   36. d   37. b   38. c
39. b   40. d   41. b   42. c   43. a   44. c   45. b   46. a   47. d   48. c   49. d   50. a